THE

EVERYTHING® MUSIC THEORY BOOK WITH CD

2ND EDITION

Dear Reader,

I can't believe it's been almost six years since the first edition of *The Everything® Music Theory Book with CD* came out. Over the years, many readers have reached out via e-mail with some small feature requests they'd like to see in a future edition. When I was approached to do a second edition of this book, I knew exactly what I wanted to change. I wanted to give you, the reader, more practice and more examples. In fact, the goal of this edition is to give you a lot more practice. Without practice, you'll lose the information as fast as you read it. Gone are the three large Etude chapters from the first edition. At the conclusion of each chapter, you'll find examples to practice what you've learned. At the end of the book, you can check your work and grade yourself. Along the way, I've freshened the information in each chapter based on feedback from readers and continued experience teaching. I'm very proud of the first edition and even more proud of this edition. I know you'll get something out if it, even if you already have the previous edition.

Cheers,

Welcome to the EVERYTHING® Series!

These handy, accessible books give you all you need to tackle a difficult project, gain a new hobby, comprehend a fascinating topic, prepare for an exam, or even brush up on something you learned back in school but have since forgotten.

You can choose to read an *Everything*® book from cover to cover or just pick out the information you want from our three useful boxes: Extra Credit, In Time, and Point to Consider.

We give you everything you need to know on the subject, but throw in a lot of fun stuff along the way, too.

We now have more than 400 *Everything*® books in print, spanning such wide-ranging categories as weddings, pregnancy, cooking, music instruction, foreign language, crafts, pets, New Age, and so much more. When you're done reading them all, you can finally say you know *Everything*®!

EXTRA CREDIT

Something to practice

IN TIME

A quick spot of music history

POINT TO CONSIDER

To clarify a musical concept

PUBLISHER Karen Cooper

DIRECTOR OF ACQUISITIONS AND INNOVATION Paula Munier

MANAGING EDITOR, EVERYTHING® SERIES Lisa Laing

COPY CHIEF Casey Ebert

ASSISTANT PRODUCTION EDITOR Jacob Erickson

ACQUISITIONS EDITOR Lisa Laing

ASSOCIATE DEVELOPMENT EDITOR Hillary Thompson

EDITORIAL ASSISTANT Ross Weisman

EVERYTHING® SERIES COVER DESIGNER Erin Alexander

LAYOUT DESIGNERS Colleen Cunningham, Elisabeth Lariviere, Ashley Vierra, Denise Wallace

THE EVERYTHING® MUSIC THEORY BOOK WITH CD

2ND EDITION

Take your understanding of music to the next level

Marc Schonbrun

Adams Media
New York London Toronto Sydney New Delhi

I want to dedicate this book to whoever has been looking out for me all these years.

Adams Media
An Imprint of Simon & Schuster, Inc.
57 Littlefield Street
Avon, Massachusetts 02322

Manufactured in the United States of America

20 19 18 17 16 15 14 13 12

Library of Congress Cataloging-in-Publication Data has been applied for.

ISBN 978-1-4405-1182-0
ISBN 978-1-4405-1204-9 (ebook)

Contents

Acknowledgments

Properly thanking everyone who has helped me over the years isn't easy. I need to thank my teachers for sharing their passion; my family for always supporting me; my friends for never giving up on me; every composer and musician for inspiring me; and my wife for changing my life.

The Top 10 Things You're Going to Learn about Music Theory

1. That music theory doesn't have to be confusing or overly complicated
2. How to spell major and minor scales in any key
3. How to recognize key signatures and name them
4. How to read and write in any clef
5. How to spell triads and seventh chords
6. How to improve your ear
7. How to write and understand traditional harmony
8. How to use modes and their origins
9. How to write and understand jazz harmony
10. How to transpose for any instrument

Introduction

WELCOME TO *The Everything® Music Theory Book with CD, 2nd Edition*! This book has a definite purpose and a defined reader. Quite simply, you are here to learn more about music. When you study a musical instrument, you typically work in stages. First, you learn the basics of your individual instrument. You can devote years to learning the techniques and practices that make your instrument work. Many times this study starts in school at an early age and typically includes learning how to read music notation. Many of you who play "traditional" instruments—that is, band and orchestral instruments like flute, clarinet, violin, and cello—got your start in public schools. If so, you got a good foundation of practical work on your own instrument, including reading music and performance. If you studied a nontraditional instrument—such as guitar, bass, and piano—chances are you received your instruction in a different setting. Many schools only offer instruction in band and orchestral instruments, although that is starting to change.

Depending on the instrument you chose, you may or may not have a strong background in reading music. For example, pianists typically are well grounded in reading, while many guitarists are not. This book is the logical follow-up to *The Everything® Reading Music Book*, whose premise was to present a logical way for all players to learn to read musical notation. This is a critical step and if you are not comfortable with it, you'd be wise to check out that book as well. While the first chapter of this book is a review of basic concepts, music reading will not be covered in-depth and you will need to understand notation. If you aren't sure of your reading, or just want a companion text, grab *The Everything® Reading Music Book* as a good start. This book could be considered a silent follow-up, but not necessarily. You can learn theory without strong music-reading skills, but strong skills will make everything easier, at every step.

Your ability to play your instrument well has led you to a common place: the "what's next" phase. After attaining some mastery of your instrument, things begin to change and the instrument becomes a simple vehicle for musical expression. You begin the transformation from (*insert your instrument here*) to *musician*. As a musician, you start to look at the larger picture of what makes music work and hold together. The word *theory* is almost always thrown around as an "elusive" second step toward understanding music. Many players constantly say, "I have got to learn more about theory." Many use the word *theory* as if it's a chore, akin to "I have to paint the house," or something task-oriented. Let me put that quickly to rest: Music theory is not a task. It actually may be one of the hardest things to define.

Theory won't necessarily make you a better player. It's not guaranteed to improve any part of your musical life. Music theory is not a prediction of music! It is an educated look at what has happened throughout music history. Music has evolved slowly, and theory reviews that journey and tries to make sense of it. Theory will put words to concepts that you have understood all of your life. Never forget that music is sound, and theory has the Herculean task of trying to make sense of sounds and then transforming them into another medium: words. Theory will no doubt help you in all aspects of your life, but it's much like buying a new instrument: In the hands of a skilled player, it can make you better, but it is just a tool.

This book is different from other theory books. Many theory books are simply too difficult. They presuppose too much information and typically overwhelm the reader. These books cater to college-level music theory, and rarely are they suitable for self-study. The other problem is their "reach." "Reach" is the ability to speak to a large cross section of readers, regardless of their instrument, ability, and style of music. Many texts focus solely on classical music and only use examples from the canon of classical music—totally ignoring the music that you have grown up with. In writing this book, I wanted it to have as much reach as possible so that you can get the most out of your experience. If your goal is to get on an advanced track to music theory, this book will give you the foundation you need to tackle a much harder book. For example, you will find examples for many different instruments. In the section on chords, you'll see guitar chord grids. Typically, theory relies on the piano, and it does so for a good reason—the piano is an excellent instrument for study. But there are a lot of guitar players out there, and if you can grab a guitar and understand how chords progress better, then this book has reached more readers—and that is exactly what it should do.

The first step is a small review of music notation. Okay, folks, it's time to learn *everything* about music theory!

CHAPTER 1

Review of the Basics

Everyone needs a good review! You may not know everything you need to know, or you may have never read a music theory book, so this chapter will give you a brief overview of some of music's visual concepts, such as notes, clefs, and rhythms, so that you can look at later examples in the book and decipher them with ease.

Ins and Outs

Since you will see the language of written music throughout this book, you must be able to read it. Using the accompanying CD will reinforce many of the concepts, but there is no way around an inability to read notation. You may be thinking, "I can read just fine," but how well do you read in other clefs?

In Europe, musical tradition began with the simple monophonic (one voice) chants of the early Christian era. This was the most common type of music during the Early Middle Ages (from about A.D. 350 to 1050). Polyphonic liturgical music, which is a more complex composition with multiple melodies, developed in the High Middle Ages (from about A.D. 1050 to 1300).

Music theory explores what has been done in other music in order to reach a greater understanding overall. You will need to read in multiple clefs, since standard notation uses treble and bass clefs at a minimum and often throws in alto clef, too. Here is a basic review to help you make sense of what you are reading. There is also a somewhat detailed review of rhythms because it can be a difficult concept to understand; even if you know how to decipher the notes on a staff, you may still be uneasy with the counting aspect. If this chapter is already scaring you, try picking up *The Everything® Reading Music Book* and keeping that around; it will help you greatly in understanding this material!

Notes

What better place to start than with notes? Here's a short sample of music; try to dissect what's going on and see if you have all the information you need.

FIGURE 1.1 Musical Elements

Grave

fp

As you can see from **FIGURE 1.1**, this is a short excerpt from a piece of solo piano music. Here is what you are seeing:

1. There are notes placed on two musical staffs: one treble staff and one bass staff.
2. The staffs are further defined by their clefs.
3. The notes are identified only by use of a clef; otherwise, they are simply dots sitting on lines and spaces.

If you want to talk about the notes, you have to talk about clefs because clefs actually define the name of the notes in a staff.

Clefs

A clef is a symbol that sits at the beginning of every staff of music. A staff contains five lines and four spaces. How do you know where the note A or the note C is? The missing element is the clef, which defines what notes go where and functions a lot like a map. Placing a treble clef at the start of the staff defines the lines and spaces with note names. **FIGURE 1.2** shows the notes of a treble staff.

FIGURE 1.2 Treble Clef Staff

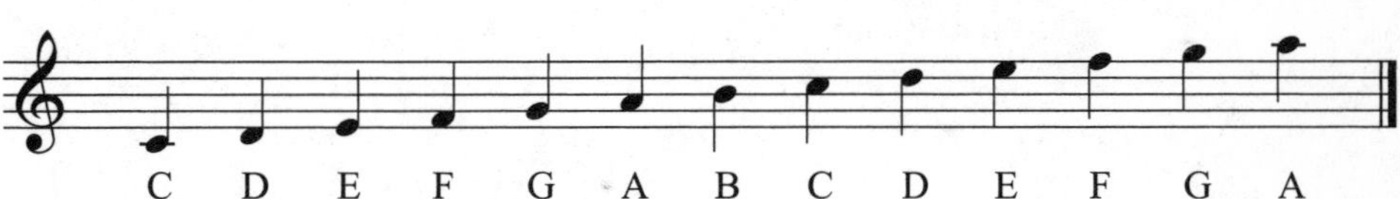

The treble clef circles around the note G. This is why it's commonly called the G clef. As for the notes, there is an important pattern. Look at the lowest line, which is designated E. Follow the musical alphabet to find where the next note is. The F is in the space just above the E. The staff ascends in this fashion—line, then space, then line—as it cycles through the musical alphabet (A–B–C–D–E–F–G).

Even though you may understand the notes on both clefs, the only way to become proficient is to read other clefs as often as you can. Set aside a few minutes each day to look at other clefs so you can easily identify their notes. Since clefs define notes, think of being able to read in many clefs as a kind of musical literacy.

The bass clef is a different clef than the treble and identifies not only different note names but also notes in different ranges. The bass clef is used for instruments that have a lower pitch, like a bass guitar. Even though the bass clef sits on the same five-line staff, it defines very different notes. Many musicians can read treble clef because it is the most common clef. It is more difficult, however, for many musicians to read bass clef. In order to make progress in understanding theory, you will need to be adept at reading all clefs. **FIGURE 1.3** shows the notes of a bass clef staff.

FIGURE 1.3 Bass Clef Staff

E F G A B C D E F G A B C

Grand Staff and Middle C

Grouping the bass clef and the treble clef together creates the grand staff. The grand staff is used in piano writing. To make a grand staff, connect a treble and a bass staff, or clef, with a brace, as shown in **FIGURE 1.4**.

FIGURE 1.4 A Brace

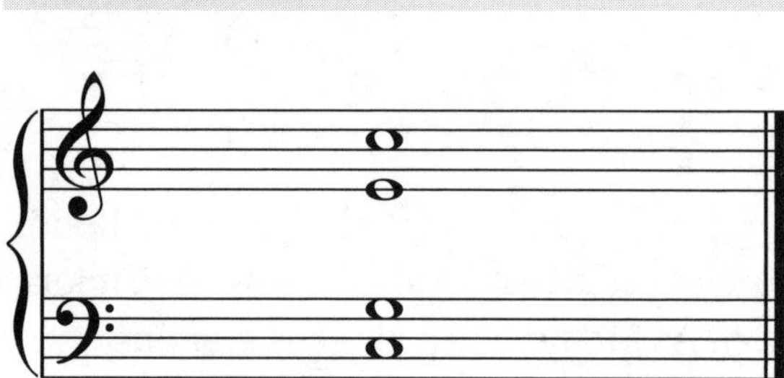

The grand staff reveals a very important note: middle C. **FIGURE 1.5** shows a middle C.

FIGURE 1.5 Middle C

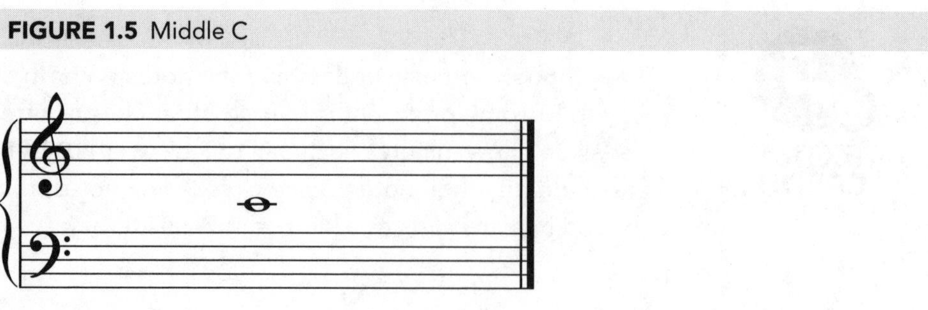

When you look at **FIGURE 1.5**, can you tell whether the note belongs to the bass clef or the treble clef? Actually, it belongs equally to both. If you trace down from the treble clef, one ledger line below the staff is a C. If you look at the bass clef notes, one ledger line above the staff is also a C. They are, in fact, the same pitch on the piano. This note is called middle C because it's right in the middle of everything. Middle C will come up throughout this book, so keep track of it!

Movable C Clefs

The last type of clef is the C clef. Typically, this clef is associated with the viola because it's the most common instrument that reads in C clef; however, other instruments read it as well. When the C clef is used with the viola, it is called the alto clef. Thankfully, this clef is very easy to read; the symbol for the C clef has two semicircles that curve into the middle of the staff and basically point toward the middle line, which is a C—and it's not just any C, it's middle C. **FIGURE 1.6** shows the notes for alto clef.

FIGURE 1.6 Alto Clef

Since this is a movable clef, you can place the clef anywhere you want; whatever lines the two semicircles point to become middle C. Some very old choral music uses a different movable C clef for each part (tenor clef, alto clef, and soprano clef). Just as long as you know that the clef always points toward middle C, you will be able to decipher the notes in this clef.

POINT TO CONSIDER

When notes use ledger lines that are extremely high or extremely low, they can be difficult to read; it's much easier to read notes that sit in the staff you are reading. Using different clefs allows you to move the location of middle C so that the majority of your notes are in and around the staff.

Accidentals

Notes can be altered with the use of accidentals. If you've heard of B-flat (B♭) or C-sharp (C♯), then you've heard of an accidental. Accidentals are used to raise and lower the pitch of a tone. There are two types of accidentals: single and double.

- A single accidental is the common ♭ and ♯ symbol.
- A ♭ lowers the pitch by one half step.
- A ♯ raises a pitch by one half step.
- A ♮ cancels an accidental (either in a measure or from the given key signature).

In addition to the simple sharp and flat symbols, you will also see double accidentals.

- A 𝄫 lowers the pitch by two half steps.
- A 𝄪 raises a pitch by two half steps.
- A ♮ cancels the double accidental in the same way it cancels the single accidentals.

Time

Even though this is a review section, time is a fundamental aspect of music theory that is often left out of formal music-theory study. Time is more than just counting beats and bars. Time can dictate the feel and flow of a piece; even harmony has a rhythm to it, aptly called harmonic rhythm. You'll start with time signatures, as they are the first time-related aspect you need to understand in detail.

Time Signatures

Music is divided into bars, or measures, for reading convenience and for musical purposes. Most music adheres to a meter, which affects the phrasing of the melody. If you don't have a lot of experience reading music, rhythm can be a very difficult concept to grasp.

The most standard time signature is $\frac{4}{4}$ time, which is also called common time and is abbreviated by this symbol . Common time looks like a fraction and signifies two things. First, the top number 4 means that every measure will have four beats in it. The bottom number 4 indicates what note value will receive the beat; in this case, 4 stands for a quarter note (♩). So common time breaks up each measure into four beats, as a quarter note receives one beat. You can, of course, further divide the measure into as many small parts as you like, but in the end, it must still add up to four beats.

Rhythm

Music is composed of pitch and rhythm. Although finer elements come into play later on, such as dynamics and expression, music can be made simply by knowing which note and how long to hold it. Without rhythm, people couldn't fully read music.

Rhythm is music's way of setting the duration of a note. Music accomplishes this task by varying the appearance of the notes that sit on the staff. Different rhythms indicate different note lengths. To get rolling, you need to hear about an essential concept: beat. Have you ever been to a concert and clapped along with 30,000 other fans? Have you noticed how everyone claps together in a steady pattern? Did you ever wonder how 30,000 people could possibly agree on anything? If you've been to a dance club, you may have noticed that there is always a steady drumbeat or bass line, usually up-tempo, to drive the music along. Those are examples of pulse and beat in music. Rhythm is a primal element, and pulse and beat are universal concepts.

Basic Rhythms

In music, changing the appearance of the notes indicates the rhythm. Remember, the location of the notes is fixed on the staff and will never change. However, the note's appearance varies, indicating how long that note should be held. Now, here are the basic musical symbols for rhythm.

Quarter Notes

A quarter note (♩) is signified with a filled-in black circle (also called a notehead) and a stem. It is the simplest rhythm to discuss. Quarter notes receive one count; their duration is one beat (see **FIGURE 1.7**).

FIGURE 1.7 Quarter Notes

Half Notes

The next in our series of simple rhythms is the half note (𝅗𝅥). As you can see, the half note looks similar to the quarter note, except the circle is not filled in. Like a quarter note, the half note has a single stem that points either up or down. The half note receives two counts; its duration is two beats. In relation to the quarter note, the half note is twice as long because it receives two counts (see **FIGURE 1.8**).

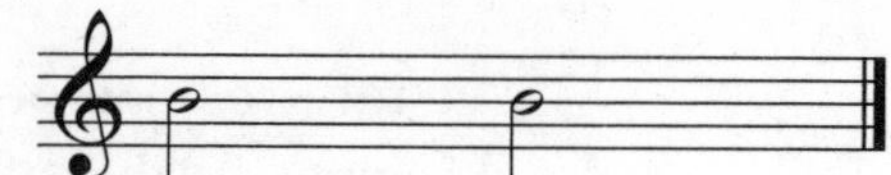

FIGURE 1.8 Half Notes

Whole Notes

A whole note (𝅝) is a rhythm that receives four beats. It's twice as long as a half note and four times as long as a quarter note—count to yourself: one, two, three, four. A whole note is represented as an open circle without a stem. It is probably the single longest rhythmic value that you will come across. Whole notes are easy to spot because they are the only notes that lack a stem (see **FIGURE 1.9**).

FIGURE 1.9 Whole Notes

Eighth Notes

The smallest rhythm you have encountered thus far is the quarter note, which lasts for one beat. Dividing this beat further allows musicians to explore faster rhythms and faster passages. Chopping the quarter note in half gives us the eighth note (♪), which receives half of one beat (see **FIGURE 1.10**).

FIGURE 1.10 Eighth Notes

Sixteenth Notes

The beat can be broken down even further for the faster note values. The next rhythm is the sixteenth note (𝅘𝅥𝅯), which breaks the quarter note into four equal parts and the eighth note into two equal parts (see **FIGURE 1.11**).

FIGURE 1.11 Sixteenth Notes

Faster Note Values

It's possible to keep chopping the beat into smaller and smaller parts. The next step beyond sixteenth notes is the thirty-second note, which breaks one beat into eight equal parts. Just like the transition from eighth to sixteenth notes, going from sixteenth to thirty-second notes will add another flag or beam to the notes. Add another flag and it will simply make the note value half the length of the previous note. **FIGURE 1.12** shows faster note values.

FIGURE 1.12 Faster Note Values

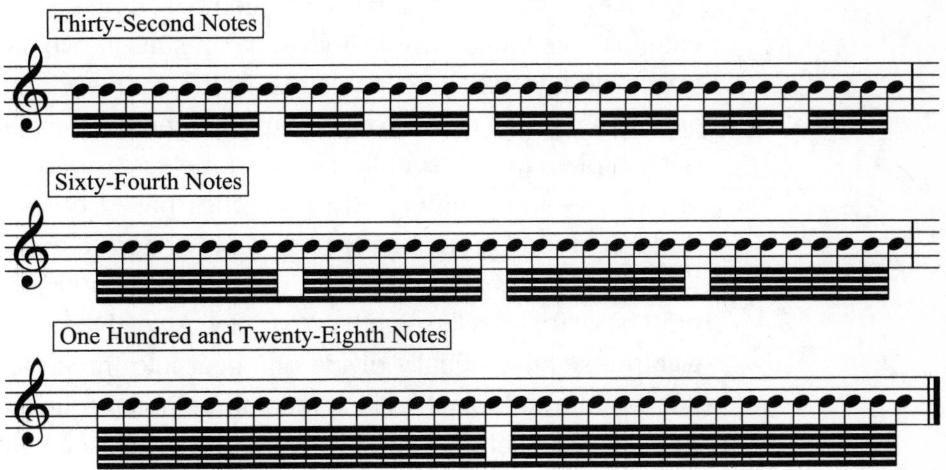

Augmentation Dots

FIGURE 1.13 Dotted Rhythms

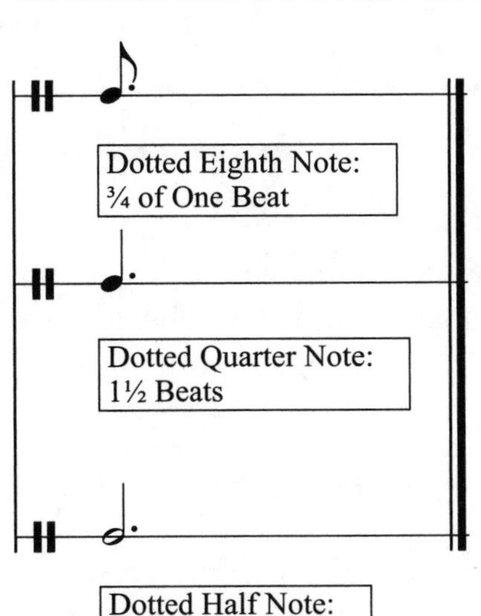

You have focused on making note values smaller and smaller, but you can also make them larger by using an augmentation dot. Placing a small dot directly to the right of any note increases its duration by one-half. For example, placing a dot after a half note makes the dotted half last for three beats. The original half note receives two beats and the dot adds half the value of the original note (a half note): The dot adds one extra beat (a quarter note), bringing the total up to three beats. Any note can be dotted. **FIGURE 1.13** is a chart of dotted rhythms and their duration.

POINT TO CONSIDER

A dot extends the value of a note. A tie also extends notes. Both do the same thing, but visually, they do it differently. A dot added to a note requires that you figure out what half of the note value is and count it. A tie is sometimes easier to read because the notes are visually glued together.

Tuplets

Up to this point, rhythms have been based on equal divisions of two. For example, breaking a whole note in half results in two half notes. In the same way, dividing a half note in two results in two quarter notes. As the divisions get smaller, going through eighth and sixteenth notes, the notes are continuously broken in half equally. However, beats can also be broken into other groupings—most importantly, groupings based on odd numbers such as three. Such odd groupings are commonly referred to as tuplets.

When you break a beat into three parts, you give birth to a triplet. The most basic triplet is the eighth-note triplet. An eighth-note triplet is simply three eighth notes that equally divide one beat into three parts (see **FIGURE 1.14**). You could also look at it like a ratio: three notes equally divided in the same space as one beat. Since there are three notes in each beat, eighth-note triplets are faster than two eighth notes taking up the same beat. The more notes per beat, the faster they progress.

FIGURE 1.14 Eighth-Note Triplets

Tuplets don't have to be in threes, although that is the most common tuplet in music. You can have tuplets that divide a beat into any number of parts: five, seven, even eleven. The number above the grouping of notes indicates how it's supposed to be divided.

Rests

All this talk about notes and rhythms wouldn't be complete without some discussion of rests. The best news of the day is that everything you've learned about rhythms also applies to rests. The only difference is that a rest tells you not to do anything! At last, you get a break.

Every pitch needs duration. Rhythm defines how long notes should be sustained. Music isn't always about sound—rests are as common as pitches. Rests indicate a spot in the music where you don't play a sound. Since a rest does not have a pitch associated with it, it requires a different symbol. Here's a chart of the rests (see **FIGURE 1.15**) and their associated notes.

FIGURE 1.15 Rests

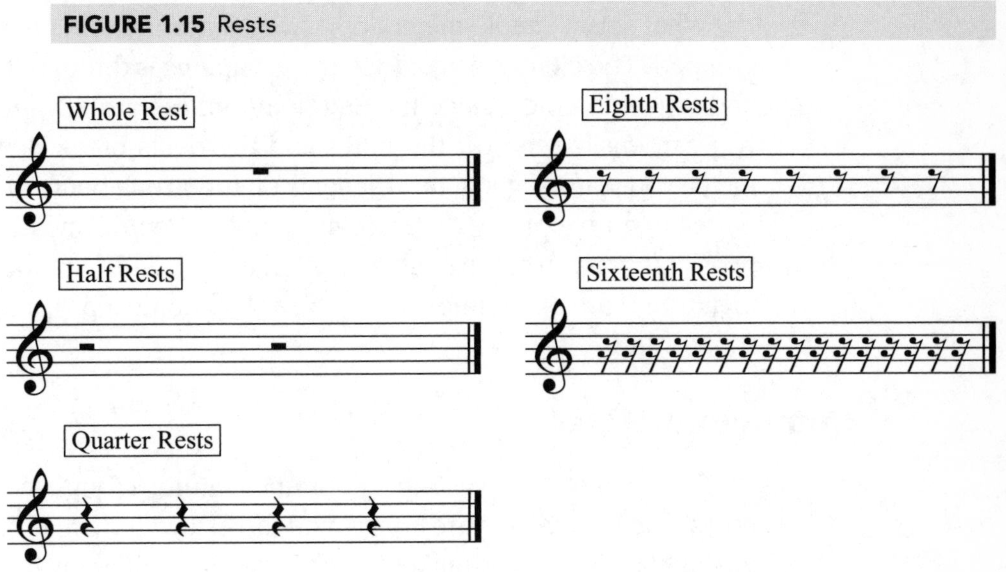

Meter

The last thing to explain is meter. You encountered one meter at the beginning of this chapter: common time, or $\frac{4}{4}$ meter. Now take a bit of time and look at the different meters.

Simple Meter

A simple meter is any meter that breaks the beat up into even divisions. This means that whatever the beat is—whether it's $\frac{4}{4}$, $\frac{3}{4}$, or $\frac{2}{4}$—each beat (which is a quarter note) is equally divided. The beat is broken into even divisions of two (eighth notes), four (sixteenth notes), or eight (thirty-second) notes.

FIGURE 1.16 Common Simple Meters

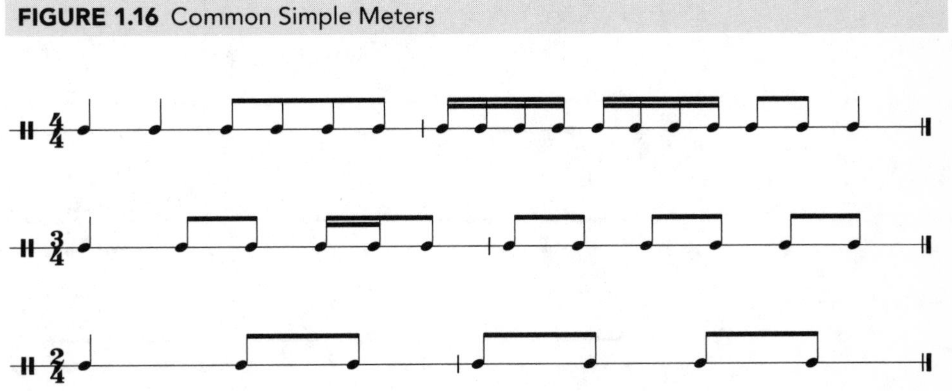

What sets a simple meter apart from other meters is how the beats are grouped. The clearest way to see the groupings is through the use of eighth and sixteenth notes. Since the flags join and are visually grouped together, you can easily see how the notes and the beats break down. In a simple meter, you place slight natural accents on the strong beats, which are always on the first note of any rhythmic grouping. Whenever notes are grouped in twos or fours, you are in simple time. Since $\frac{4}{4}$, $\frac{3}{4}$, and $\frac{2}{4}$ are the most common meters and are all in simple time, you will become a pro at simple meters in short order!

Compound Meter

Simple meters have one important feature: groupings of two or four notes. The next meters are compound meters, which are broken into groups of three. This is what makes compound time different from simple time. Common compound meters are $\frac{3}{8}$, $\frac{6}{8}$, $\frac{9}{8}$, and $\frac{12}{8}$. Compound meters usually have an 8 in the lower part of the meter because the meter is based on eighth notes receiving the beat.

Compound time relies on groupings of three notes, so you need to adjust how you view beat durations. A click on the metronome does not always signify a quarter note. What it does signify is the pulse of the music. In common time, that click could be a dotted quarter note, so keep your concept of time elastic.

FIGURE 1.17 Common Compound Meters

FIGURE 1.17 illustrates the three-note groupings of compound meters. That is, $\frac{3}{8}$ simply contains one grouping of three, $\frac{6}{8}$ two groupings of three, and so on. Counting in $\frac{4}{4}$ and other simple meters hasn't been such a big deal. Simply set your metronome or tap your foot along with the quarter notes. In compound time, your beat becomes a grouping of three notes—more specifically, a grouping of three eighth notes (although if you were in $\frac{3}{16}$, three sixteenth notes would get the beat, but since time is all relative, it all works out the same).

The combination of simple and compound time signatures will get you through most music you'll encounter. Even so, composers and musicians love to stretch the boundaries. All of the meters you've learned about so far have been divided into easy groupings. Other music exists in unusual groupings, called odd time.

Odd time or an odd meter is a meter that is asymmetric or has uneven groupings. Odd time can be expressed whenever 5, 7, 10, 11, 13, and 15 are the top value in a time signature. The bottom of the signature can be any rhythmic value; the top number determines if it's symmetric (simple) or asymmetric (odd) time. Take a look at a basic odd meter like $\frac{5}{4}$ in **FIGURE 1.18**.

FIGURE 1.18 Odd Time

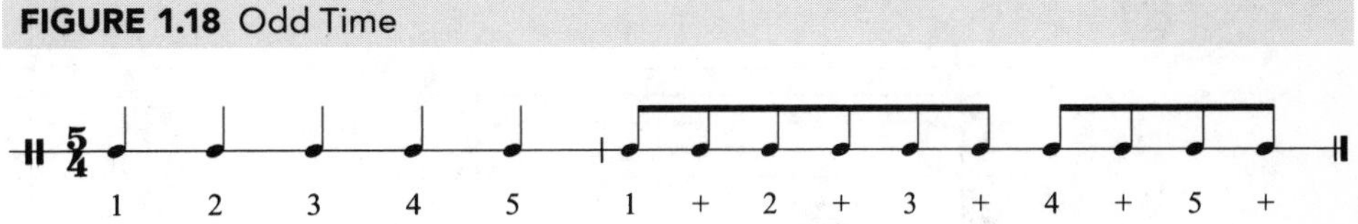

ETUDES

At the end of each chapter, you'll have the chance to practice the concepts you've just read about. Each chapter will have five pages of exercises to help you hone your skills. Appendix D contains the completed examples so you can check the accuracy of your work. If possible, write the etudes in pencil in the book, or on scrap music paper so that you can revisit them later.

ETUDE 1.1 Etude One

Name the following treble clef notes

ETUDE 1.2 Etude Two

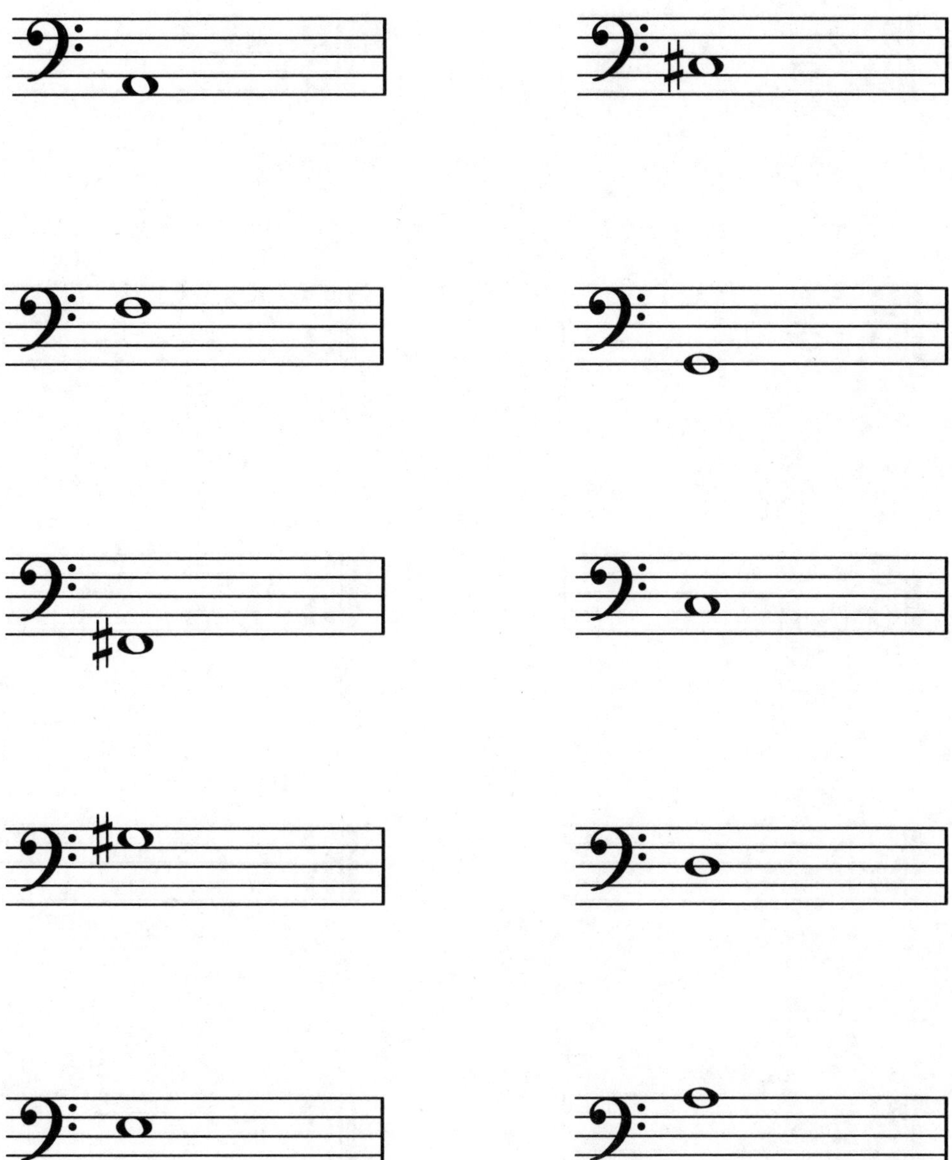

ETUDE 1.3 Etude Three

Name the following alto clef notes

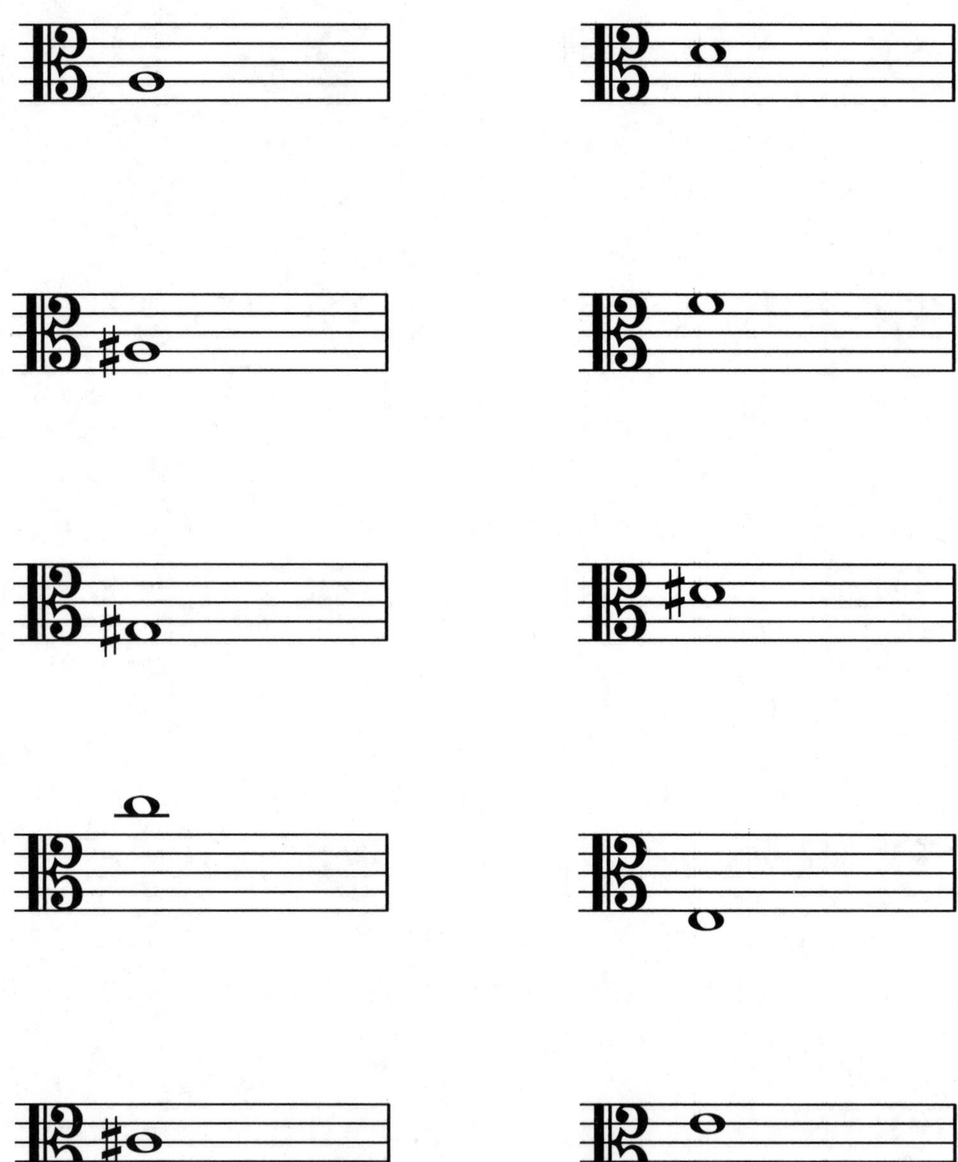

ETUDE 1.4 Etude Four

Count the beats in the following measures.
Circle if the measure has too few or too many notes
for the given time signature.

ETUDE 1.5 Etude Five

CHAPTER 2

Intervals

The most elemental part of music theory is to understand the relationships between single notes. The distance between those notes is an interval, which will serve as the foundation for practically every concept that you will explore throughout this book. Understanding intervals is extremely important.

Go the Distance

Defined as the distance from one note to another, intervals provide the basic framework for everything else in music. Small intervals combine to form scales. Larger intervals combine to form chords. Intervals aid in voice leading, composition, and transposition. There are virtually no musical situations that don't use intervals (barring snare drum solos). Even in some of the extremely dissonant music of the twentieth century, intervals are still the basis for most composition and analysis.

There are five different types of intervals:

1. Major intervals
2. Minor intervals
3. Perfect intervals
4. Augmented intervals
5. Diminished intervals

You will learn all about the five types of intervals in this chapter, but before you go any further, you need a visual helper, like a musical slide rule: the piano keyboard. Intervals can seem like an abstract concept; having some visual relationships to reference can make the concept more concrete and easier to grasp. **FIGURE 2.1** shows the piano keyboard.

FIGURE 2.1 The Piano Keyboard

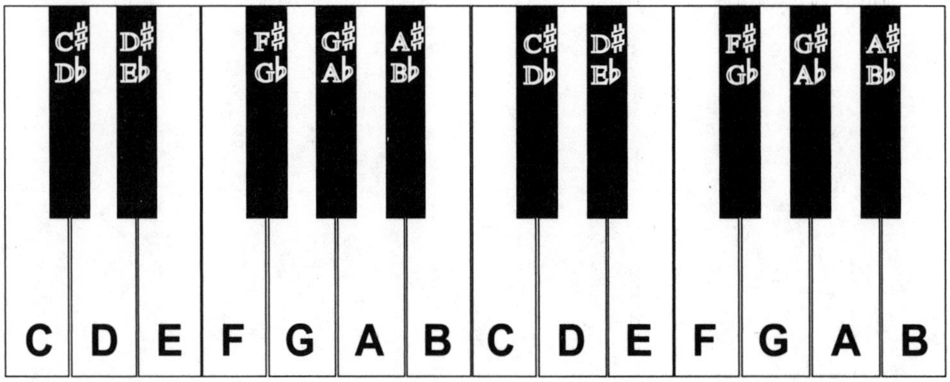

This image will be repeated at different times throughout this book, but earmark this page for reference because you're going to need it.

The keyboard shows you the location of all the notes within one full octave. It also shows you all the sharps and flats on the black keys.

Notice how C♯ and D♭ occupy the same key. This situation, in which one key can have more than one name, is called an enharmonic. This occurs on all black keys. The white keys have only one name, whereas the black keys always have a second possibility. This will be explained further along in this book.

Half Steps

The first interval to look at is the half step. It is the smallest interval that Western music uses (Eastern music uses quarter tones, which are smaller than a half step), and it's the smallest interval you can play on the majority of musical instruments. How far is a half step? Well, if you look at a piece of music, a great example of a half step is the distance from C to C♯ or D♭—remember that C♯ and D♭ sound the same. **FIGURE 2.2** shows the half step in a treble staff.

FIGURE 2.2 Half Step

Now that you have been given a rudimentary explanation of a half step, go back to the piano. Stated simply, the piano is laid out in successive half steps starting from C. To get to the next available note, you simply progress to the next available key. If you are on a white key, like C, for example, the next note is the black key of C♯/D♭. You have moved a half step. Move from the black key to the white key of D and you've moved another half step. When you've done this twelve times, you have come back around to C and completed an octave, which is another interval.

Now, this is not always a steadfast rule. It is not always the case that you will move from a white key to a black key, or vice versa, in order to move a half step.

As you can see in **FIGURE 2.3**, the movement between E and F and the movement between B and C are both carried out from white key to white key, with no black key between them. This means that B and C, and E and F, are a half step apart. This is called a natural half step, and it is the only exception to our half-step logic. The good news is that if you keep this in mind, all intervals will be much easier to define, not just half steps.

FIGURE 2.3 Hidden Half Steps

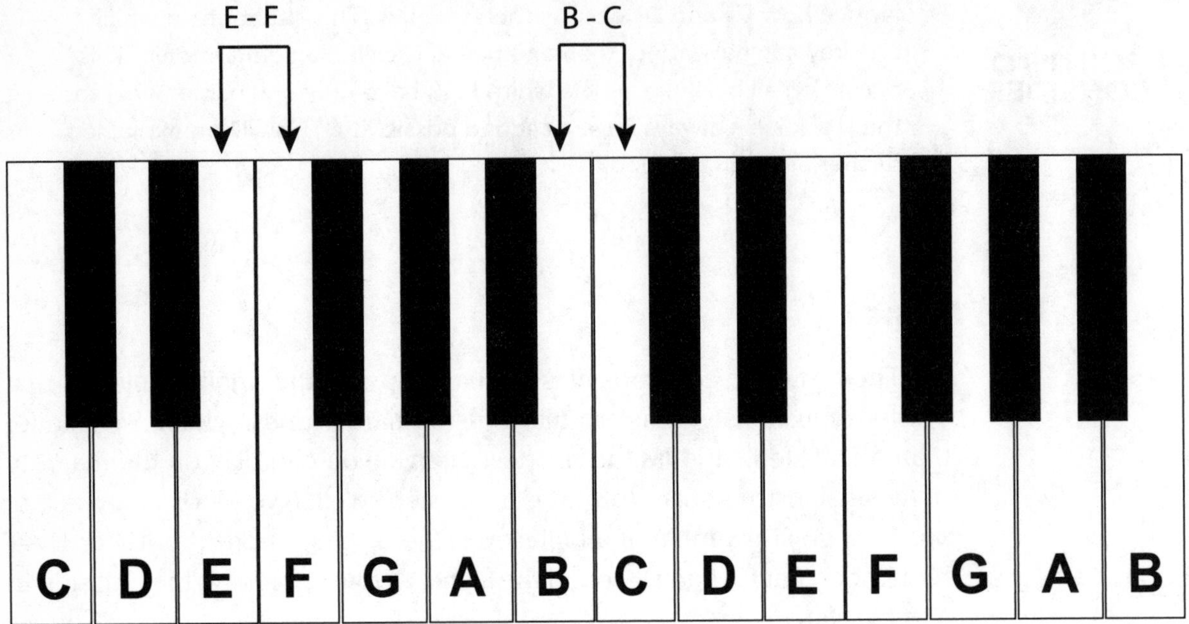

Why is there a half step between B and C and E and F when everywhere else it takes a whole step to get to the next letter name? The answer is simpler than you think. The sound of the C major scale (C–D–E–F–G–A–B–C) came first. The scale happened to have a half step between E and F and B and C. When the system of music was broken down and actually defined, that scale was laid out in white keys and had to fit the other half steps between the other notes. It really is arbitrary and provides another argument for the fact that sounds come first and then they are named or explained.

Whole Steps

A whole step is simply the distance of two half steps combined. Movements from C to D or F♯ to G♯ are examples of whole steps. If you are getting the hang of both whole and half steps, you can take this information a bit further. You could skip to scales, which would, in turn, lead you to chords.

The intervals between E and F and B and C are still natural half steps. **FIGURE 2.4** gives an example.

FIGURE 2.4 Unusual Whole Steps

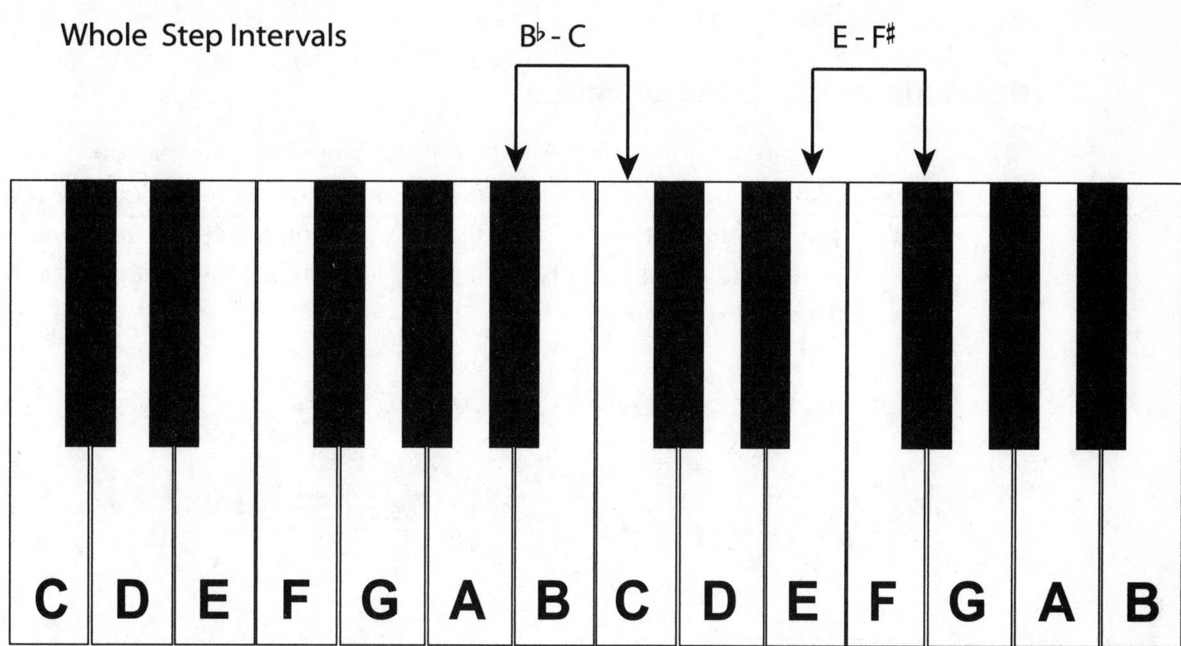

A whole step from E ends up on F♯ because you have to go two half steps to get to F♯, passing right by F♮. The same holds true for B♭ to C.

Now that you have gone through half and whole steps, the next step is the C major scale to see some of the other intervals out there.

Intervals from Scales

You may be wondering why a discussion of the C major scale appears in the interval chapter, when, according to the plan of the book, scales appear in the next chapter. Simply put, once you know whole and half steps, you can spell any scale, but more important, the other intervals are much easier to see and learn through the use of a scale.

Usually when musicians name a large interval, they don't count the numbers of half steps they need to figure out the answer. They are so familiar with scales that they use that information to solve their puzzle. Scales are such useful bits of information, and they are, of course, made up of simple intervals!

Consider this a sneak peek at scales; you will get the full scoop in the next chapter.

Intervals in the C Major Scale

Forming a C major scale is pretty simple: You start and end on C, use every note in the musical alphabet, and use no sharps or flats. Because the C major scale contains no sharps or flats, it's very easy to spell and understand. It's the scale you get if you play from C to C on just the white keys of a piano. **FIGURE 2.5** shows the scale.

FIGURE 2.5 The C Major Scale

Look at the distance between any two adjacent notes in the scale, and you will see that this is simply a collection of half and whole steps. Now try skipping around the scale and see what intervals you come up with. Start with C as a basis for your work for now. Every interval will be the distance from C to some other note in the C scale.

To start simply, measure the distance where there is no distance at all. An interval of no distance is called unison. See **FIGURE 2.6.**

TRACK 1

FIGURE 2.6 Unison Interval, C to C

Unison is more important than you think. While you won't see it in a solo piano score—you couldn't play the same key twice at the same time—when you learn to analyze a full score of music, it's handy to be able to tell when instruments are playing exactly the same notes and not other intervals, like octaves.

The movement from C to D is a whole step, but the interval is more formally called a major second. Every major second comprises two half steps' distance. See **FIGURE 2.7.**

TRACK 2

FIGURE 2.7 Major Second, C to D

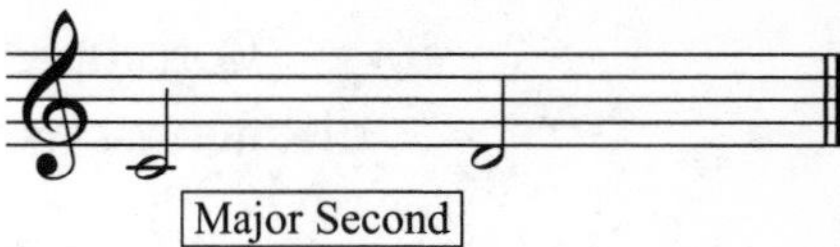

The next interval is from C to E, which is four half steps' distance. It is more formally called a major third (**FIGURE 2.8**).

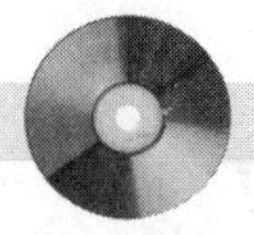
TRACK 3

FIGURE 2.8 Major Third, C to E

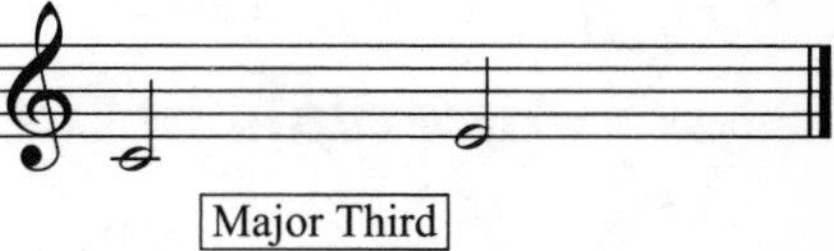

Next up is the distance from C to F, which is five half steps. It is formally called a perfect fourth, as seen in **FIGURE 2.9.**

TRACK 4

FIGURE 2.9 Perfect Fourth, C to F

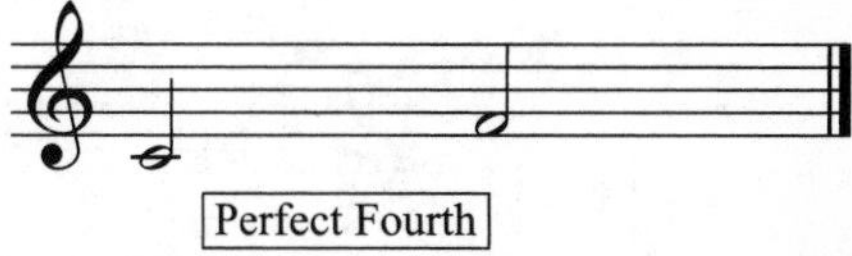

Perfect fourth? Are you confused yet with the naming of these intervals? Hang in there! Before you get to why this is so and the logic behind it, finish the scale. You have only begun to chip away at intervals.

The next interval is the distance from C to G. It is seven half steps and is formally called a perfect fifth (**FIGURE 2.10**).

TRACK 5

FIGURE 2.10 Perfect Fifth, C to G

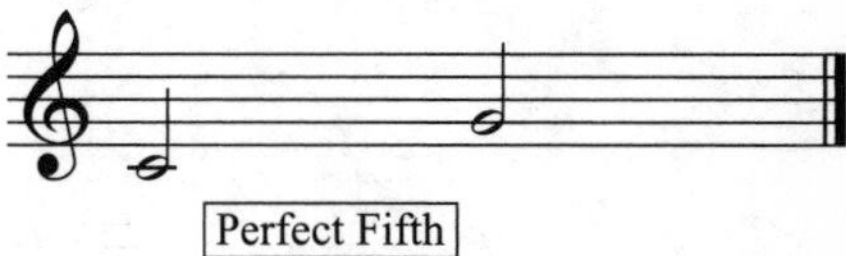

The interval from C to A, which is nine half steps, is formally called a major sixth. **FIGURE 2.11** presents a major sixth.

TRACK 6

FIGURE 2.11 Major Sixth, C to A

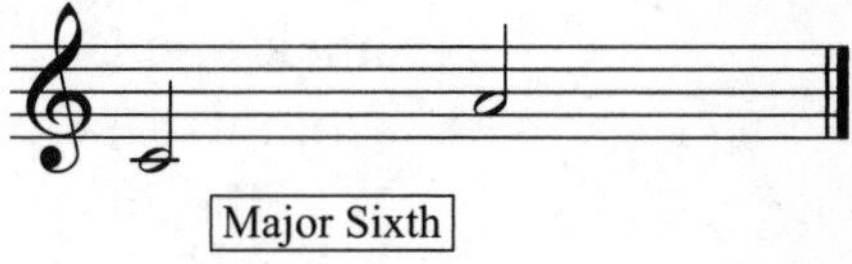

The next interval, from C to B, is eleven half steps. It is formally called a major seventh (see **FIGURE 2.12**).

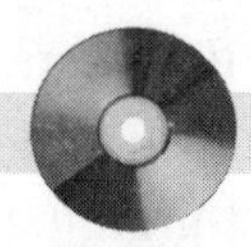
TRACK 7

FIGURE 2.12 Major Seventh, C to B

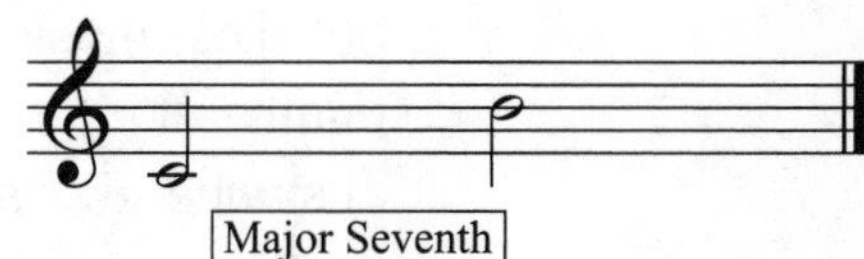

To complete this scale, the last interval will be C to C. This interval is a distance of twelve half steps, or an octave (see **FIGURE 2.13**).

FIGURE 2.13 Octave, C to C

Intervals in the C Minor Scale

Now that you've seen the intervals in the C major scale, here is the whole C minor scale and all of its intervals. Look at **FIGURE 2.14**. What do you see?

FIGURE 2.14 Minor Scale Intervals

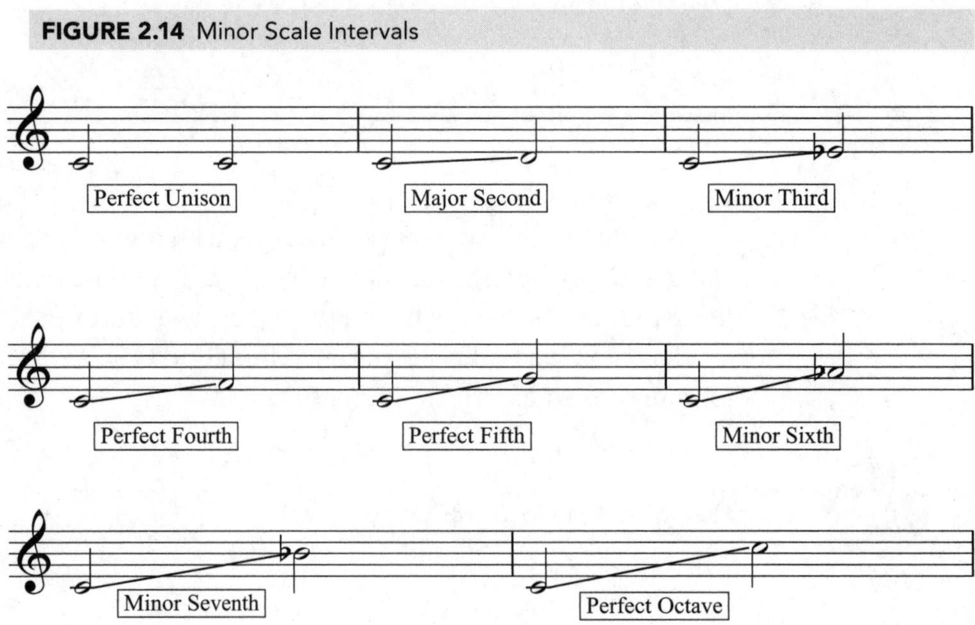

For starters, the third, sixth, and seventh intervals are now minor. That makes sense because those are the three notes that are different when you compare a C major and a C minor scale side by side, as in **FIGURE 2.15**.

The intervals that were perfect in the major scale remain the same between both scales. However, the second note of the scale (C to D) remains the same in both scales, yet that interval is called a major second.

Why are scales so important when dealing with intervals? Can't intervals be measured on their own, separately from a scale? Of course, that's right, but most musicians become very comfortable with scales and use them to figure out intervals because scales are a point of reference. If you ask a musician what the interval is between A and F, it's likely that he will think first of an A major scale and then determine if F♯ is in the A scale. Since it is, he will

FIGURE 2.15 Major and Minor Scale Comparison

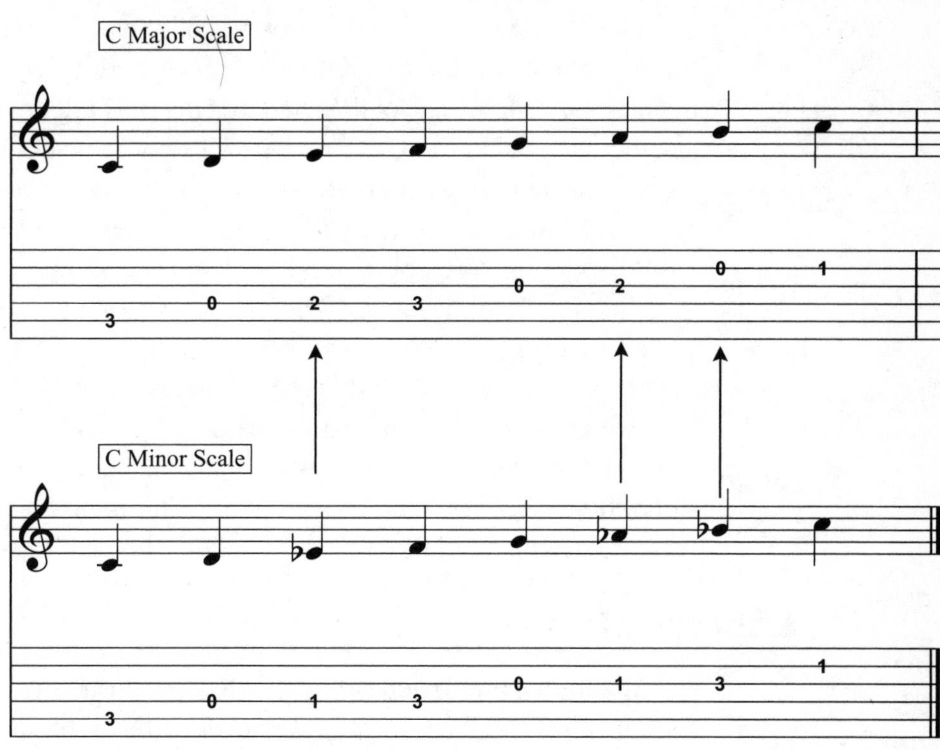

quickly lower the F♯ from a major sixth down to a minor sixth, and that's the answer. Otherwise, he would have to count half steps (a tedious process), or memorize every possible interval combination in music, and that has its own obvious disadvantages. (It might happen naturally over time but not overnight.) Certain intervals are easy to memorize, but most musicians remember scales since they know them so well. What you don't see in either the major or minor scale is diminished or augmented intervals. That's not to say they aren't there; it just depends on how you look at it. Suffice it to say that major, minor, and perfect intervals are the most basic intervals, and they are the easiest to spell and understand because they naturally occur in the major and minor scales that you play so much. Augmented and diminished intervals are less common but are equally important to know and understand.

POINT TO CONSIDER

When you measure a musical interval, *always* count the first note as one step. For example, C to G is a fifth because you have to count C as one. This is the most common mistake students make when they are working with musical intervals. They often come up one short because they forget to count the starting spot as one.

Quality and Distance

Intervals have two distinct parts: quality and distance. Quality refers to the first part of an interval, either major or perfect, as you saw from the C major scale intervals. Now, these are not the only intervals in music, these are just the intervals in the C scale; you will see the rest of the intervals shortly. Distance is the simplest part—designations such as second, third, and fourth refer to the absolute distance of the letters. For example, C to E will always be a third apart, because there are three letters (C, D, and E) from C to E.

The numerical distance is the easiest part of intervals: Simply count the letters! Determining the quality of an interval is a different story. In the C major scale, there are two different qualities of intervals: major and perfect. Why were some of them major and what's so perfect about the fourth and the fifth? At first, learning all of these rules is challenging, but when you understand the basics, you can do so much. As for interval quality, it's only when you understand all of the different qualities that you can name any interval.

Enharmonics

An interval has to determine the distance from any note to another note. As you can see in the C major scale, every interval has a distance and a quality to it. Confusion arises because notes can have more than one name. You might recall enharmonics (it was mentioned at the beginning of the chapter), where C♯ and D♭ sound the same yet are different notes when written.

In analyzing written music, you have to deal with what you are given. When you listen to any interval, you hear the sound—you don't listen to the spelling—so the distance from C to D♯ will sound just like C to E♭. What you hear is the sound of those notes ringing together, but if you had to analyze it on paper, you'd be looking at two different intervals (one is a minor third and the other is an augmented second) with two different names. The system of intervals has evolved somewhat strangely and with a certain amount of ambiguity because enharmonics is built into written music.

IN TIME

Many modern theorists and composers don't use the traditional intervallic system. Instead, they use a more numerically based system of organization, called set or set theory, which bases intervallic measurements on pure distance-based relationships in half steps. This system solves the ambiguity with enharmonic intervals. So, instead of a major third, it would be a five because a major third is five half steps.

The Simple Intervals

As previously mentioned, there are five distinct types of interval qualities: major, minor, perfect, diminished, and augmented. The distance of an interval always consists of the quality first, followed by the numerical measure of how many notes you are traveling, for example, major sixth. The simple intervals—major, minor, and perfect—are presented first, followed by diminished and augmented intervals in the next section.

Major Intervals

Major intervals apply only to distances of seconds, thirds, sixths, and sevenths. A quick trick to spell any major interval is to look at the major scale being used. For example, if you wanted to find out what a major third was from the note E, you could spell the scale, name the third note of the E major scale, and that would be your answer. Many musicians use this method to spell intervals and scales.

The other way to figure out an interval is to look at the distance in half steps (or whole steps). This method precludes knowing the scale (which this book doesn't officially get to until next chapter). **TABLE 2.1** presents all the major intervals and their intervallic distances.

▼ **TABLE 2.1: MAJOR INTERVALS**

Type	Distance in Half Steps	Distance in Whole Steps
Major Second	two	one
Major Third	four	two
Major Sixth	nine	four and one half
Major Seventh	eleven	five and one half

That's all there is to major intervals!

Minor Intervals

Minor intervals are closely related to major intervals, as they also only exist as seconds, thirds, sixths, and sevenths. So, what's the difference between a major and a minor interval? Simply, a minor interval is exactly one half step smaller than a major interval. Look at **TABLE 2.2** on minor intervals and compare it to **TABLE 2.1** on the major intervals.

▼ TABLE 2.2: MINOR INTERVALS

Type	Distance in Half Steps	Distance in Whole Steps
Minor Second	one	one half
Minor Third	three	one and a half
Minor Sixth	eight	four
Minor Seventh	ten	five

You can name any major interval simply by looking at a major scale and counting. This works for the minor scale, but it's not perfect. If you spell out the minor scale, you do, in fact, get the minor third, minor sixth, and minor seventh, but beware of the second. A minor scale's second note is a major second from the root. If you need to measure a minor second, just remember that a minor second is the smallest interval in music: the half step.

Minor intervals are always exactly one half step lower than their major counterparts. So, if you have to name a minor interval and you're fast at the major intervals, simply lower any major interval exactly one half step and you will be there. **FIGURE 2.16** shows how this works.

FIGURE 2.16 Major Intervals to Minor

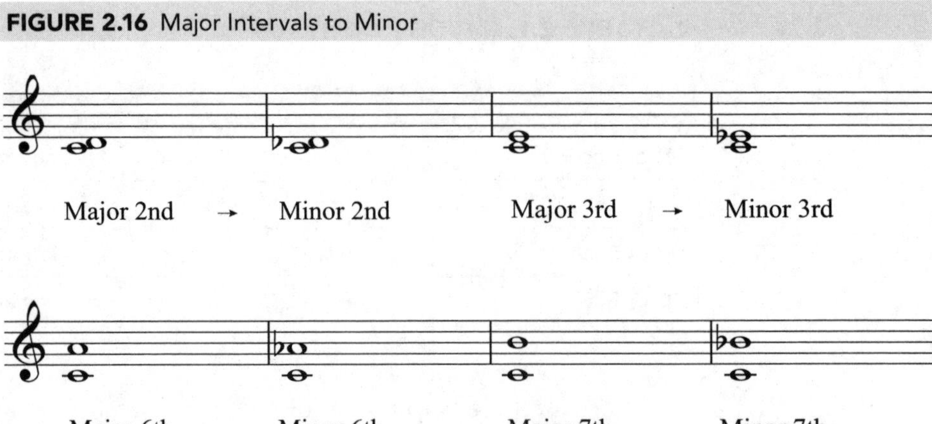

See, that isn't so bad! Just remember that major intervals are the larger of the two intervals when you compare major and minor intervals.

Strengthen your vocabulary! Instead of talking about half and whole steps, call them by their proper names. A half step is a minor second and a whole step is a major second.

Perfect Intervals

So far, the logic to naming interval quality has made sense: Major intervals come from major scales, and minor intervals (all except one) come from the minor scale. Now you come to perfect intervals, and you may be wondering what is so perfect about them. Here is a brief history lesson. As music was evolving, most music was monophonic, meaning that only one line was sung or played at a time. When musicians became daring enough to add a second line of music, they considered only certain intervals consonant and those were the ones that could be used. In the early days of polyphony, fourths and fifths were commonly used, so *perfect* seemed to fit because they almost never sounded bad. To modern ears, fourths and fifths don't always sound as nice as thirds or sixths do, but that's just a matter of taste. Back to the intervals! Perfect intervals encompass the following distances: unison (no distance at all), fourth, fifth, and octave.

Perfect intervals are fairly easy to spell because all the perfect intervals appear in both the major and the minor scales, so no matter what you are more comfortable spelling in, you'll find all the perfect intervals there. If you're up for counting in steps, look at **TABLE 2.3.**

▼ TABLE 2.3: PERFECT INTERVALS

Type	Distance in Half Steps	Distance in Whole Steps
Unison	N/A	N/A
Perfect Fourth	five	two and a half
Perfect Fifth	seven	three and a half
Perfect Octave	twelve	six

In contrast to major intervals that can be made into minor intervals by simply lowering them a half step, the perfect intervals are stuck. If you do anything to a perfect interval (flat or sharp one of the notes), you are changing the interval type away from being perfect. It always becomes something else. What it actually becomes is something discussed in the next section.

See, this isn't that bad. Intervals are fairly concrete and have an absolute distance; you can name them based on those parameters. Remember, though, naming an interval includes two parts: quality and distance. You have two more qualities to explore: augmented and diminished.

The term *octave* has the root *oct* like *octagon. Oct,* of course, is the prefix indicating eight, and an octave is the distance spanning eight notes. More important, an octave is the same letter name repeated at a higher part of the musical spectrum.

Advanced Intervals

The basic intervals of music are major, minor, and perfect. If you stopped there, you would have more than just a cursory understanding of intervals; you could do more than just get by. However, there are two more types of intervals that deal with the issue of enharmonic spellings of notes and other anomalies: augmented and diminished intervals.

As you know, the intervals of C to E♭ and C to D♯ sound exactly the same. The only thing that's different is the spelling of the D♯ and the E♭. That's called an enharmonic.

Now, the spelling of those intervals will change as the note changes its name—this is regardless of whether those intervals sound exactly the same. For example, if the interval is spelled C to E♭, the interval is called a minor third. If the interval is spelled C to D♯, you can't call it a minor third anymore. Third intervals are reserved for intervals of three notes (C to E). Since this interval is from C to D, it must be called a second of some sort. In this case, the correct name is an augmented second. Enharmonic spellings give birth to the need for terms like augmented and diminished intervals.

Augmented Intervals

An augmented interval is any interval that is larger than a major or perfect interval. **FIGURE 2.17** shows a few examples of augmented intervals.

Traditionally, you can only augment second, third, fourth, fifth, or sixth intervals, and you can only use augmented intervals when the notes are spelled in an unusual way. The logic is "if it's three notes apart, I have to call it some sort of third, and it's larger than a major third." The deciding factor is how the interval is spelled on paper. Use the distance between the notes as your guide. Again, augmented intervals are used when an interval is too large to be called major or perfect.

FIGURE 2.17 Augmented Intervals

Augmented 2nd

Augmented 3rd

Augmented 4th

Augmented 5th

Augmented 6th

Diminished Intervals

Diminished intervals are more specialized. A diminished interval is an interval that has been made smaller. Typically, diminished intervals are used only to make perfect intervals smaller. In reality, this is just another spelling convention. You can make a fourth or a fifth diminished by lowering any of the perfect intervals one half step. You can also make a minor interval diminished by simply lowering a minor interval one half step. The interval of C to E♭ is a diminished third. The interval of a diminished fifth is commonly called a tritone because, at six half steps, it splits the octave evenly in half (twelve half steps in an octave).

Both the diminished fifth and the augmented fourth are considered tritones—the spelling is not important, only the distance. The tritone is such a dissonant interval it was called *diablo en music* (the devil in music) during the Middle Ages and was something to avoid at all costs. Things have changed, and tritone intervals do occur in modern music, but they still sound dissonant.

Chromatic Intervals

The chromatic scale includes all twelve tones (including all the half tones) in the octave. Thus, chromatic intervals are a semitone apart.

FIGURE 2.18 provides a full chart of every possible interval and enharmonic spelling in one octave to show you how all this lays out. Notice how the number of half steps an interval has is not always the deciding factor in its name. Because of enharmonic spellings, there are pluralities. Always remember to look at the distance between the written notes, and then look for the quality.

Here is another way to understand intervals. If the top note of the interval exists in the major scale of the bottom note, the interval is major or perfect. If not, it's minor, diminished, or augmented. Here is a little chart to help you. Arrows indicate movement of a half step in either direction.

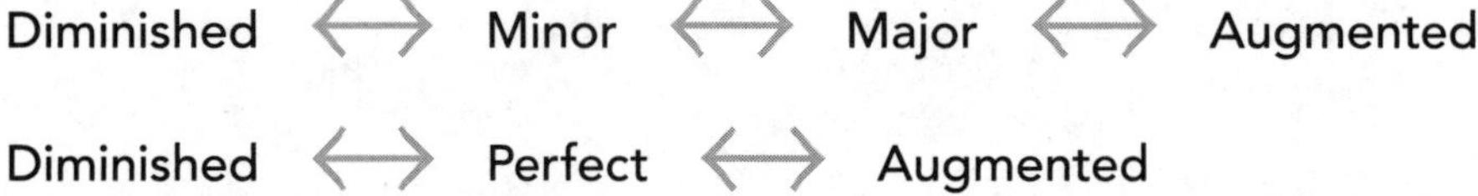

FIGURE 2.18 Chromatic Intervals

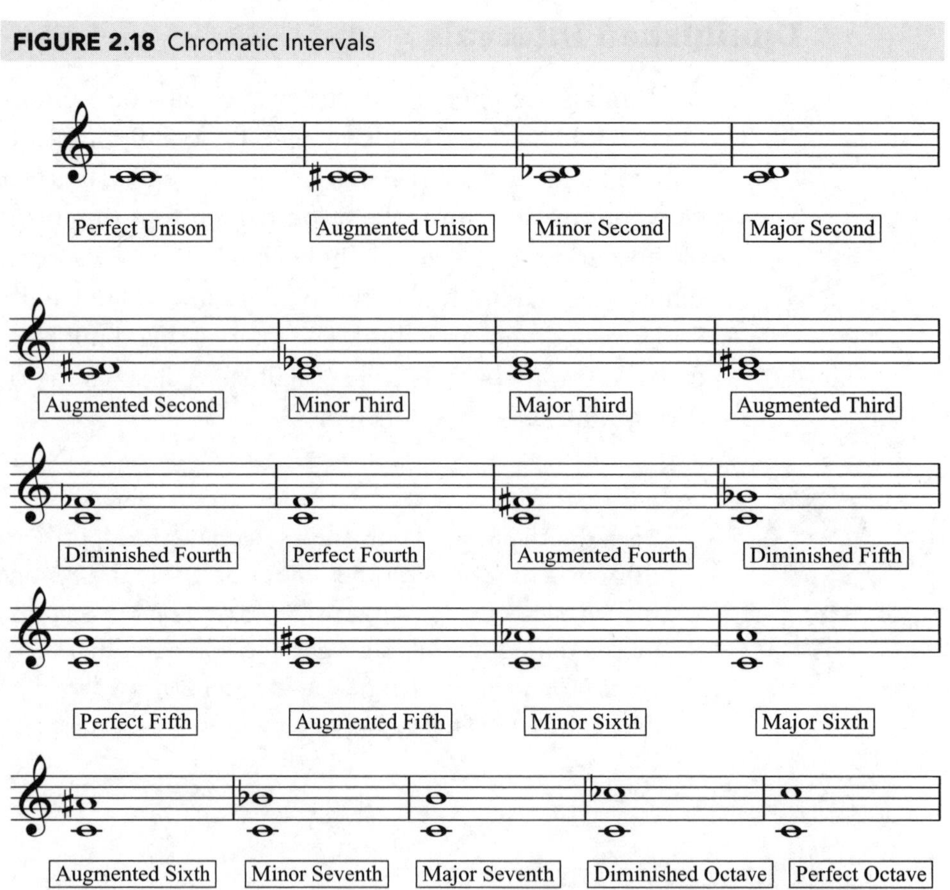

Inverted and Extended Intervals

How far is it from C to G? You might say a perfect fifth. You might be right. However, what if the interval went down? What if the C were written higher on the staff than the G? Would it still be a perfect fifth? In this case, it would actually be a perfect fourth.

So far, this text has dealt with ascending intervals. But what happens when you read a descending interval? When you name any interval, such as C to G, you must specify if it's an ascending interval or if it's descending. If the interval ascends, no worries, you've been trained to handle that without a problem. On the other hand, if the interval descends, it's not spelled the same way. A fifth interval, when flipped around, is not a fifth anymore because the musical scale is not symmetrical.

Interval Inversion

Any interval that ascends can be inverted (flipped upside down). **FIGURE 2.19** looks at the example of C to G from the last section. When you flip the perfect fifth, it becomes a perfect fourth. Wouldn't it be great if there were a system to help you invert any interval? Thankfully, there is. You are going to learn to use the rule of nine to invert any interval with ease.

FIGURE 2.19 Inverted Intervals

The Rule of Nine

The rule of nine is defined as: When any interval is inverted, the sum of the ascending and descending intervals must add up to nine. Using the first example, the interval from C to G is a perfect fifth. The interval from G to C is a perfect fourth. When you add up 5 and 4, you get 9. Test this in a few notation examples in **FIGURE 2.20**. What's the inversion of a third? It's a sixth, because 3 and 6 add up to 9. This rule works on any interval.

FIGURE 2.20 Inverted Intervals and the Rule of Nine

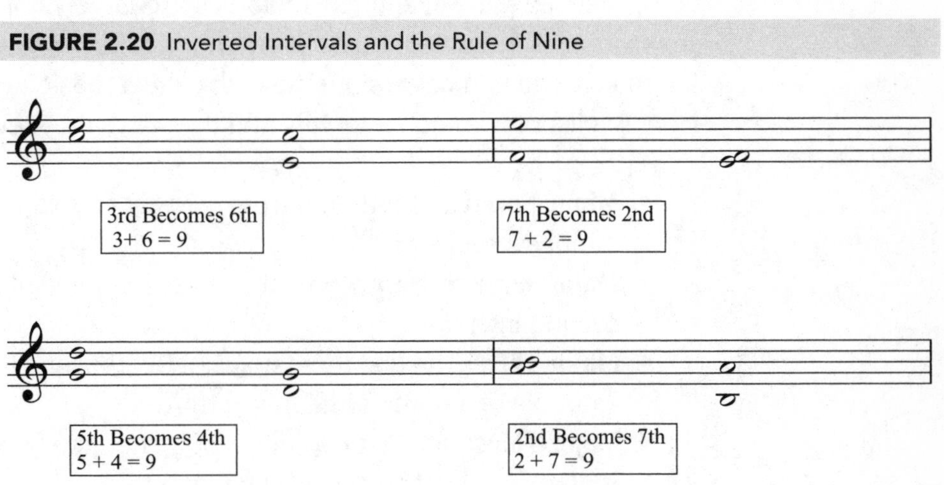

Inverted Qualities

When using the rule of nine, it's easy to flip the intervals over and get the correct inversion. But the type, or quality, of the interval also changes as you invert it. The rule of nine tells you the name of the interval numerically, but the type of interval that it becomes (major, minor, perfect) will change as the interval is flipped over. This problem has a simple solution. Here is what happens to interval qualities when the intervals invert.

- If the interval was major, it becomes minor when inverted.
- If the interval was minor, it becomes major when inverted.
- If the interval was perfect, it remains perfect when inverted.

This is easy to remember. Major becomes minor, minor becomes major, and perfect stays perfect. As you can see, by using the rule of nine and changing the type of interval accordingly, you can invert intervals like a pro!

Learning to Hear Intervals

Music theory doesn't just have to exist on paper. It can also be measured by ear. We're talking about the amazing human perception known as relative pitch and its elite cousin, absolute or perfect pitch. One way that you can accelerate your music theory ability is to use your ears. While perception is very hard to teach, you can still learn some tricks to make your hearing more acute. One technique that's used in teaching aural acuity is to relate intervals to famous songs. Can you sing the first few notes of "Here Comes the Bride"? If you said yes, then you can sing a perfect fourth at will. There are several well-known songs that can help you identify musical intervals completely by ear. Since these melodies are largely copyrighted, you won't see examples in written music. If you need to relate these melodies to written music, you can always purchase the sheet music and study from there. Here is a list of common intervals and the songs they relate to.

- **Minor Second:** The theme from *Jaws* is an example of an ascending minor second.
- **Major Second:** "Happy Birthday" is an example of an ascending major second interval.
- **Minor Third:** The first three notes of Beethoven's Fifth Symphony is an example of a descending minor third.
- **Major Third:** The first two notes of "When the Saints Go Marching In" is an example of an ascending major third.

- **Perfect Fourth:** The first two notes of "Here Comes the Bride" and "Amazing Grace" are examples of ascending perfect fourth intervals.
- **Tritone (Diminished 5th/Augmented 4th):** The first two notes of "Maria" from *West Side Story* and the theme from *The Simpsons* are examples of ascending tritone intervals.
- **Perfect Fifth:** The first four notes of "Twinkle, Twinkle Little Star" are an example of an ascending perfect fifth.
- **Minor Sixth:** Minor sixth intervals are hard, as the songs are bit more obscure. The first two melody notes of the theme to *Dr. Who* are an ascending minor sixth.
- **Major Sixth:** The theme music from the NBC chimes is an example of an ascending major sixth interval.
- **Minor Seventh:** The first two notes from the theme to *Star Trek* are an example of an ascending minor seventh.
- **Major Seventh:** The first two notes to the chorus of "Take On Me" by A-Ha and the first two notes to "Don't Know Why" by Norah Jones is an example of an ascending major seventh.
- **Perfect Octave:** The first two notes of "Somewhere over the Rainbow" from *The Wizard of Oz* is an example of an ascending perfect octave.

Relative Pitch Versus Perfect Pitch

What's the difference between relative pitch and perfect pitch? Relative pitch is the ability to discern intervals, qualities, and sounds by ear. You may not know the name of the individual pitches, but you can learn to hear a perfect fourth, or sing it out of thin air. Someone who possesses perfect pitch can identify note names by ear. They can hear single notes or chords/multiple notes at once and identify the names of each of the notes.

ETUDES

ETUDE 2.1 Etude One

Name or write the following major intervals

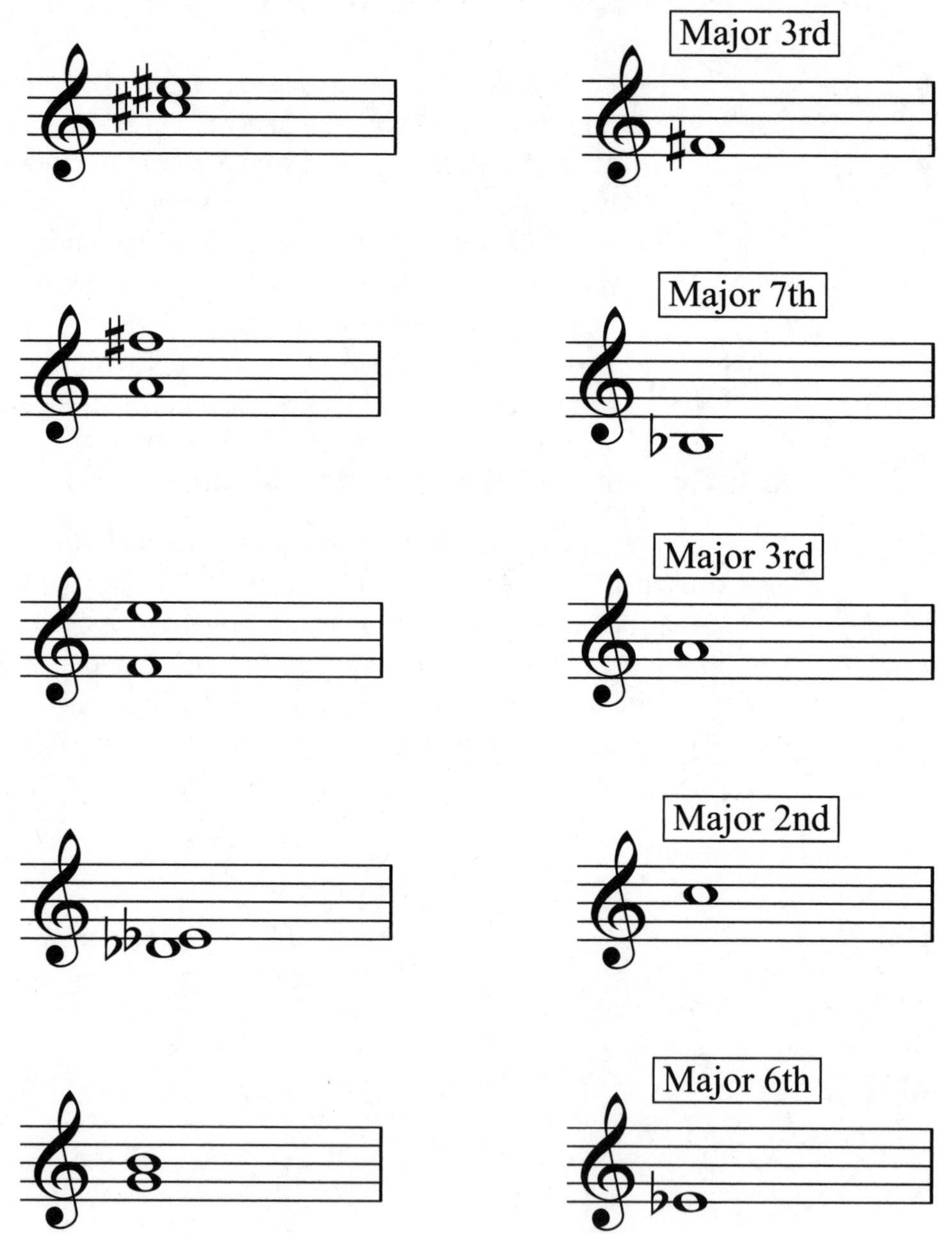

ETUDE 2.2 Etude Two

Name or write the following minor intervals

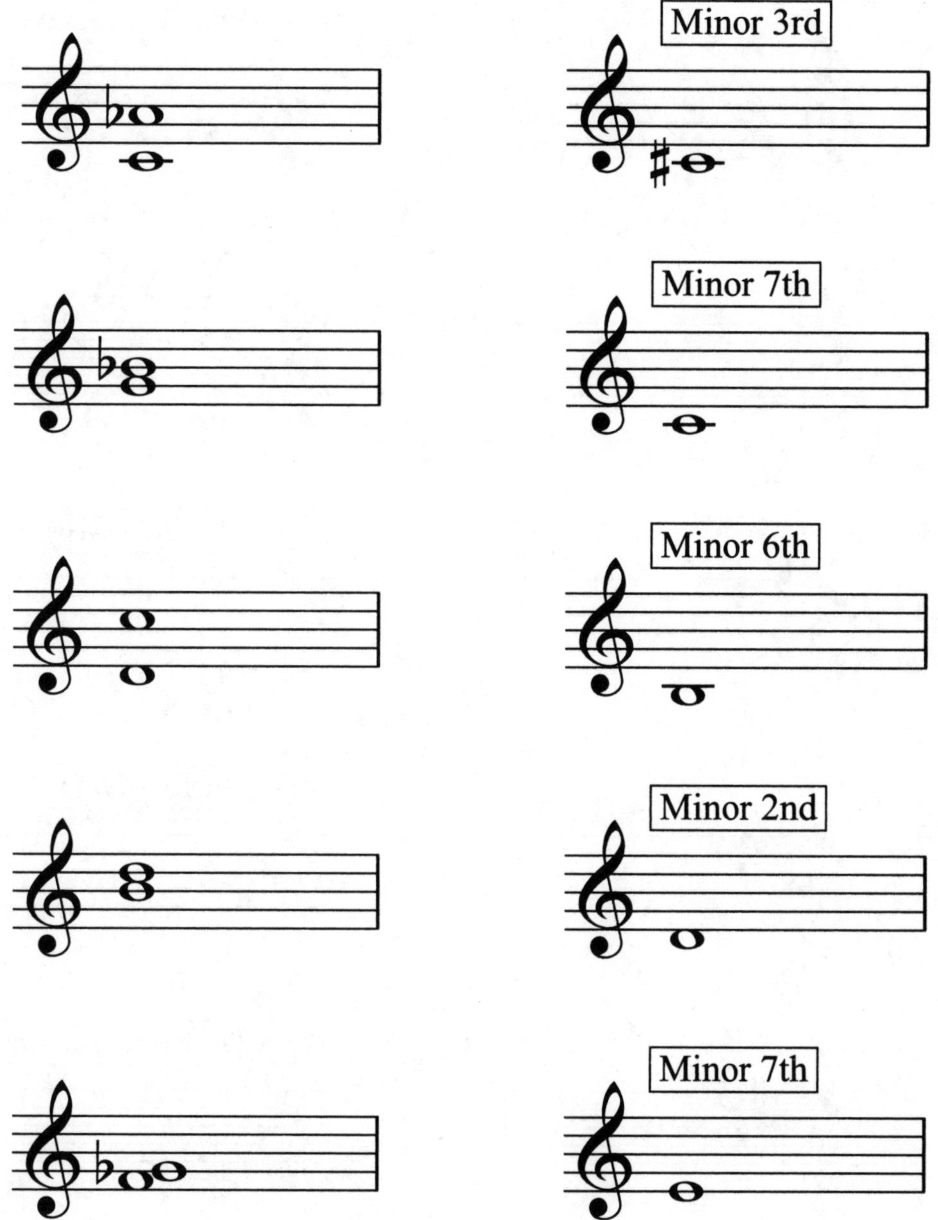

ETUDE 2.3 Etude Three

Name or write the following perfect intervals

ETUDE 2.4 Etude Four

Name or write the following augmented & diminished intervals

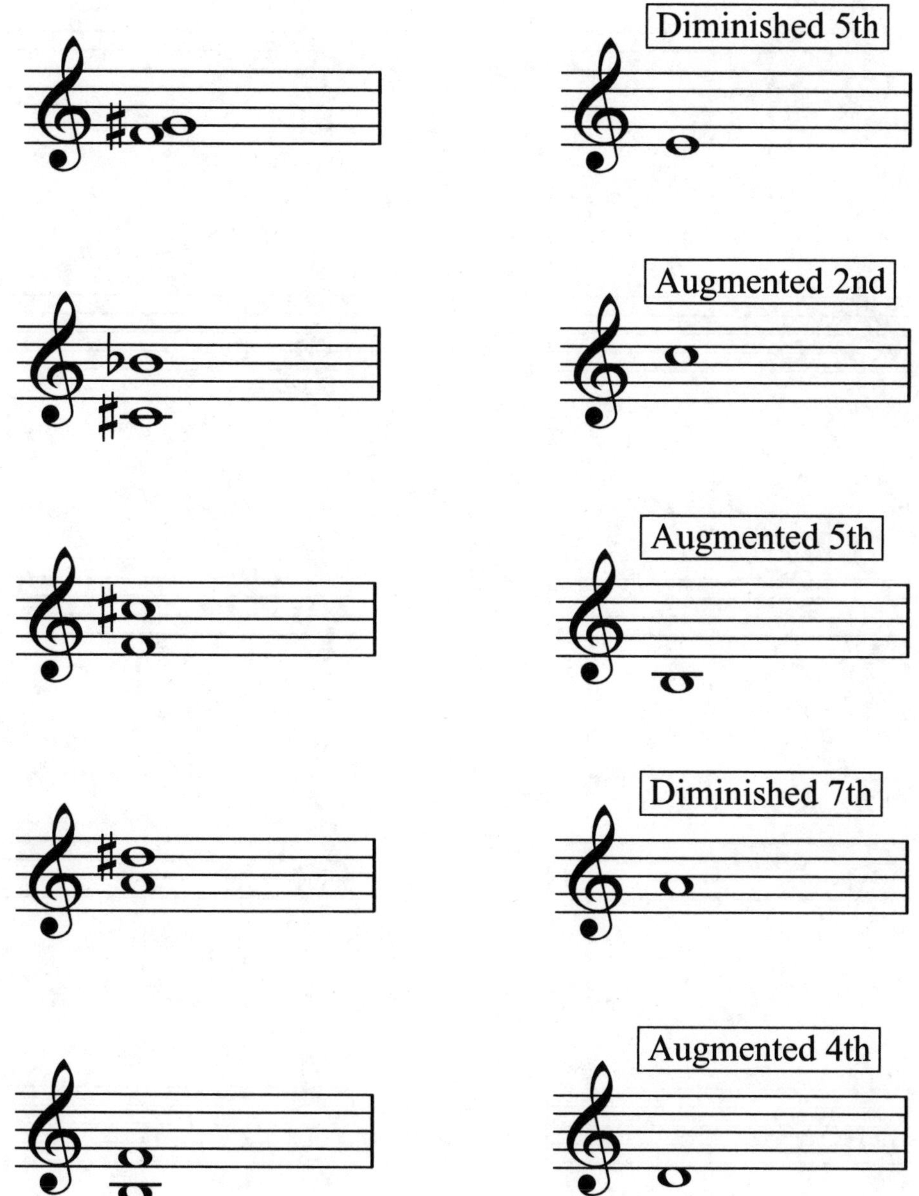

ETUDE 2.5 Etude Five

Name the original and inverted intervals

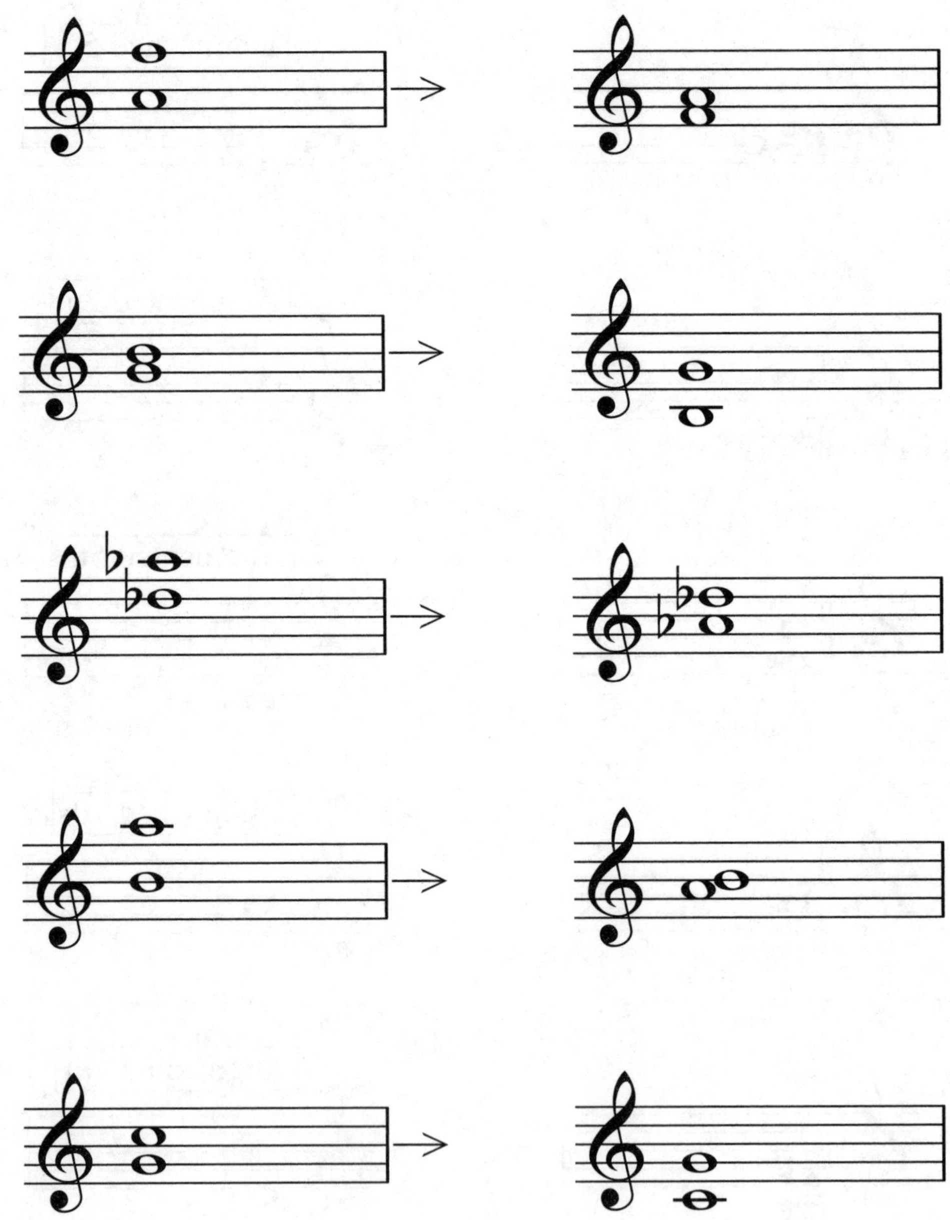

CHAPTER 3

The Major Scale

A simple formation of notes can bring you into the mind of the composer, allowing you to see what elements are used in composition. The major scale is one of the first such structural elements that you should study in music. Major scales are multifaceted and are used for melodies and harmonies. If you are interested in music theory, you should know as much as possible about the major scale.

Scales Defined

You've probably heard the term *major scale* many times. Many of you play scales in some shape or form and may not even realize it. Although scales were mentioned earlier, now it's time to look at them more closely. For starters, a scale is a grouping of notes that makes a key. Most of the scales you will encounter have seven different pitches (but a total of eight notes, including the repeated octave). Some scales contain more than seven notes, and some contain fewer. A scale is defined as a series of eight notes (seven different pitches) that start and end on the same note, which is also called the root. The root names the scale. If a scale starts and ends on C, the root is C and the scale's name is the C something (major, minor, etc.) scale. What that something is depends on its intervallic formula. Aren't you glad you know a thing or two about intervals? Since this chapter focuses on major scales, take a look at a very basic C major scale in **FIGURE 3.1**.

TRACK 9

FIGURE 3.1 The C Major Scale

As you can see, the scale starts and ends on C and progresses up every note in order. Since C major contains no sharps and no flats, it's an easy scale to understand and remember. On the piano, it's simply all the white notes. The C scale contains seven different notes: C, D, E, F, G, A, and B. Although the last C isn't counted because it's a repeated note, the major scale has eight notes in total.

What makes this a major scale is not the fact that it uses the notes C–D–E–F–G–A–B–C. That only tells you that it's one particular key. Music theory looks for larger-scale ideas and tries to tie them together. What makes that scale a major scale are the intervals between the notes. If you look at the distance from each note in the scale to the next, you see a pattern of half or whole steps in a series. This series, which you can also call a formula, is exactly what you are going to learn about now. **FIGURE 3.2** shows the C major scale with the intervals defined.

FIGURE 3.2 Intervals of the C Major Scale

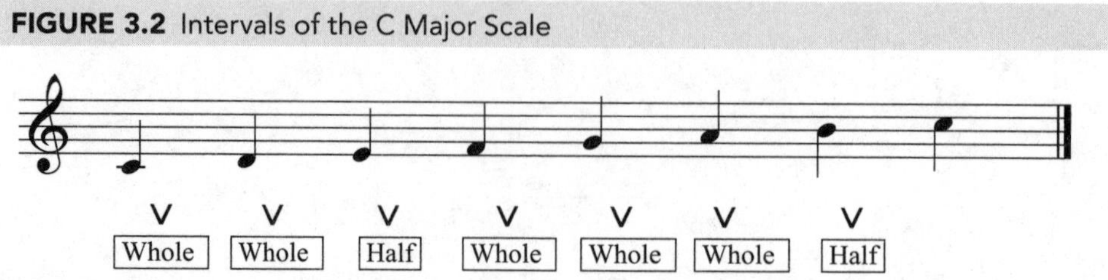

What you come up with is the interval series of Whole, Whole, Half, Whole, Whole, Whole, Half, or WWHWWWH. This is what makes one scale different from any other: the formula of the intervals. As long as that interval formula is present, you have a major scale. It's a perfect system, because you can start on any of the twelve chromatic notes and follow these rules:

1. Pick a root note.
2. Progress up seven notes until you reach the octave.
3. Use the formula of WWHWWWH between your notes to ensure that you have the correct spelling.
4. Make sure that you use any letter only once before the octave.

If you can follow these rules, you can spell any scale. Here's how.

Spelling Scales

Start out with a root note; in this example it will be A♭, as seen in **FIGURE 3.3**.

FIGURE 3.3 Building a Scale: *Step One*

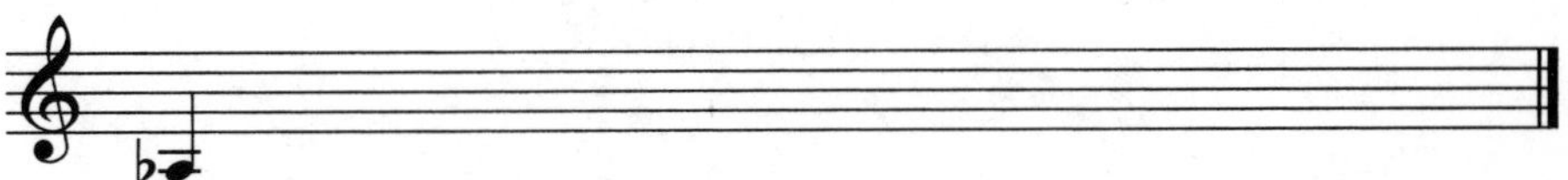

Next, place the rest of the notes on the staff. Now, don't be too concerned about whether you have the correct intervals or even the right spellings, you just need to have one of each letter name, in order, up to the octave. So simply add B–C–D–E–F–G–A to **FIGURE 3.4**.

FIGURE 3.4 Building a Scale: *Step Two*

Now that you have added in the raw notes, you need to add the intervals. The formula is WWHWWWH, so add the intervals between the notes of the scale, as seen in **FIGURE 3.5**.

FIGURE 3.5 Building a Scale: *Step Three*

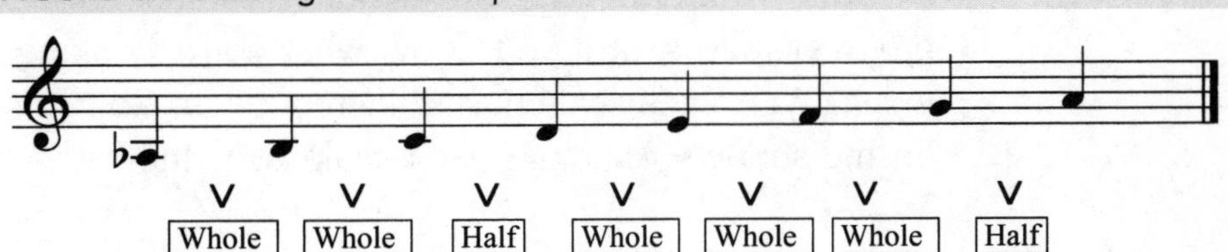

You're nearly done. Now just engage the intervals and make sure your scale is spelled correctly. Follow this process:

- You need a whole step from A♭. A whole step away would be B♭. Add a B♭ to the scale.
- You need a whole step from B♭. A whole step away would be C, which you already have written down, so you don't have to change anything.
- You need a half step from C. A half step away would be D♭, so put a flat in front of the D to make it D♭.
- You need a whole step from D♭. A whole step away is E♭, so make the E an E♭.
- You need a whole step from E♭. A whole step away is F, which you already have, so no change is needed.
- You need a whole step from F. A whole step away is G, which you also already have, so no change is needed.
- You need a half step from G. A half step away is A♭. Change the A to A♭. (Coincidentally, since this is a ♭ scale; every A in this scale is flat, so you could have just made it flat.)

Now, look at **FIGURE 3.6**.

FIGURE 3.6 Building a Scale: *Step Four*

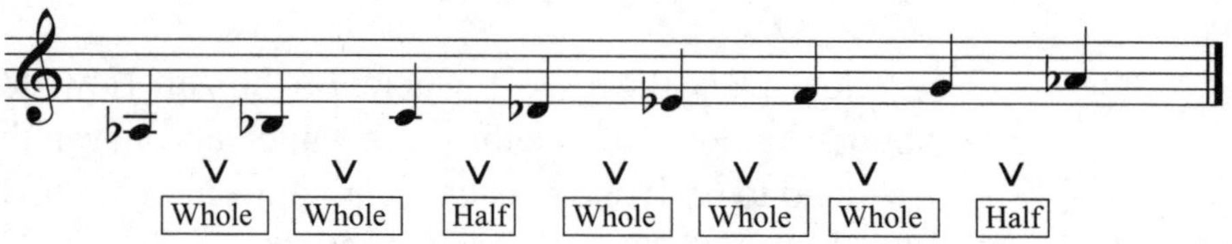

Whole Whole Half Whole Whole Whole Half

That's it! You have an ascending scale that uses every letter of the musical alphabet once. The scale follows the pattern of WWHWWWH, which all major scales follow. Play it on your instrument just to be sure, and that familiar sound will tell you that you're correct.

Some Thoughts

You have now seen a couple of major scales in this chapter. This is a good time to pause and point out some very interesting characteristics about scales.

First, scales are unique. They are a bit like DNA and that makes them pretty easy to spot if you know what you're looking for. What does that mean? Well, each scale has a different pitch. No two scales look the same on the surface. Although each scale uses the same interval pattern, that fact is not clear until you analyze the scale. The fact that each scale uses a unique set of pitches is what makes each one unique, and that is something that you can clearly see.

Ludwig van Beethoven (1770–1827) composed in almost every genre of music, including piano sonatas, chamber music, nine symphonies, and an opera. Although born in Bonn, Germany, he moved to Vienna, Austria, as a young man, where he wrote his most celebrated works, including the famous *Ode to Joy*.

Second, did you notice that the scales that contain sharps use only sharps and never throw in a flat or two? Also, the scales that contain flats use only flats and never sharps? That's right, when you spell scales or analyze in music, you will notice that scales have either flats or sharps; you rarely see both sharps and flats in the same scale (see Chapter 4 for the rare exceptions to this rule, posed by the harmonic and melodic minor scales). These two points will help you understand scales so much better and make your life in music theory so much easier.

Based on which chromatic note the scale starts on, you may get a scale that spells pretty easily. On the other hand, certain scales contain double flats or double sharps in order to keep the WWHWWWH pattern going and use each note in the alphabet. Some spell easily and others are a pain. As a result, some chromatic major scales don't appear often; you typically see scales that spell without constant use of double sharps and double flats.

Due to enharmonic notes, scales can have the same sound but be spelled differently. A good example is A♭ and G♯. The key of A♭ has four flats and isn't too hard to spell or read in. The key of G♯ has six sharps and a double sharp. Which would you rather read in if both scales actually sounded the same? Even though there are twenty-four possible scales, there are only twelve chromatic notes in the scale, and you will find yourself reading in the easiest twelve keys. Remember, music isn't just for the composer; it has to suit the player as well.

Knowing that flats and sharps are mutually exclusive items in scales should help you spell your scales more accurately. If you're spelling a scale and you see a mixture of flats and sharps, something's wrong. If you see mostly flats and one sharp, something's wrong. Scales will always look cohesive, and that will make your job a bit easier.

Scale Tones

Each scale has seven tones (eight, if you include the octave). There are two ways to talk about tones: by number and by degree.

Scale Tones by Number

In a C major scale, the note C is given the number one because it's the first note of the scale. Then, each of the scale tones, one through seven, can be assigned a different note. This is useful for several reasons. First, the distance of an interval is measured with a number, which is often taken from a scale. Second, since all major scales are made of the same pattern, music theory uses a universal system for naming these scales. If a piece starts on the third note of a scale, you can take that idea and use it in any key. If you simply say, "It starts on E," you lose the context of what scale or key you are in and need extra information in order to work with the idea. Using numbers is a handy way to think about scales and scale tones. A numbering system is also useful in the discussion of chords and chord progressions, since in music theory chord progressions are only labeled with Roman numerals.

Scale Tones by Degree

You can also describe the tones of the major scale by giving a name, instead of a number, to each degree. This method is traditionally used in classical or academic music-theory contexts, but some of the terms have become universal and you should at least be aware of them. One example is the term *tonic*, which is used to refer to the root (that is, the first chord or tone) of any scale. The chart below gives the names of each note in the major scale.

▼ NAMES OF NOTES IN THE MAJOR SCALE

Scale Degree	Name
First	Tonic
Second	Supertonic
Scale Degree	Name
Third	Mediant
Fourth	Subdominant
Fifth	Dominant
Sixth	Submediant or Superdominant
Seventh	Leading Tone
Eighth (the Octave)	Tonic

These names are also used when talking about chords and chord progressions, so knowing them will aid you in understanding progressions. Although these terms aren't used nearly as much as numbers for the tones, certain names such as tonic, dominant, and leading tone are prevalent in musicians' vernacular. Formal theory, however, uses the names of scale degrees, so now you know what they mean.

IN TIME

Originating in the thirteenth century, the motet (derived from the French *mot,* meaning "word") is an early example of polyphonic (multivoice) music. Motets were generally liturgical choral compositions written for multiple voices. Johann Sebastian Bach wrote many motets, seven of which still exist today.

How Scales Are Used in Music

Scales are really important. As you're going to see, they spin off into all sorts of directions. By itself, a scale is an organization of pitches, which are called sounds. This organization makes scales more than just a set of random pitches; it turns them into a set of sounds that musicians and theorists call a key. A key is a concept you will see in much more detail throughout this book.

A key is like a family: Everyone's related in some way. When you use a scale to compose a melody, those notes sound as though they belong together. When you stay exclusively in a scale, or a key, you get a very regular and expected sound. Composers use scales to construct melodies. Because keys already have the built-in feeling of belonging together, or better yet, sounding together, it isn't hard to make a scale into a memorable melody. Hundreds of well-known melodies come from a scale of some sort. So think of a scale as a vocabulary for musical phrases, much like letters form words, which in turn form sentences—see the parallels?

When you play a scale one note at a time, you get a melody. When you take notes from scales and combine them by playing them together, you get harmony, which will be discussed in more depth later in this book. For now, just accept that you can break the vast majority of music down into melody and harmony. Now that you know that scales can give you melodies and harmonies, you can begin to understand how important scales are. Practice your skills with the next etudes, which are all based on major scales.

ETUDES

ETUDE 3.1 Etude One

Spell major scales from the starting note

ETUDE 3.2 Etude Two

Spell major scales from the starting note

1

2

3

4

5

ETUDE 3.3 Etude Three

Can you find the mistake in each major scale?

ETUDE 3.4 Etude Four

In the following examples, find the half steps

ETUDE 3.5 Etude Five

In the following examples, notate the scale tones (1-7) beneath the notes

Major scales are not the only scales in the musical universe. The major scale is very important, but a true understanding of music would be incomplete without a look at the minor scale, the other basic scale of music. Now it's time for some minor exploration.

CHAPTER 4

The Minor Scale

The next stop on your journey into musical understanding is a closer look at the minor scale. Minor scales have their own distinct pattern, construction, order, and, more important, their own sound, which is darker and heavier than major scales. Major and minor constitute the two fundamental elements of musical scales used most often in musical theory, writing, and performance.

Minor Colors

By this point, you have learned a lot about the major scale. It is one of the two main musical scales and represents a certain color or type of sound. The minor scale, which represents a different color, a darker sound, is the other main musical scale. You'll encounter the minor scale often as well.

Certain pieces of music can convey mood and feeling based on the key and type of scale in which they're written. Major scales have a bright and cheery sound. Since music is all about contrast, the minor scale and its darker sound are needed in juxtaposition to the major scale. Think of it as another flavor in your spice rack.

There are a few ways to look at the minor scale. One is a definitive approach, and the other is the derivative approach. You will explore the derivative approach later in the chapter. For now, treat the minor scale as a separate entity that has its own formula, intervals, and usage. Later on, you can look at the bigger picture and make some fun connections.

The Definitive Approach

In Chapter 2, in the explanation of intervals, the example of the C minor scale illustrated some minor intervals and also showed a contrast against C major. **FIGURE 4.1** shows the C minor scale.

FIGURE 4.1 The C Minor Scale

TRACK 10

By now, you should know that C major has no sharps or flats; that's what makes it such an easy key to work with. Now, if you look at **FIGURE 4.1** again, you'll notice that it's different. Sure, it's a different scale, even though it has the same root, C. You learned about the differences in the intervals in this scale in Chapter 2, but now you need to learn the underpinnings of the intervals between the notes so you can understand a formula that enables you to spell any minor scale. Remember that theory is an attempt to find universal parts of music—that is, elements that apply over the entire range of music. Simply knowing that a C minor scale is spelled C–D–E♭–F–G–A♭–B♭ allows you to recognize, spell, and work with only one key. However, if you look at the scale for its intervallic content, you can take that information and apply it anywhere. It's time to break the scale into pieces. **FIGURE 4.2** shows the pattern of half and whole steps that are present in the C minor scale.

FIGURE 4.2 The Intervallic Pattern of the Minor Scale

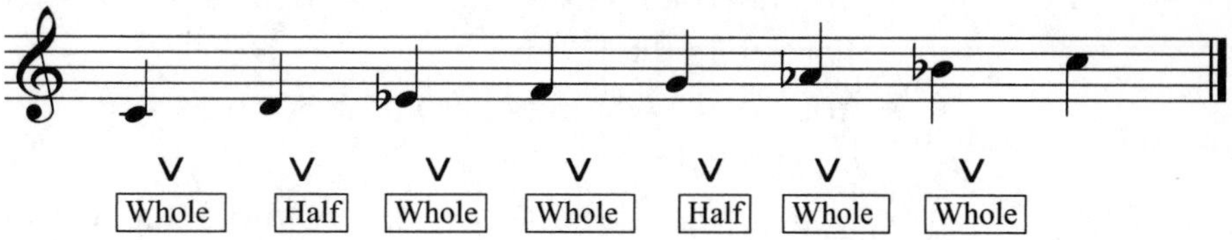

Whole Half Whole Whole Half Whole Whole

Not surprisingly, there is a different interval pattern here than in the major scale. It is WHWWHWW. You can use that interval pattern as a construction blueprint and spell any scale you want. Now take a step-by-step look at how to create any minor scale.

First, start out with a root note, such as C, as seen in **FIGURE 4.3**.

FIGURE 4.3 Building a Minor Scale: *Step One*

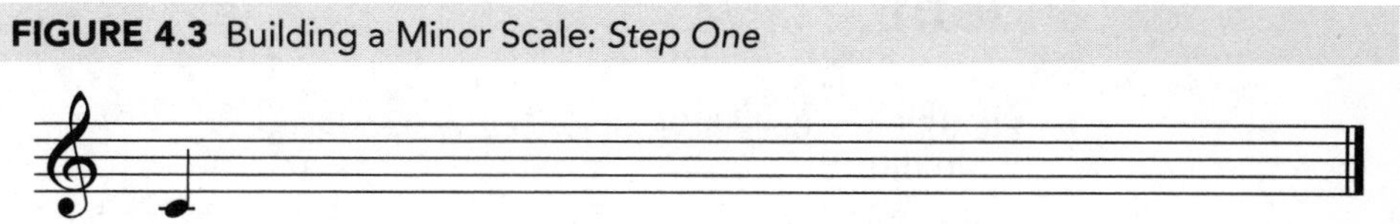

Now place the rest of the notes on the staff. Don't be concerned with whether you have the correct intervals or even the right spellings. You just need to have one of each letter name, in order, up to the octave. So simply add a D–E–F–G–A–B to **FIGURE 4.4**.

FIGURE 4.4 Building a Minor Scale: *Step Two*

You have the raw notes in; next you need to add the intervals. The formula is WHWWHWW, so add the intervals between the notes of the scale, as seen in **FIGURE 4.5**.

FIGURE 4.5 Building a Minor Scale: *Step Three*

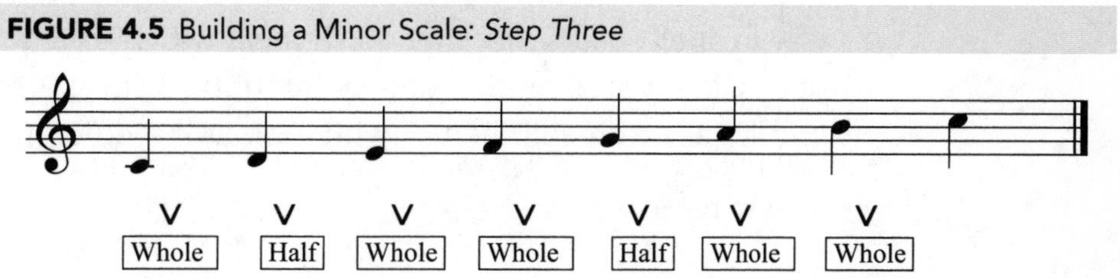

You're nearly done. All you have to do is engage the intervals and make sure your scale is spelled correctly. Here's the process:

- You need a whole step from C. A whole step away would be D, which you already have.
- You need a half step from D. A half step away would be E♭, so add a flat before the E.
- You need a whole step from E♭. A whole step away would be F, which you already have.
- You need a whole step from F. A whole step away is G, which you also already have.
- You need a half step from G. A half step away is A♭, so add a flat before the A.
- You need a whole step from A♭. A whole step away is B♭, so place a flat before B.
- You need a whole step from B♭. A whole step away is C.

Now to see your full scale, look at **FIGURE 4.6**.

FIGURE 4.6 Building a Minor Scale: *Step Four*

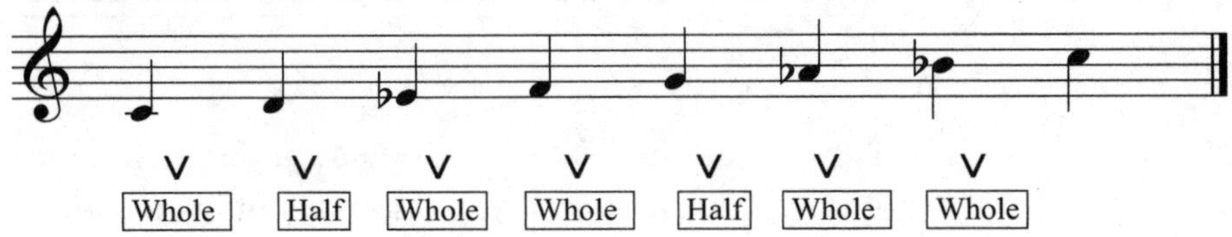

Whole Half Whole Whole Half Whole Whole

That's it! You now have an ascending scale that uses every letter of the musical alphabet once. Your scale follows the pattern of WHWWHWW, which all minor scales follow.

Now it's your practice time. Start on each note and spell your minor scales. You can use the method just described or go your own way. Just remember that you have to use the WHWWHWW interval pattern, otherwise they won't be minor scales.

The Derivative Approach

Being able to form scales from pure intervals is a common and useful way to spell scales. Another convenient way is to derive them from major scales. Many students become comfortable with spelling major scales and find it easy to recall them. If you look at the difference between a major scale and a minor scale with the same root, you can form another way to spell minor scales: deriving them from modifications to the major scales. **FIGURE 4.7** shows a C major scale on the top line and a C minor scale on the bottom line.

FIGURE 4.7 Major and Minor Scale Differences

C Major Scale

C Minor Scale

The Highlighted Notes Are The Only Changes Between C Major and C Minor

The scales are very similar. The notes C, D, F, and G stay the same. Only the third, sixth, and seventh note are changing from the major scale to the minor scale. More specifically, the third, sixth, and seventh scale degrees are lowered exactly one half step from their spelling in the major scale to make the minor scale.

Since you have dealt with intervals in detail, take a closer look at what happened when you went from the major scale to the minor scale. Simply, the intervals of the major third, major sixth, and major seventh (when measured from the root of C) are all changed from major intervals to minor intervals simply by lowering each of the intervals one half step. Remember from the discussion of intervals, the only difference between a major interval and a minor interval is that the minor interval is one half step smaller than the major interval, or vice versa.

This means that any major scale can become a minor scale by lowering the third, sixth, and seventh scale degrees one half step. This method derives the minor scale from the spelling of the major scale—using the derivative approach. This is one more way to look at spelling the minor scale. It is important to be comfortable with all the different ways to spell scales because you never know which one will work the best for you!

Degrees in Minor Scales

As explained in Chapter 3 on major scales, minor scales can also have scale degrees. As with major scales, you can refer to the tones in the minor scale numerically, just as you did when looking at the derivative approach for spelling minor scales (talking about the third, sixth, and seventh scale degrees). In case you skipped Chapter 3, here is an explanation of scale degrees.

The other way to describe the tones of the minor scale is to give a distinct name to each degree. This method is traditionally used in classical and academic music-theory contexts, but some of the terms have become universal, and you should at least be aware of them. The term *tonic*, used to refer to the root of any scale, is an example of the names given to each note in the minor scale. The table below shows how to name each note in the minor scale.

▼ NAMES OF NOTES IN THE MINOR SCALE

Scale Degree	Name
First	Tonic
Second	Supertonic
Third	Mediant
Fourth	Subdominant
Fifth	Dominant
Sixth	Submediant or Superdominant
Seventh	Leading Tone
Eighth (the Octave)	Tonic

These names are also used when discussing chords and chord progressions, so knowing them will aid you in understanding progressions. Although these terms aren't used nearly as much as numbers, musicians commonly refer to certain names such as tonic, dominant, and leading tone. Formal theory uses the names of scale degrees, so now you'll know what they mean.

Multiple Scales—Scale Clarity

In contrast to the major scale, which comes in only one variety, the minor scale comes in a few different forms. What you have begun to explore is the natural minor scale. When people talk about minor scales, they are typically talking about the natural minor scale, which has the formula of WHWWHWW. However, there are two other minor scales that have different interval patterns than the natural minor scale: harmonic and melodic minor.

The natural minor scale is a naturally occurring extension of the major scale, also called a related or relative minor. Relative minors will be discussed in Chapter 5. The other minor scales (harmonic and melodic minor) are derivatives of the natural minor scales.

Harmonic and melodic minor scales are slightly controversial in traditional music theory. Some theorists argue that they are not true scales because they are not naturally occurring patterns. But music theory is about identifying what is seen and heard in music, and whether you believe that scales should have their own names, these minor scales are found in music often enough that it is important to know about them. In any case, harmonic and melodic minor scales are part of the basic level of theory knowledge.

Harmonic Minor

The harmonic minor is the first variation of the minor scale you should know. It's a simple change of the natural minor scale, formed by raising the seventh note one half step. Doing so creates a leading tone to the scale. It simply gives a very strong pull from the last note of the scale back to the tonic. All major scales have a built-in leading tone, but natural minor scales do not; they have a whole step between the sixth and seventh tones. Interestingly, this is not why composers use the harmonic minor scale. The name of the scale gives some insight into why the scale exists. The raising of the seventh tone gives composers a slightly better harmonic palette to work with; it gives better chords. The harmonic minor scale provides a major chord on the dominant degree and a diminished chord on the leading-tone degree. Both of these chords are extremely important to composers and musicians and are used so frequently that the harmonic minor scale actually became a scale.

The D harmonic minor scale is shown in **FIGURE 4.8**.

FIGURE 4.8 The D Harmonic Minor Scale

The formula of the scale is interesting as it is no longer strictly kept to whole and half steps. In fact, between the sixth and seventh tone, there is a step and a half (an augmented second to be more exact). That large leap is awkward melodically.

If you play the scale by itself, you may imagine the Middle East and the traditional melodies of the Jewish religion, which uses the harmonic minor scale as material for melodies. It's hard to use the scale by itself and not have it sound ethnic.

Melodically, the harmonic minor scale is awkward to work with. So composers created the melodic minor scale to solve this dilemma.

Melodic Minor

The melodic minor scale is created by raising the sixth and seventh tones of a natural minor scale one half step each. The whole point is to smooth out the skip between the sixth and the seventh tones in the harmonic minor scale. The raised seventh tone in harmonic minor is crucial to minor scale harmony, but the scale played alone sounds strange. By raising the sixth as well, the melodic minor scale works better for melodies and harmonies. The augmented second interval between the sixth and seventh tone disappears, and it's back to whole and half steps.

Because the change in the scale makes it melodically smoother, it's called the melodic minor scale. Both the harmonic and melodic minor scales fall under the umbrella of basic music theory, which is important to understand in order to read music. **FIGURE 4.9** presents the melodic minor scale in the key of D minor.

TRACK 12

FIGURE 4.9 D Melodic Minor

T
A
B
0 2 3 0 2 0 2 3

Classical Melodic Minor Versus Jazz Melodic Minor

The melodic minor scale when used and practiced in a classical setting has some odd usage rules. When you play the scale and ascend with it, you sharp the sixth and seventh tones, just as in the construction of the melodic minor scale. The odd part is, when you descend with the same scale, you return the sixth and seventh tones to their natural minor spellings. This method is taught in classical music traditions. If you study an instrument with a classical teacher, you may practice your scales that way: ascending one way and descending another way. **FIGURE 4.10** shows that scale:

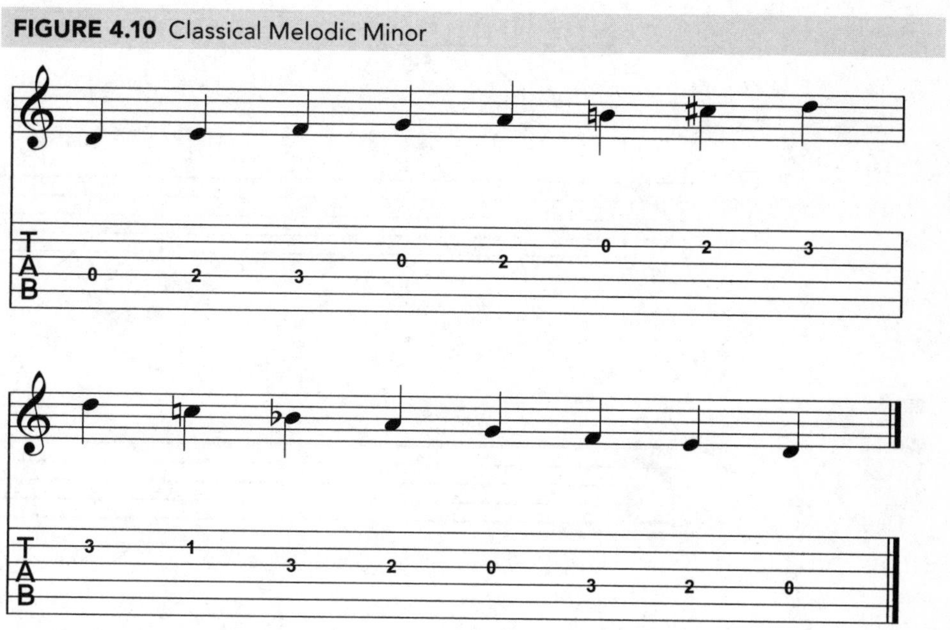

FIGURE 4.10 Classical Melodic Minor

Nowadays, especially in jazz circles, the melodic minor scale is not altered depending on its direction. It is the same scale no matter which direction it's played in (the sixth and seventh remain raised the whole time).

Variant Variables

One of the points made about scales earlier in this book is that they are composed of half and whole step intervals. The harmonic minor has proved, however, that scales don't always have that interval pattern. Adding the augmented second (a step and a half) breaks that pattern. Do you remember reading that all scales use either flats or sharps but not both? In the case of the harmonic and the melodic minor scales, that rule doesn't apply to some of the scales. On a positive note, anomalies like this make the scales easier to spot when you analyze music. Mixtures of sharps and flats can be the calling cards of these scales.

Take the time to play through all of these scales on your own instrument on a regular basis. Being able to play these scales and recognize them visually and aurally will help you understand them on a deeper level. For your reference, all of the chromatic minor scales are included in Appendix C.

ETUDES

ETUDE 4.1 Etude One

Spell minor scales from each note

ETUDE 4.2 Etude Two

Spell harmonic minor scales from each note

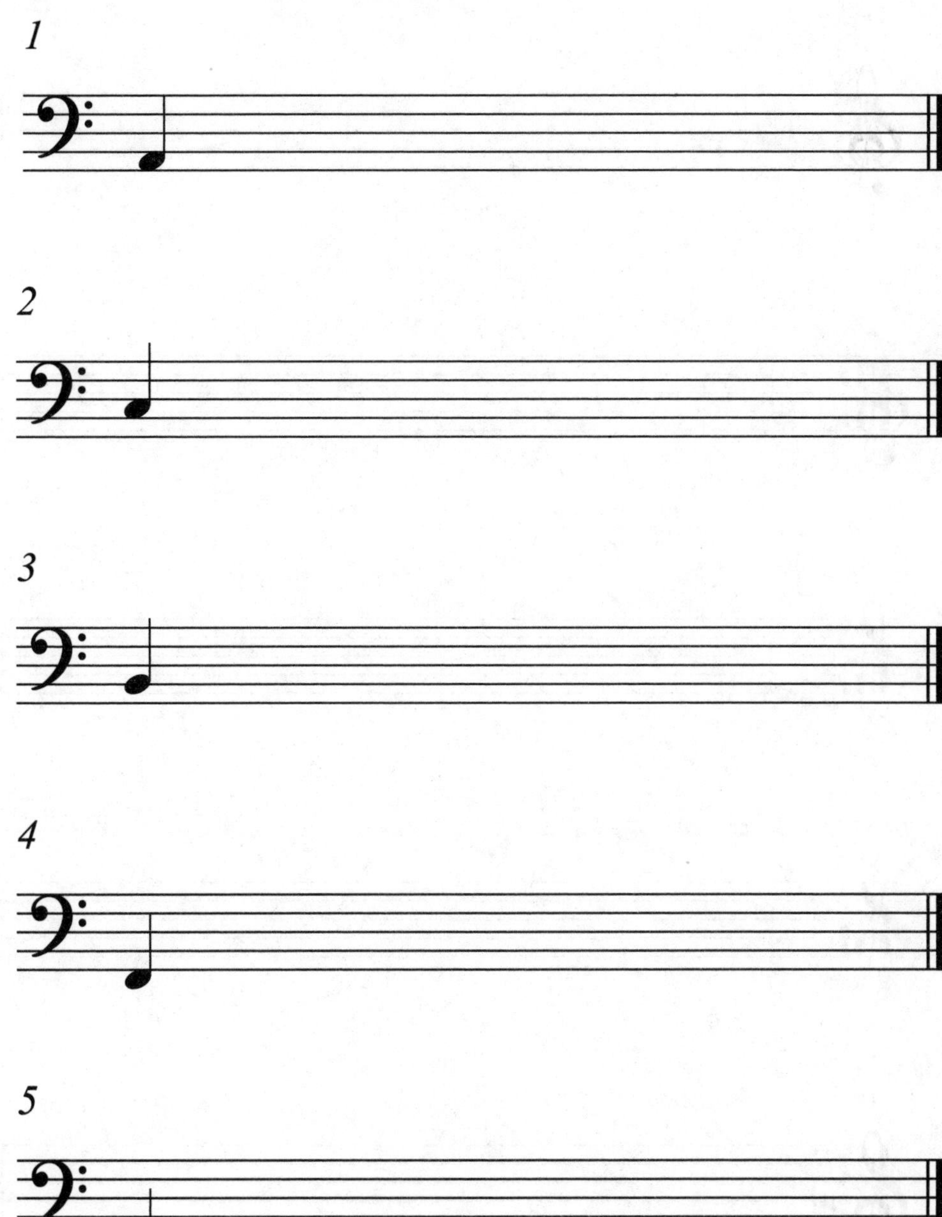

ETUDE 4.3 Etude Three

Spell melodic minor scales from each note

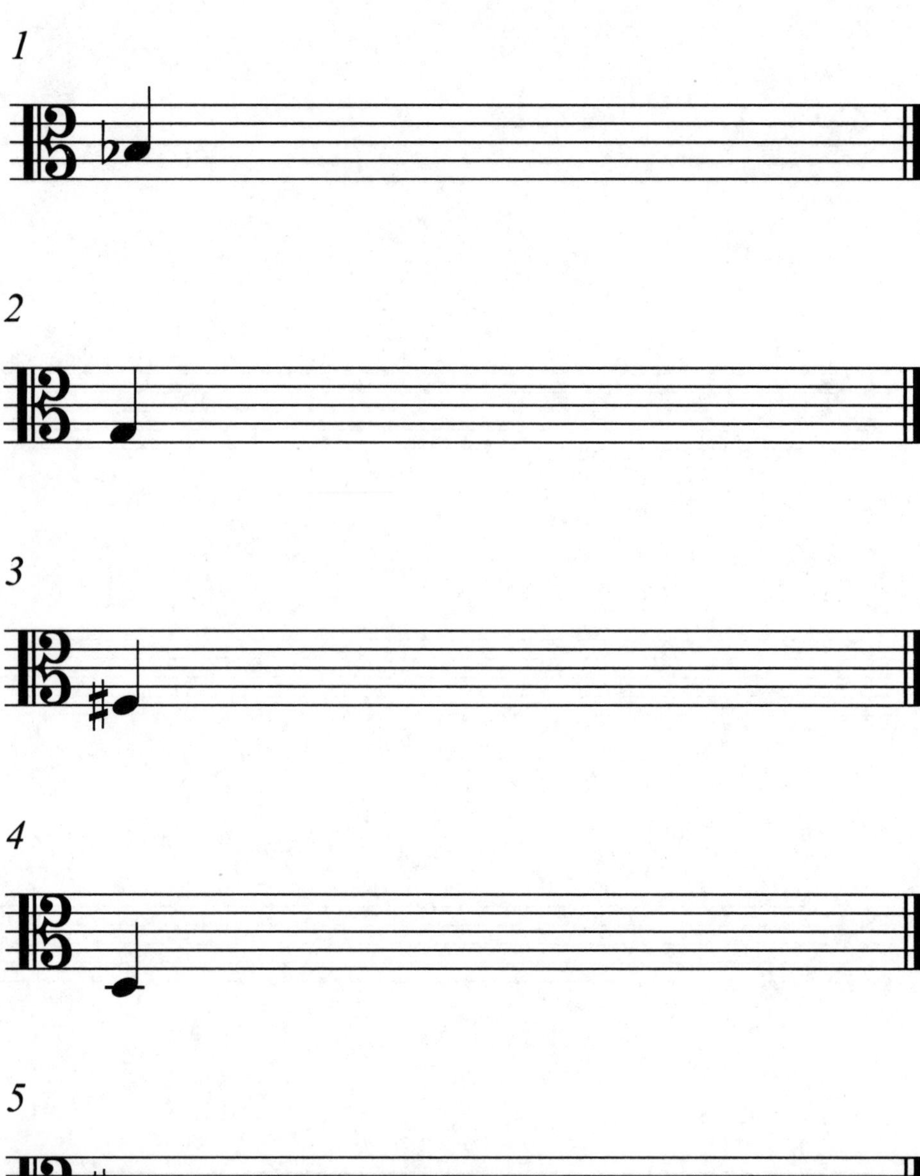

ETUDE 4.4 Etude Four

Find the mistakes in the following minor scales

ETUDE 4.5 Etude Five

Change the following major scales to minor

CHAPTER 5

Musical Keys and Key Signatures

As you learned earlier in this book, intervals are the smallest element of music. Intervals combine to form scales. Scales, in turn, make up melody and harmony, the lifeblood of music. The key is the next major level of organization and one of the major elements of musical analysis. In this chapter, you will learn what makes a key, how to identify a key, and why you should care about the musical key.

Musical Organization

Now that you have explored the primary scales that make up music, it's time to explore the key. The key is the first level of organization in tonal music—that is, music that is composed of keys, chords, and scales. Of course, there are forms of music that do not rely on keys, such as modern and atonal music. For the purpose of this book, tonal music makes up the majority of music from the common-practice period (circa 1685–1900) and is still very much in use today. The study of theory starts in the common-practice period and moves forward. If you want to study tonal music, keys are going to be very important.

The concept of musical keys is closely tied to scales, both major and minor. A key defines the basic pitches for a piece of music. It does not have to use those notes exclusively, but the majority of the notes will come from the scale of that key. You know from studying the major and minor scales that no two scales are ever spelled alike. Because each scale/key is unique, it is fairly easy to spot them in music and understand some of the musical structure involved. You can think of keys as the DNA of music.

POINT TO CONSIDER

Key signatures correspond to major and minor scales. Since a great deal of written music adheres to major and minor scales, key signatures are a convenient way to indicate the keys and scales that are frequently used. Key signatures are also a visual method of determining the key of a piece of music.

A key is a slightly abstract concept, which can be a challenge to describe. A key defines what notes can be used to create an expected sound, such as consonant and not dissonant. As you progress as a musician, keys and key signatures will become more important than just defining what notes to play. Keys can give you a glimpse into the mind of the composer and help you unravel how music is composed. In any event, you need to know a lot about keys and their key signatures if you want to be a competent music theorist.

What Is a Key Signature?

You know all about sharps and flats and can comfortably spell scales in any key. That knowledge is one step removed from real music and how it functions. Observe the spelling of the A major scale in **FIGURE 5.1** versus the same scale with a key signature shown in **FIGURE 5.2**. Instead of spelling each sharp and flat, you can use a key signature to make all the Fs, Cs, and Gs sharp. Most musicians would rather read **FIGURE 5.2** any day of the week.

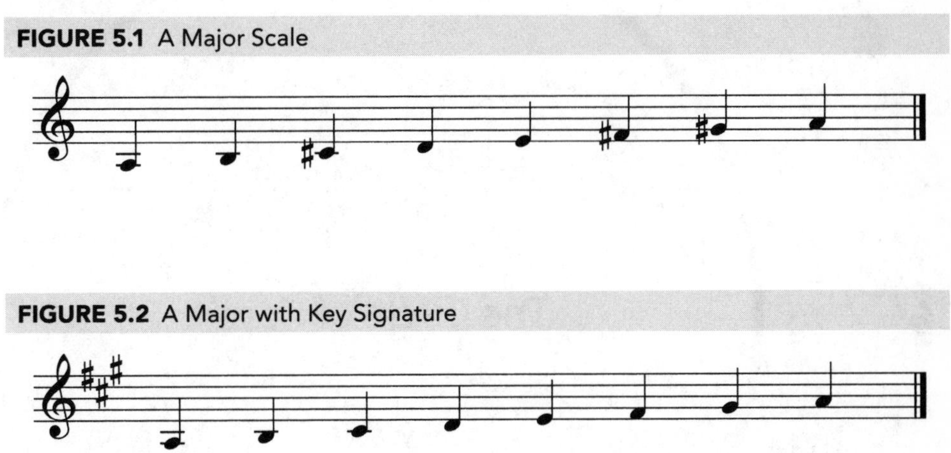

FIGURE 5.1 A Major Scale

FIGURE 5.2 A Major with Key Signature

In other words, a key signature is used to indicate that a certain note or notes are going to be sharp or flat for the entire piece. It cleans up the written music for the reader and eliminates the need for the sharp and flat symbols that would otherwise appear throughout. A good reader is used to reading in key signatures and prefers them.

The Key Signatures

In Appendix C, you can see every possible scale in existence, even the really odd and rare enharmonic keys like F♭ major. Key signatures apply to the common keys/scales and rarely deal with the enharmonic keys. Students often encounter the circle of keys, a graphic representation of the typical keys. Since every key or scale has its unique spelling, each of the keys looks different as well. Each single key signature corresponds to one single major key. Here is the circle of keys (**FIGURE 5.3**).

FIGURE 5.3 The Circle of Keys

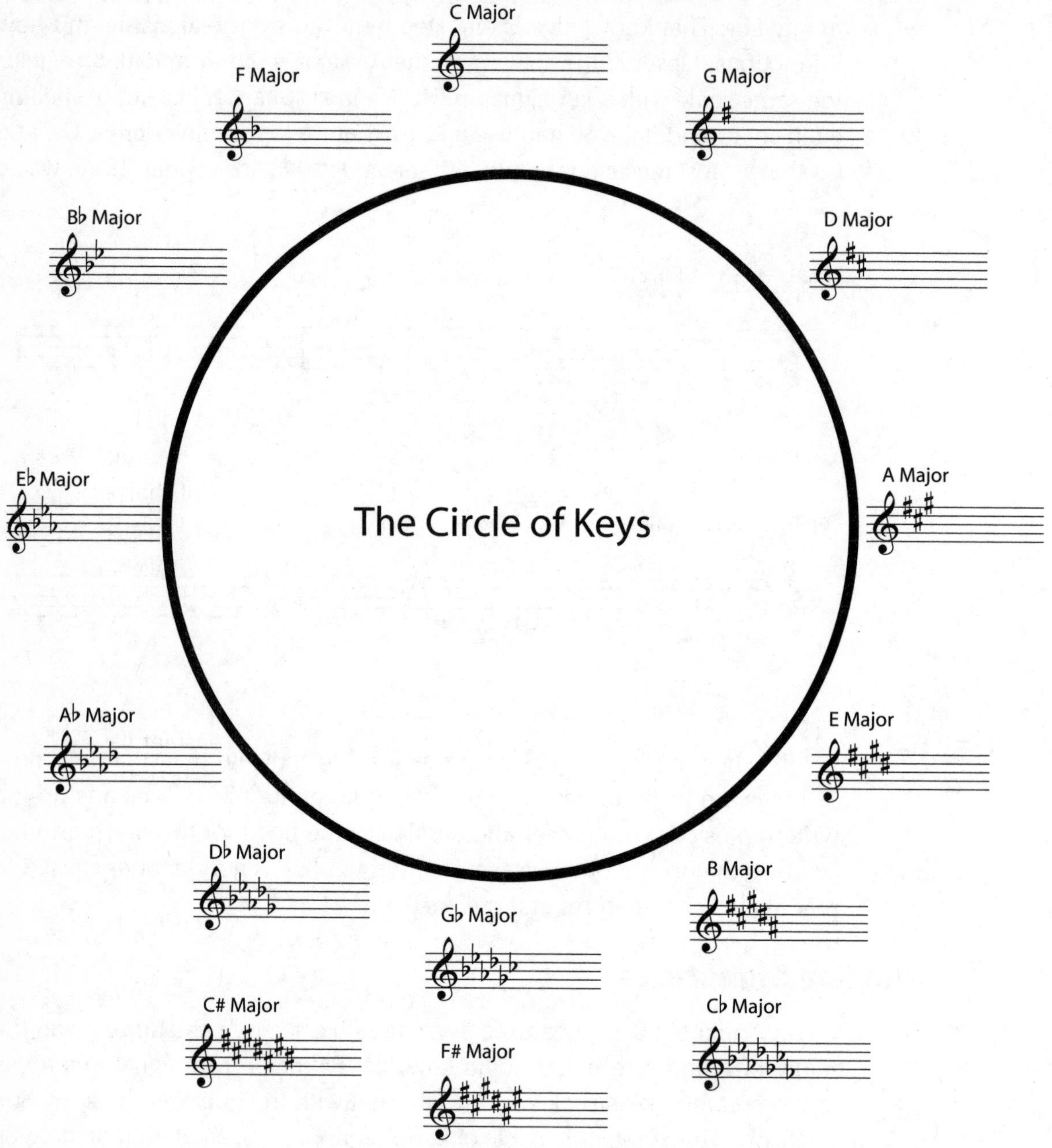

The System of Key Signatures

Key signatures use a specific system. Not just any note can appear in a key signature. There is an order and a logic that makes key signatures understandable. There are two varieties: sharp key signatures and flat key signatures (excluding C major, which has no sharps or flats). A key signature displays only sharps or only flats, never both. Within these groupings of sharps or flats, there is an order to how individual notes appear. Take a look at sharps and flats separately.

Do you remember reading that proper scale spellings also result in either sharps or flats? Scales and key signatures show you the same information, which is exactly why they help you understand more about the music.

Sharps appear in key signatures in a specific order: F♯, C♯, G♯, D♯, A♯, E♯, B♯.

They always follow that order. If a key has one sharp, it will be an F♯. If a key has two sharps, it will have F♯ and C♯. It always works through the pattern in the same way. A great way to remember the order of sharps is to use a little mnemonic device: <u>F</u>ather <u>C</u>harles <u>G</u>oes <u>D</u>own <u>A</u>nd <u>E</u>nds <u>B</u>attle. The first letter of each word corresponds to the sharps as they appear. It's a silly mnemonic, but it might just help.

> Even though key signatures may appear confusing at first, most musicians would have a hard time reading without them. Constant flats and sharps placed throughout music are more challenging to read than a single key signature.

Just like sharps, flats appear in a specific order every time. Here is the order: B♭, E♭, A♭, D♭, G♭, C♭, and F♭.

There is also an easy way to remember the order of flats: Just reverse the mnemonic for sharps! <u>B</u>attle <u>E</u>nds <u>A</u>nd <u>D</u>own <u>G</u>oes <u>C</u>harles' <u>F</u>ather. One saying gets you both sharps and flats—pretty convenient!

Learning the Key Names

If you stare at the circle of keys long enough, you might memorize what each key represents. There are a few tricks that can help you. On the flat side, the first key is F, which starts with the same letter as the word *flat*. After that, BEAD contains the names of the next four flat keys. That's a handy way to learn some of the keys. The sharp side is a bit harder. BEAD appears again on the right side. However, there are two little tricks you can learn for instantly naming a key just by looking at it.

The Sharp Key Trick

For any key that has a sharp in it, naming the key is as simple as following two easy steps. First, find the last sharp (the one all the way to the right). Once you've found and named the note that corresponds to the same line or space the sharp is on, go one note higher, and you've named the key. Look at **FIGURE 5.4**. The last sharp in this key is A♯. Going one note above this is the note B. Five sharps is, indeed, the correct key signature for the key of B major. You can check the trusty circle just to make sure.

FIGURE 5.4 Name This Signature

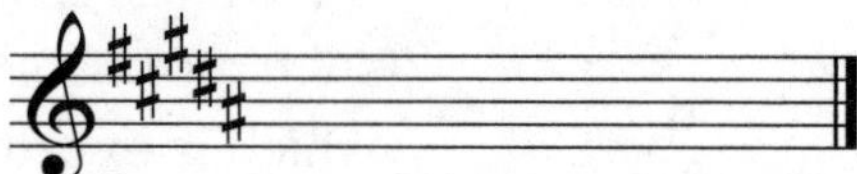

The good news is that this trick works on every key that has a sharp in it. To find the name of a sharp key:

1. Name the last sharp, the one all the way to the right.
2. Go one note higher than the last sharp, and that's the name.

Unfortunately, it works only when you're looking at a key. If someone asks you, "How many sharps are in the key of E major?" you're stuck. For everything else, refer to the circle of keys and the order of sharps and flats.

The Flat Key Trick

The flat keys have a different naming trick. When you see a piece of music that has flats, find the second-to-last flat. The name of that flat is the name of your key. Look at the example in **FIGURE 5.5**. This key has two flats and the second-to-last flat is B♭. The name of the key with two flats is B♭. This is an easy trick.

FIGURE 5.5 Name This Key

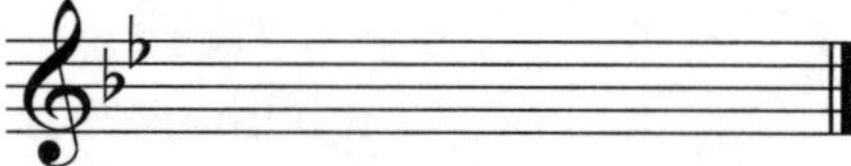

There is one exception: the key with one flat, F major. Since this key has only one flat, there is no second-to-last flat. In this case, you'll just have to memorize that F has one flat (which is B♭).

To find the name of a flat key:

1. Find the second-to-last flat (from the right).
2. The name of the flat note you find is the name of the key.

Just remember the exception—the key of F major has one flat and therefore the rule does not work for it. For the other keys, it works like a charm!

The Circle Moves in Fourths and Fifths

The name of this section says it all. The circle of keys is often referred to as the circle of fifths or the circle of fourths. The keys are arranged in the circle in a fairly logical way. The key of C, with no sharps or flats, sits squarely in the center, and the sharp keys move around the right side, each key increasing the number of sharps by one. The flat keys move to the left, increasing their flats by one as they progress.

EXTRA CREDIT

Even before you memorize the entire circle of fifths, you can construct it using intervals. Draw a C at the top of a piece of paper. Now draw a few fifths to the right to name the sharp keys. To the left, draw a few fourths for the basic flat keys. Across the bottom of the page, spell the order of sharps from F, in fifths, and the order of flats from B, in fourths. As you move away from the key of C, each key increases by one flat or sharp (depending on which direction you move). You can match up the flats and sharps from the bottom of the page.

If you move to the right from C, each key is a perfect fifth apart. In addition, the order of sharps as they appear in the key signatures is also in perfect fifths starting from F♯.

If you move to the left from C, each key is exactly a perfect fourth apart. Conveniently, the flats as they appear in the key signature are also a perfect fourth apart, starting from B♭.

Think about these two points:

1. Sharp keys move in fifths around the circle, and the sharps are fifths apart.
2. Flat keys move in fourths around the circle, and the flats are fourths apart.

When you move in one direction in the key circle, you move in fifths; when you move in the opposite direction, you move in fourths. Remember the explanation in Chapter 2 about interval inversion: A perfect fifth becomes a perfect fourth when inverted. A fifth up is the same as a fourth down. The same explanation applies to the order of sharps and flats. The sharps are spaced a fifth apart starting from F, and the flats are spaced a fourth apart starting from B. Interestingly, when you spell out all the sharps and read them backward (backward = inverted = in fourths), you get the order of flats.

Relative Minor Keys

Up to this point, you have learned solely about major key signatures and their related major scales; the circle of keys and the tricks for naming the keys all refer to major keys.

Of course, you know about minor scales, and where there are scales, there are keys. The good news is that all of the minor scales and keys share the same key signatures, which you already know. The bad news is that they aren't the same as the major keys. Never fear, there are some easy ways to learn the minor keys as well.

Shared Signatures

Every major key and its corresponding key signature serve a dual function. Not only do they indicate a major key, they indicate a minor key as well. The concept is called relative keys and related minor. Simply put, every major scale/key has a minor scale/key hiding inside it. For now, you'll learn how to figure out the name of the minor keys. **FIGURE 5.6** shows the key signature for E♭ major. The same key signature can signify the key of C minor.

FIGURE 5.6 Dual-Function Key Signature/Relative Minor

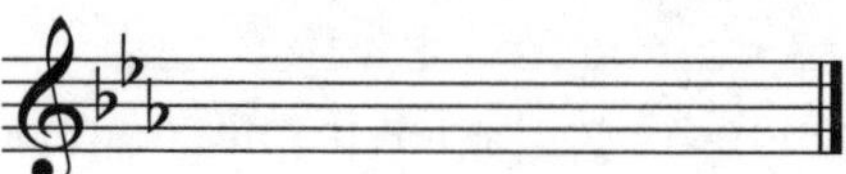

Is this E♭ or C Minor?

How is this possible? Well, simply put, if you spell the E♭ major scale and the C minor scale, you will see that they share the same key signature. The other thing that you are seeing is a mode: The minor scale is a mode of the major scale. Modes come up in the next chapter, but for now, just accept that since they share the same pitches, even if they are in a different order, they are related.

POINT TO CONSIDER

Looking at a key signature alone won't tell you whether your piece is in the major or the minor key. You need to investigate the piece of music itself.

Naming Minor Keys

To name a minor key signature, first name the major key. Then count up six notes (up a major sixth) or down three (down a minor third). Either way, you arrive at the same note. In the case of C major, counting up six notes brings you to A. C major and A minor share the same key signature and are referred to as related keys. When you look at a piece without sharps or flats in the signature, it could just as easily be in A minor as C major. You won't know for sure by just looking at a key signature because music isn't that easy. You have to look at the harmony and that comes later in this book. For now, concentrate on being able to name minor keys from major key signatures.

When naming a minor key, be careful to look at the key signature when you are doing so. Simply counting up six notes or down three notes may not give you the correct key. If the note you pick has a sharp or a flat in that key, the name of the minor key needs to reflect that. You're not just counting up six letters; you have to mind the key signature. It's much easier to use the interval of a major sixth, which has a clear name. Look at **FIGURE 5.7**. In this case, the sixth note is not just C, but C♯, so the name of the key has to reflect that. The key of E major has a relative minor of C♯ minor.

FIGURE 5.7 The Relative Minor of E Major

FIGURE 5.8 shows the full circle of keys with both the major and the minor keys.

FIGURE 5.8 Circle of Keys with Minor Keys

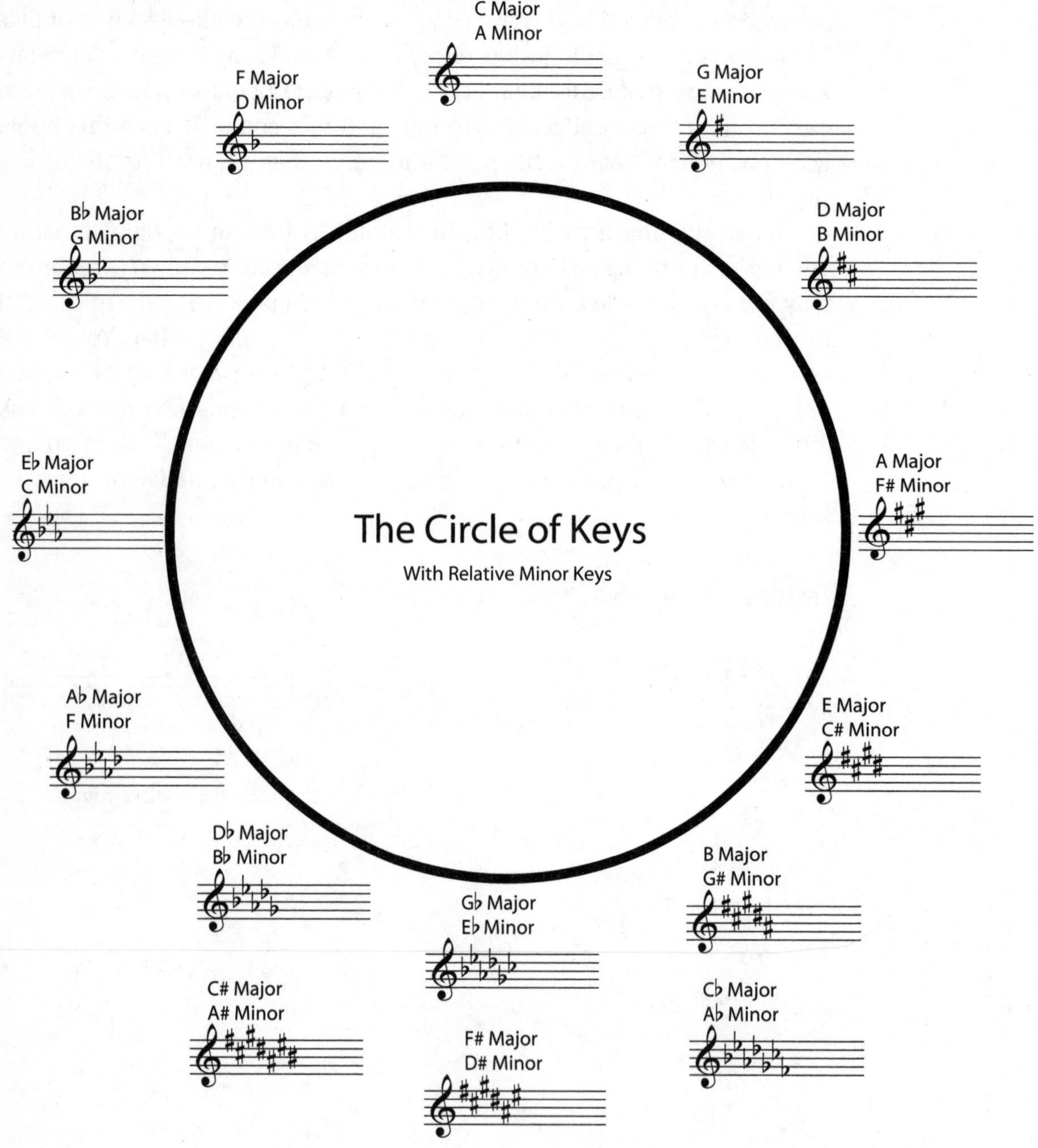

Determining the Key

You can determine the key by looking at the signature and checking your circle of keys. This action will give you at least two answers: the major and the relative minor key. In a way, this is your first step toward musical analysis, but it is more than just looking at a key signature. The answer is rarely that simple. Or is it?

One old trick suggests that you can look at the first and last notes of any piece to determine the key. Now, although this rarely works because music involves so many variables, sometimes it does work. If you look at a key signature and your choices are either a minor or a major key (C major or A minor, for example), you could scan the piece for Cs or As and that may answer your question. Then again, it may not. While it is true that many pieces conclude on the tonic note of the key, that fact only tells you where the piece ended not where it went in the middle.

Composer Antonio Vivaldi was born in Venice, Italy, on March 4, 1678, and died in Vienna, Austria, on July 28, 1741. He was the son of a professional violinist and an accomplished violinist as well. Ordained as a priest in 1703, he soon stopped celebrating Mass on account of his poor health. Today Vivaldi is most famous for his work *Le Quattro Stagioni* (The Four Seasons).

If you are trying to decipher what key you're in, the first and last note (or chord) may give you a basic answer. The answer that works in every piece can only be found by looking at the details of the piece—and that involves the key signature, the harmony, and the per-note changes that exist throughout the piece. Since you know about scales in detail now, you can work on one more aspect of keys based on minor scales and their typical visual patterns.

Minor Keys on Paper

In a great deal of music, you rarely see the natural minor scale; instead you see the harmonic or melodic minor scales. When you are looking at a piece of music and the key signature gives you two possible answers, look inside the music itself for more clues.

Both the harmonic minor scale and the melodic minor scale have alterations via accidentals. For a minor scale to function in the traditional sense, it needs this alteration. More specifically, the leading tone needs to be raised, which will cause a subsequent sharp, flat, or natural where it doesn't normally belong.

If the piece is in the major key, it won't need any additional accidentals (sharps or flats) to function. That's not to say that pieces in major keys never have accidentals, but minor keys have very specific accidentals. If you know what to look for, you should have no problem finding out the answer.

A leading tone is the seventh note of a scale. In the case of the harmonic and melodic minor scale, it's raised one half step higher than in the natural minor scale. For example, in A minor, the leading tone in the natural scale is G; if you raise it, it becomes a G♯. Now, remember that A minor and C major share a key signature that has no sharps or flats. So, you're looking at a piece with no key signature and scattered throughout the piece are a bunch of G♯s. The final note of the piece is A. Chances are that you are in A minor, or at least you were in A minor for a part of that piece and concluded there. By the same token, if you see a piece with no key signature and nothing but G♮s, you're in C major, because the G♯ is the leading tone of A minor.

Look at **FIGURE 5.9**. What key do you think it is?

TRACK 13

FIGURE 5.9 What Key Are We In?

At first glance, the key signature has one sharp, so it could be G major or E minor. The first thing to do is look for accidentals. Do you have any? Yes, there is a D♯ throughout the piece. The next step is to determine if that is just an accidental or if it is a minor-scale leading tone. In the key of E minor, the leading tone is a raised seventh note, which happens to be D♯. The fact that the piece starts and ends on E drives home the point that you are in the key of E minor.

See, that wasn't so hard. It shows you that you cannot judge the key based on the signature alone—you must look at the material within the piece to be absolutely sure. Knowing what the leading tones are will make it much easier to understand the differences between key signatures and their relative minor scales.

To find the leading tones for minor keys, just find the seventh note of the scale. Rather than go seven notes up, go one note down. Then make sure it's a half step away. For example, the leading tone for C minor is B♮ because B and C are a half step apart. In D minor, the leading tone is C♯.

Keys Change

Music does not need to stay in one key; key changes happen frequently in music. The way to change keys and identify key changes will become much clearer when you understand harmony. For now, go back to the circle of keys and make a few assumptions that will be explained as the book progresses.

Here are the rules:

- When music changes keys, it changes to a closely related key.
- The closest related key is the relative minor.
- The other close keys that you can modulate to are next to the original key on the key circle (either one key to the left or one key to the right).
- The other modulation you can make is from a major to a parallel minor; for example, C major to C minor.

FIGURE 5.10 Circle of Keys with Minor Keys

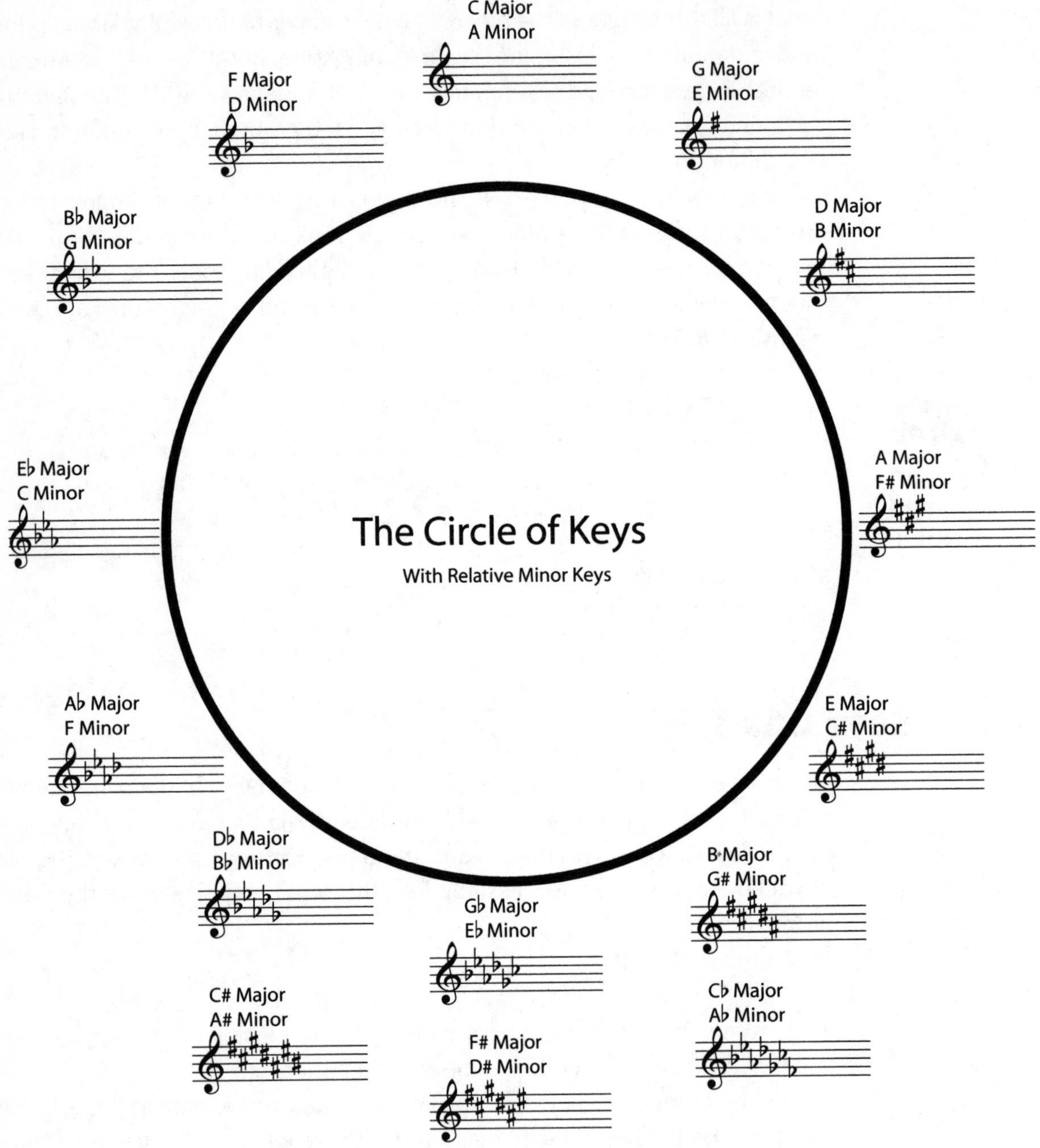

Talking about common and simple ways to change keys does not mean that the more difficult and uncommon ones are not used; just the opposite is true. Composers love to break the rules and find interesting and musically compelling ways to do so. Part of learning about theory is trying to understand what the majority of music did when the piece was written. What were the norms of the times and why did the composers use them? There will always be musicians who push the boundaries of music to new levels.

Keys are more than just scales and key signatures, so you need to keep moving into the rest of the scales and chords and harmony to fully grasp what keys mean and how you will use them. For now, you have the basic groundwork to name and spell keys, which was the goal for this chapter. The next step is to look at the last group of scales and modes in this book, and then on to bigger things: chords and harmony.

ETUDES

ETUDE 5.1 Etude One

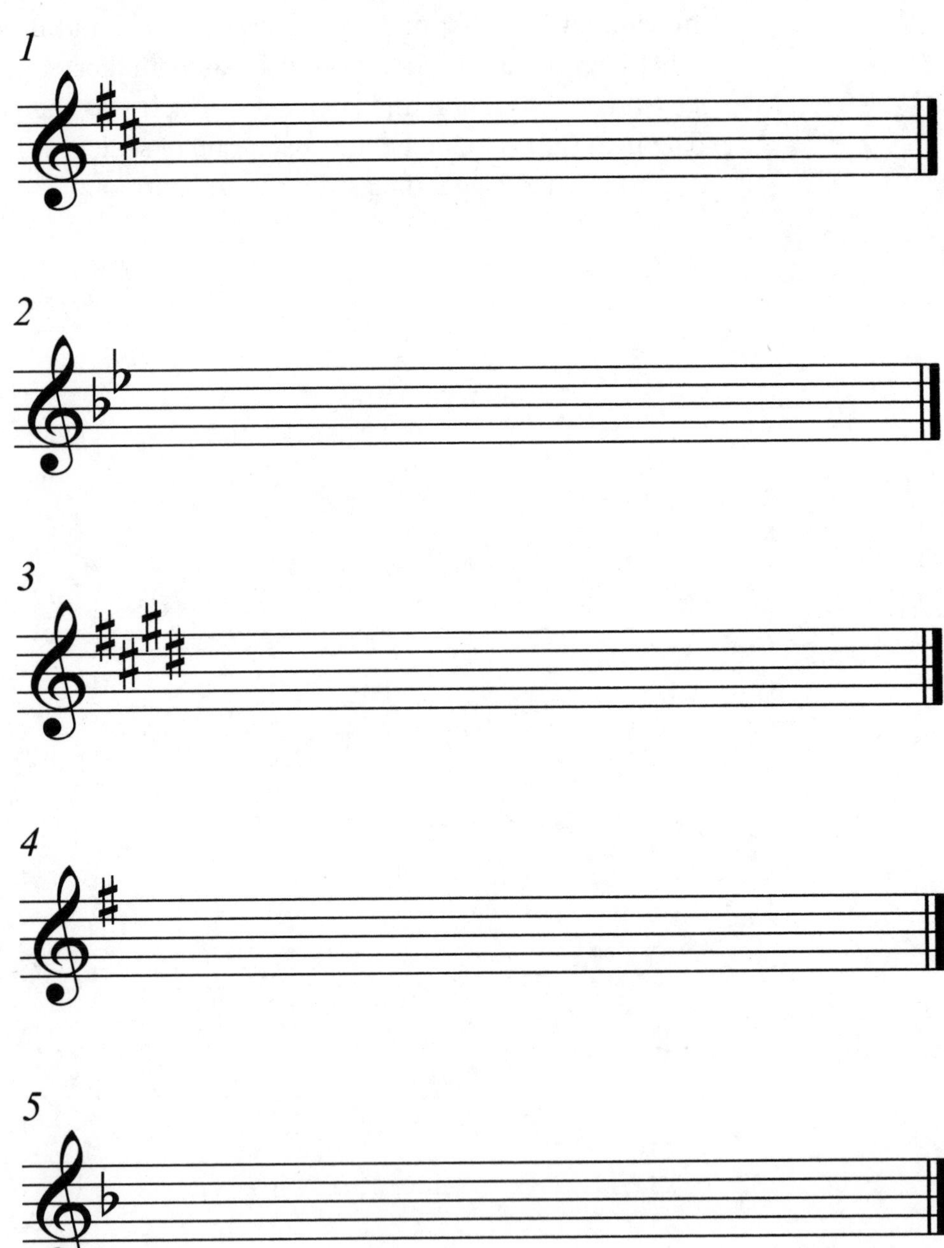

ETUDE 5.2 Etude Two

Name the following minor key signatures

1

2

3

4

5

Draw the following major key signatures

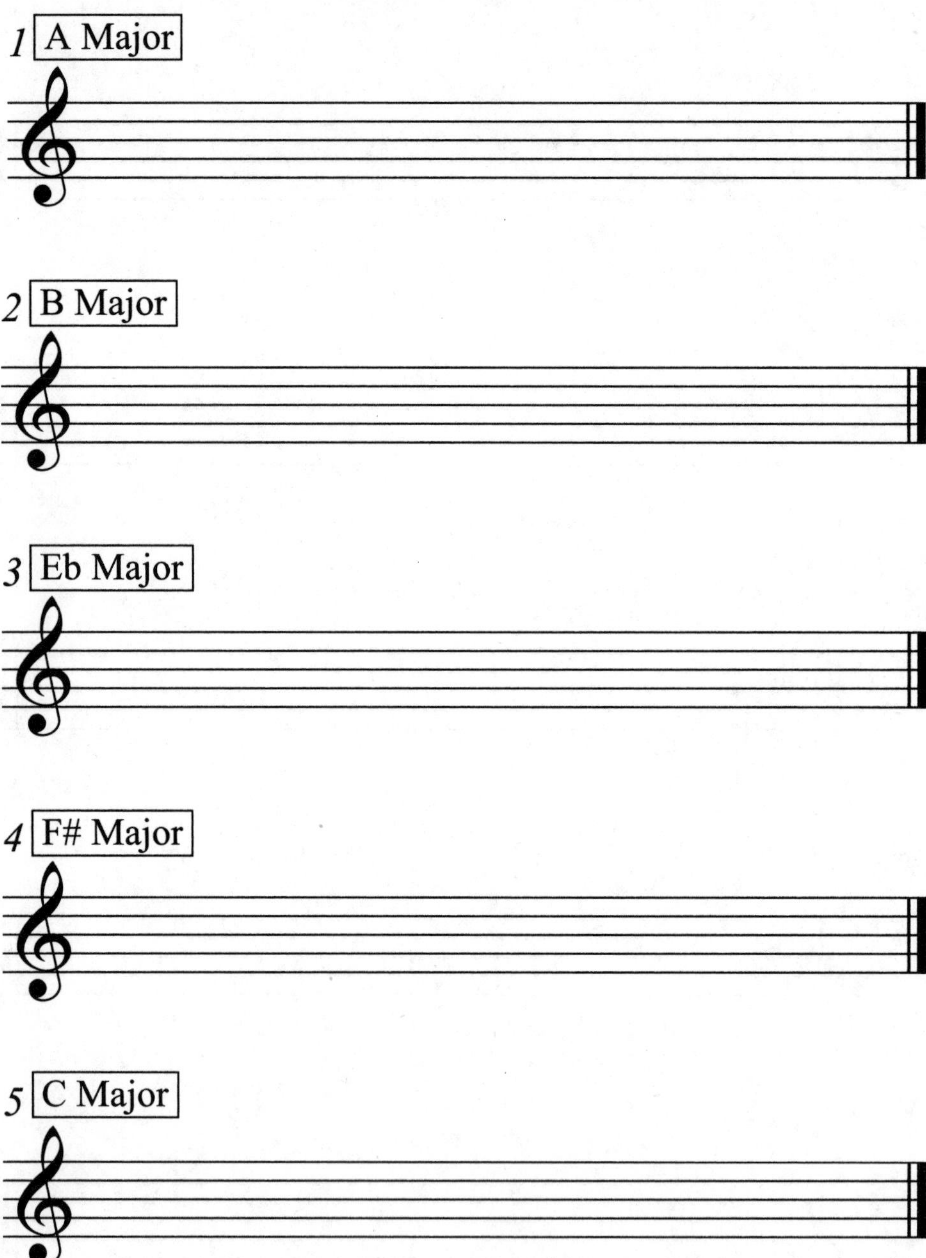

ETUDE 5.4 Etude Four

Draw the following minor key signatures

1 D Minor

2 B Minor

3 C# Minor

4 Bb Minor

5 G# Minor

ETUDE 5.5 Etude Five

First, name the key signature on the left.
Then, draw the parallel key signature on the right
(e.g. D major ↔ D minor)

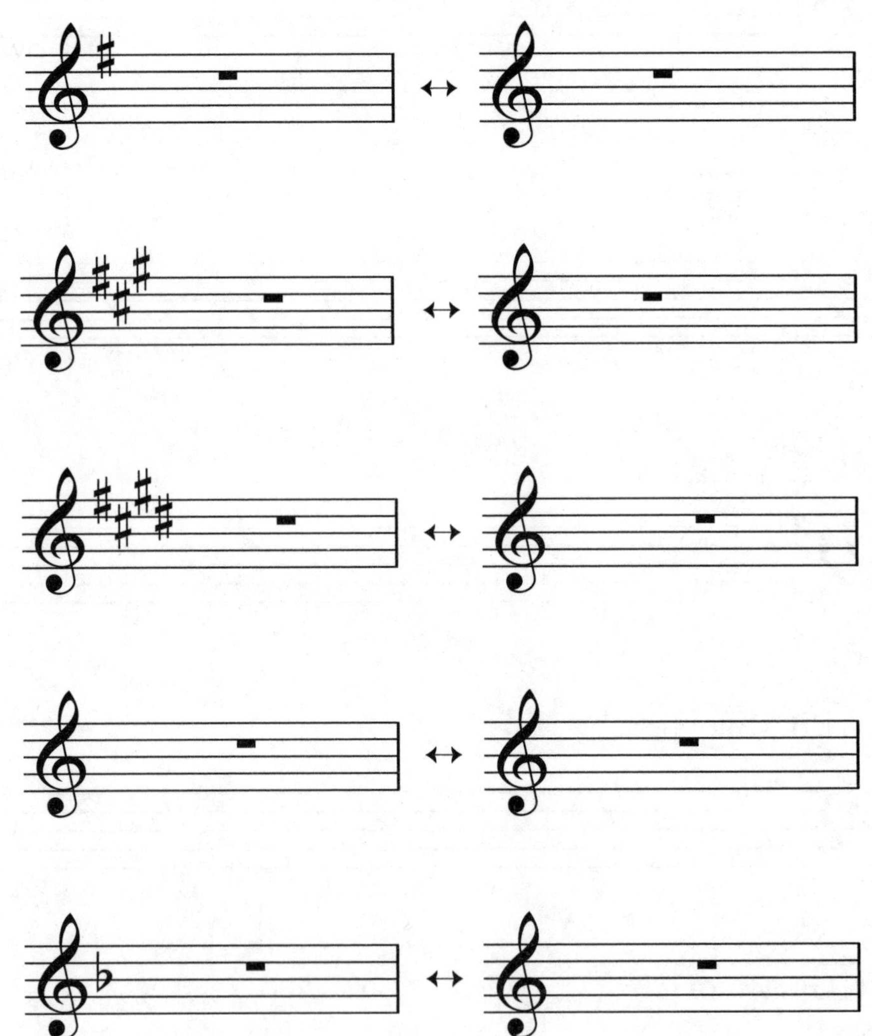

CHAPTER 6

Modes and Other Scales

It is true that major and minor scales make up the majority of the scales that you encounter in everyday life. However, both traditional and modern music theory include other scales as well. Mode is a term that students hear often and rarely understand. In addition, you'll hear about pentatonic, diminished, and whole-tone scales.

Modes—The Other Side of Scales

The first place to deepen your understanding of scales is right back at the major scale. As a musician, you may have heard the term *modes*. Many classical musicians don't deal with modes early on in their study, but jazz and rock players do. There are several reasons for this musical divide, which will become clear as you learn more about modes.

Defining Modes

The simplest definition of a mode is that it is a displaced major scale. First, what does the term *displaced* mean? Take the F major scale: F–G–A–B♭–C–D–E–F. As you know, what makes it an F major scale is that the note F (the tonic degree) has the most weight; the scale wants to stop on the high F when you play it.

Now, what if you were to use the same vocabulary—that is, use the same F–G–A–B♭–C–D–E–F pitches (the F major scale)—but make a different note the root? What if the scale looked like this: D–E–F–G–A–B♭–C–D? If the D sounded like the root note (which is based on the context of the piece), then you have an official mode. You have a bit more than a mode, actually.

If you reread the last paragraph, you'll notice that an F scale is spelled from D. Is there a special relationship between F and D? Well, they are a sixth apart. Hmm, sixth note of a major scale, where have you heard that before? Try Chapter 5, in the section "Naming Minor Keys." Remember the trick you learned there, to find the relative minor by going up six notes. Using this example, you can spell an F major scale starting from D, its sixth note, and it's called a mode. It's the D minor scale and a mode of F major.

So, you see that minor scales are also modes. The notes D–E–F–G–A–B♭–C–D form a D minor scale. A mode is formed when you call any other note besides the original root of the scale the root. The minor scale is just one example of a mode, one that you already know. But wait, there's more. Because a major scale has seven notes, there are seven modes.

Modal History

Modes gained prominence during the golden age of the Gregorian chant, circa A.D. 900, when they were used to compose the melodies of vocal plainchant. Modes stayed in use throughout the medieval era with some modification. The baroque and prebaroque periods used major and minor scales exclusively instead of modes. For all intents and purposes, modes lay dormant throughout the baroque era, the classical era, and most (but not all) of the romantic era.

Even though impressionist composers revived modes, it wasn't until jazz musicians started using them in improvisation and composition that modes became a useful part of music curricula. Today, all music students learn about modes, but the rock and jazz players tend to utilize them more frequently.

Seven Modal Scales

Each and every major scale can be looked at from seven different angles—one mode starting from each note in the scale. While modes theoretically come from parent major scales, it's easiest to think of them as their own entities.

In a classical music-theory class, modes are commonly referred to as church modes because of their widespread use in sacred music—especially Gregorian chant. Relegating modes to historical learning is a disservice, however. Modes are alive and well in modern music, especially jazz.

Ionian

Ionian is the first mode to learn about, and you already know it. The Ionian scale is simply the major scale. It follows the interval pattern WWHWWWH. **FIGURE 6.1** shows an F Ionian mode. Since the Ionian mode is simply the traditional major scale, think of Ionian as the proper name for a major scale. It's great to know what the proper name is, but you don't have to be caught up in its usage and refer to every major scale as an Ionian mode; the terms are interchangeable.

FIGURE 6.1 Mode One: *The Ionian Mode* (Major Scale)

Dorian

The Dorian mode, the first of the displaced scales, is a major scale played from its second note. If you continue to use F major as the parent scale, the Dorian mode in this key starts from the note G and progresses up the same notes. **FIGURE 6.2** shows the G Dorian scale. The G Dorian scale uses the interval pattern WHWWWHW.

TRACK 15

FIGURE 6.2 Mode Two: *The Dorian Mode*

There is a very important aspect to understand about modes. The G Dorian scale comes from the F major scale and shares all the same notes. This is an important learning tool, but all musicians need to learn the modes as "their own thing." The Dorian mode is a scale unto itself, with its own distinct sound. If you look at the notes of G Dorian (G–A–B♭–C–D–E–F–G), you might notice that the G Dorian scale looks a lot like the traditional G minor scale (G–A–B♭–C–D–E♭–F–G)—and you're right. The only difference is that the G Dorian scale contains an E♮ and the G minor scale contains an E♭.

You could look at the Dorian scale as a minor-type scale, with an altered sixth note. In this case, the sixth note is raised up a half step. It's very much like a flavored minor scale. Today modes are used to spice up traditional major and minor scales that may sound overused and dated. As you'll see, all of the rest of the modes will closely resemble either a traditional major or a traditional minor scale.

POINT TO CONSIDER

When you think of the parent-scale relationship between each mode, don't fall into the trap of thinking that each mode has to be related to its parent scale. Using the minor scale as an example again, you don't have to think about its related major scale, do you? No, it can stand on its own. The same holds true for all of the modes. Learn to see them on their own if you plan to use them quickly.

Phrygian

Phrygian, the third mode, is the result of forming a scale starting from the third note of the parent major scale. Using F major as the parent scale, the Phrygian scale is an A Phrygian scale. It uses the interval pattern HWW-WHWW (see **FIGURE 6.3**). Phrygian has a distinct sound and sometimes recalls the music of Spain, as Spanish composers often use this scale.

TRACK 16

FIGURE 6.3 Mode Three: *The Phrygian Mode*

The A Phrygian scale (A–B♭–C–D–E–F–G–A) looks very much like a traditional A minor scale (A–B–C–D–E–F–G–A). The only difference is that the A Phrygian scale lowers the second note a half step. You could say that Phrygian is just a minor scale with a lowered second note—and you'd be right.

Lydian

The fourth mode of the major scale is the Lydian mode. Using F as a parent scale, you come to the B♭ Lydian scale. Lydian uses the interval pattern WWWHWWH. See **FIGURE 6.4**.

TRACK 17

FIGURE 6.4 Mode Four: *The Lydian Mode*

The Lydian mode is a striking, beautiful, and bright sound. It's used by film composers to convey uplifting spirit and is a favorite of jazz and rock composers. The Lydian scale is so bright and happy that it's no surprise it's closely related to the major scale. The B♭ Lydian scale is spelled B♭–C–D–E–F–G–A–B♭, which resembles a traditional B♭ major scale (B♭–C–D–E♭–F–G–A–B♭). The only difference between B♭ Lydian and B♭ major is that a Lydian scale raises the fourth note of the major scale a half step. So, B♭ Lydian is a B♭ major scale with a raised fourth note. The raised fourth tone results in a bright and unusual sound and allows the plain major scale to have a unique overall effect.

Mixolydian

The fifth mode of the major scale is called the Mixolydian mode. Using the parent scale of F, our fifth mode is C Mixolydian. C Mixolydian, or Mixo as it's commonly abbreviated, uses the interval pattern of WWHWWHW. See **FIGURE 6.5**. The Mixolydian mode is a mainstay of jazz, rock, and blues music.

TRACK 18

FIGURE 6.5 Mode Five: *The Mixolydian Mode*

The Mixolydian mode is closely related to the major scale but is slightly darker sounding. The C Mixolydian scale (C–D–E–F–G–A–B♭–C) closely resembles the C major scale (C–D–E–F–G–A–B–C). The only difference is that the Mixolydian scale lowers the seventh note of the major scale a half step. The lowered seventh note gives the Mixolydian mode a bluesy, dark color, leading away from the overly peppy major scale. Because of this, it's a staple of blues, rock, and jazz players who want to darken the sound of major scales. It also coincides with one of the principal chords of jazz, blues, and rock music: the dominant seventh chord (C7, which you're going to learn all about in Chapter 8).

Aeolian

The sixth mode of the major scale is the Aeolian mode. In Chapter 4, you learned that minor scales are derived from the sixth note of a major scale.

That's right, the Aeolian mode is the natural minor scale. This is another mode that you already know. Aeolian is the proper name for natural minor. You can refer to it as Aeolian at parties and look smarter. Using the parent key of F major, our sixth mode brings us to D Aeolian. You'll also remember that the keys of F major and D minor are related keys—F Ionian and D Aeolian are related modes from the same parent scale. The D Aeolian scale uses the interval formula WHWWHWW. See **FIGURE 6.6**.

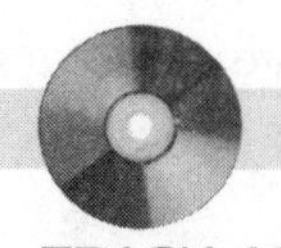

TRACK 19

FIGURE 6.6 Mode Six: *The Aeolian Mode* (Minor Scale)

Since the Aeolian scale is an exact minor scale, there's no need to compare it to another major or minor scale. Some players are still more comfortable with major scales. If this applies to you, just look at Aeolian as a major scale with lowered third, sixth, and seventh notes.

Locrian

The seventh and final mode is called the Locrian mode. In our parent scale of F major, the seventh mode is E Locrian. E Locrian mode uses the interval pattern HWWHWWW. See **FIGURE 6.7**. The Locrian mode has a very distinct sound that you won't encounter often. Actually, you may go your whole life without ever hearing it or using it. Nevertheless, it completes your knowledge of modes, so it's good to know it.

TRACK 20

FIGURE 6.7 Mode Seven: *The Locrian Mode*

The E Locrian scale (E–F–G–A–B♭–C–D–E) looks a lot like an E minor scale (E–F♯–G–A–B–C–D–E). The only difference is that the Locrian scale has a lowered second and a lowered fifth note.

Looking at Modes on Their Own

You now know modes in relation to a parent scale. If someone were to ask you to spell a C♯ Lydian scale, however, you might have quite an ordeal. First, you have to remember which number mode it is, then you have to backtrack and find the parent scale, and then you can spell the scale correctly. It's much more convenient to think of the modes on their own, which is how they are commonly used. It's much easier to understand modes than to have to take several steps to puzzle them out. Looking at modes as almost major or minor scales will help you understand them.

Here is a recap of the modes, their interval formulas, and easy ways to relate the scales:

▼ MODES, SCALES, AND INTERVAL FORMULAS

Mode	Scale	Interval Formula	Description
Mode 1	Ionian	WWHWWWH	Ionian is the major scale.
Mode 2	Dorian	WHWWWHW	Dorian is a minor scale with a raised sixth note.
Mode 3	Phrygian	HWWWHWW	Phrygian is a minor scale with a lowered second note.
Mode 4	Lydian	WWWHWWH	Lydian is a major scale with a raised fourth note.
Mode 5	Mixolydian	WWHWWHW	Mixolydian is a major scale with a lowered seventh note.
Mode 6	Aeolian	WHWWHWW	Aeolian is the minor scale.
Mode 7	Locrian	HWWHWWW	Locrian is a minor scale with lowered second and fifth notes.

By learning these formulas, you will be able to learn modes as their own scales and spell and relate to them quickly and easily.

Other Important Scales

Major scales, minor scales, and modes make up the majority of the scales encountered in Western music. However, they are not the only important scales; scales come in many different shapes and sizes, especially as you move throughout history.

Major Pentatonic

Pentatonic scales contain only five notes per octave as opposed to major and minor scales, which contain seven. The name *pentatonic* reflects this distinction as the prefix of pentatonic is *penta*, Greek for "five"—*tonic* means "tones" or "notes." The pentatonic scales are widely used in folk, liturgical, rock, and jazz music. Pentatonic scales come in two varieties: major and minor.

The familiar old sea chantey "What Do We Do with the Drunken Sailor?" is actually composed using a modal scale: the Dorian mode. Another famous example of modes is the theme to *The Simpsons,* which uses the Lydian mode for its main theme. Modes are all around us; they are often used in film and TV soundtracks as well.

The major pentatonic is a five-note scale derived from the major scale. It simply omits two notes—the fourth and seventh tones—from the major scale. In the key of G, the major pentatonic scale is G–A–B–D–E. Stated another way, the G major pentatonic is the first, second, third, fifth, and sixth notes of a major scale. See **FIGURE 6.8**.

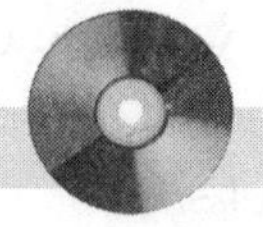

FIGURE 6.8 The Major Pentatonic Scale

TRACK 21

The major pentatonic is a mainstay of folk, blues, rock, and country music. Famous melodies such as "Mary Had a Little Lamb" and "London Bridge" were composed using only the major pentatonic scale. If you like to improvise solos, the major pentatonic is a basic and essential scale for improvisation over major tonalities found in music genres such as rock, jazz, and blues.

Minor Pentatonic

The minor pentatonic scale is also derived from a scale with two notes omitted (just not the same ones as the major pentatonic). A minor pentatonic scale leaves out the second and sixth tones from a natural (or more formally, Aeolian) minor scale. In the key of D, a minor pentatonic scale is D–F–G–A–C. You could also say that the scale is the first, third, fourth, fifth, and seventh notes of a natural minor scale. See **FIGURE 6.9.**

TRACK 22

FIGURE 6.9 The Minor Pentatonic Scale

Whole Tone

The whole-tone scale is built entirely with whole steps. Because it uses the same intervals, the whole-tone scale is considered a symmetric scale. Using whole steps from C, a C whole-tone scale is C–D–E–F♯–G♯–A♯. Note that the whole-tone scale is a six-note scale (see **FIGURE 6.10**). Not five notes like our pentatonic scales, or seven notes like major and minor scales, but six.

TRACK 23

FIGURE 6.10 The Whole-Tone Scales: *C and D♭*

C Whole Tone

D♭ Whole Tone

There are only two different whole-tone scales. Forming whole-tone scales from anywhere other than C or D♭ will yield the same notes as the C or D♭ whole-tone scales. See for yourself in **FIGURE 6.11**.

FIGURE 6.11 C and D Whole-Tone Scales

Both Scales Use the Same Pitches

Notice how both the C and D whole-tone scales contain the same notes. This makes them very easy to learn and play. You see whole-tone scales in romantic music and jazz music.

IN TIME

Jazz pianist Thelonious Monk loved the whole-tone scale and used it in many of his recorded improvised jazz solos. The whole-tone scale was his trademark. He wasn't the first to use it, but boy, did he like it!

Diminished/Octatonic Scales

The last scale is also symmetric and is built using repeating intervals. The diminished scale is based on repeating intervals, always half steps and whole steps. There are two varieties of diminished scales: one that starts with the pattern of whole step, half step intervals, and one that uses a half step, whole step interval pattern. **FIGURE 6.12** shows the two varieties of diminished scales, both starting from C. Diminished scales are also called octatonic, which is Greek for eight-note scale. This is the first scale that exceeds seven individual notes.

FIGURE 6.12 The Two Types of Octatonic/Diminished Scales

TRACK 24

There are only three unique diminished scales. Diminished scales spelled from C, C♯, and D are the only diminished scales that utilize unique tone sets. Spelling diminished scales from other roots will yield repeating scales, with the identical tones from C, C♯, or D diminished. Composers, theorists, and jazz players use diminished scales primarily.

ETUDES

ETUDE 6.1 Etude One

Spell modal scales from each note

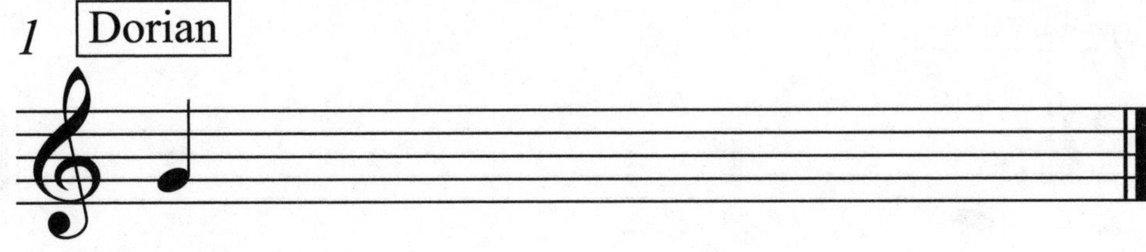

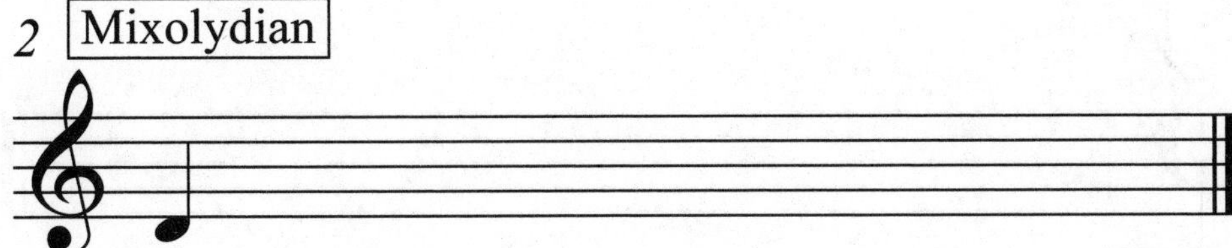

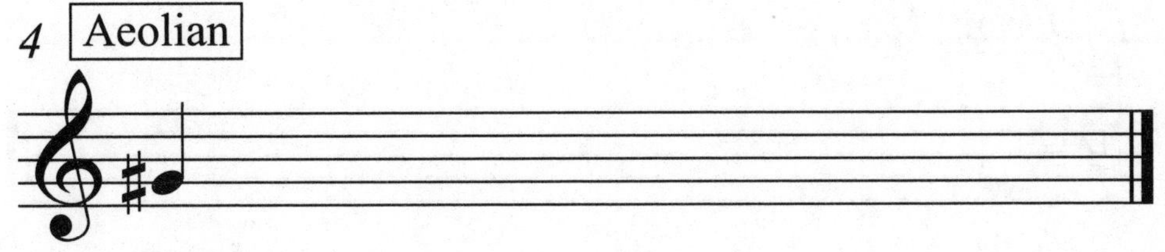

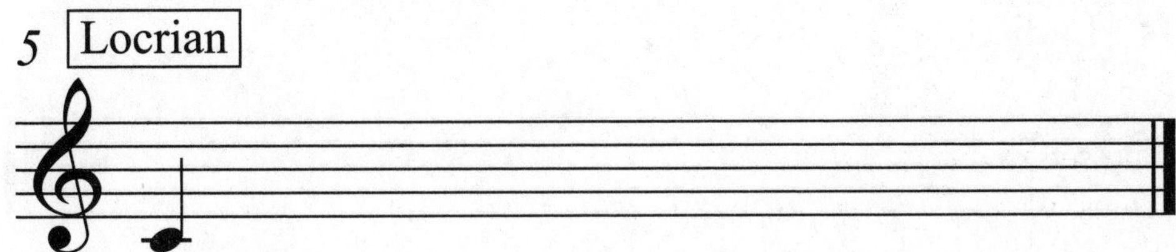

ETUDE 6.2 Etude Two

Spell modal scales from each note

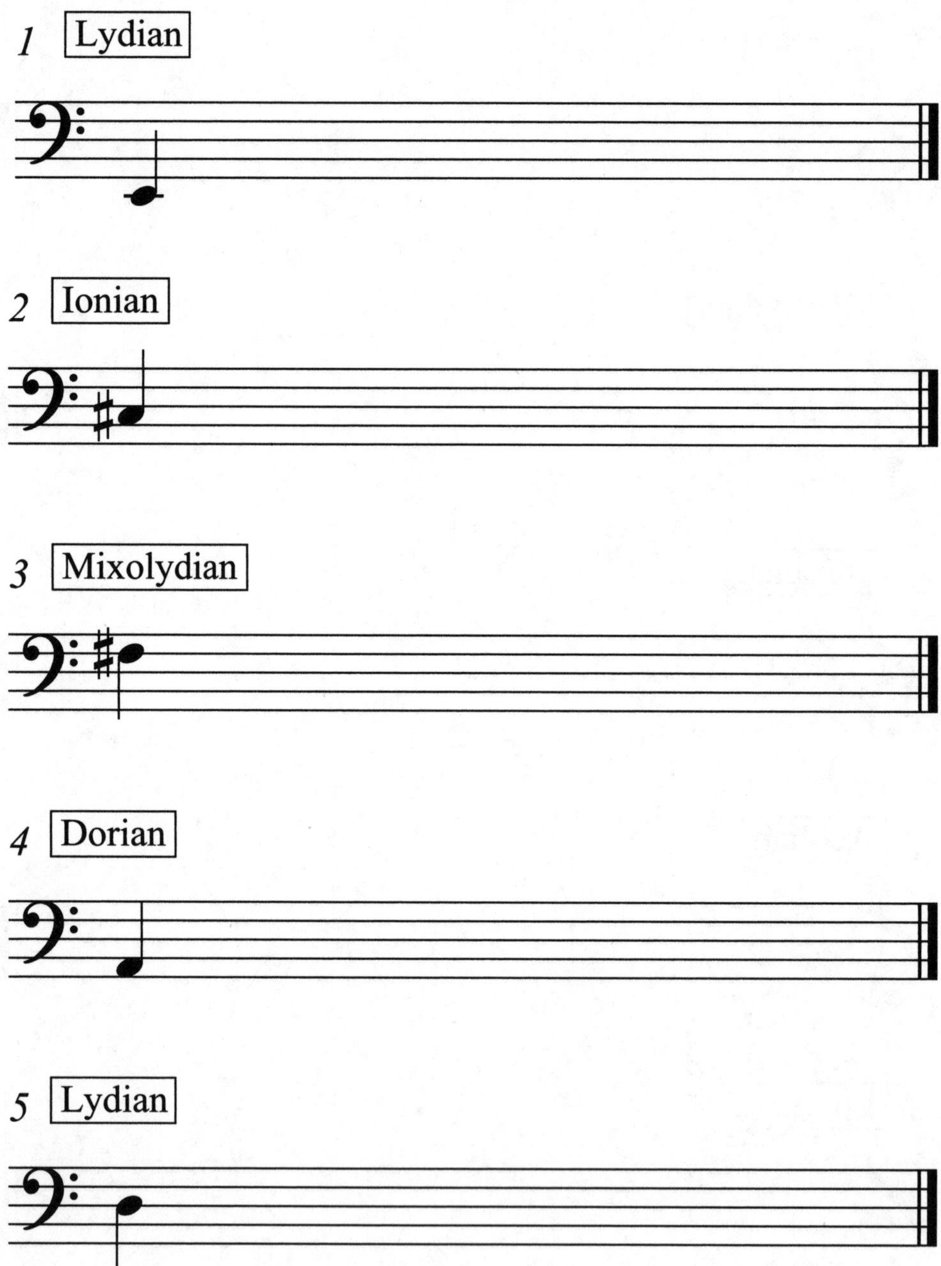

ETUDE 6.3 Etude Three

Spell major pentatonic scales from each note

ETUDE 6.4 Etude Four

Spell minor pentatonic scales from each note

ETUDE 6.5 Etude Five

Spell the following scales from each note

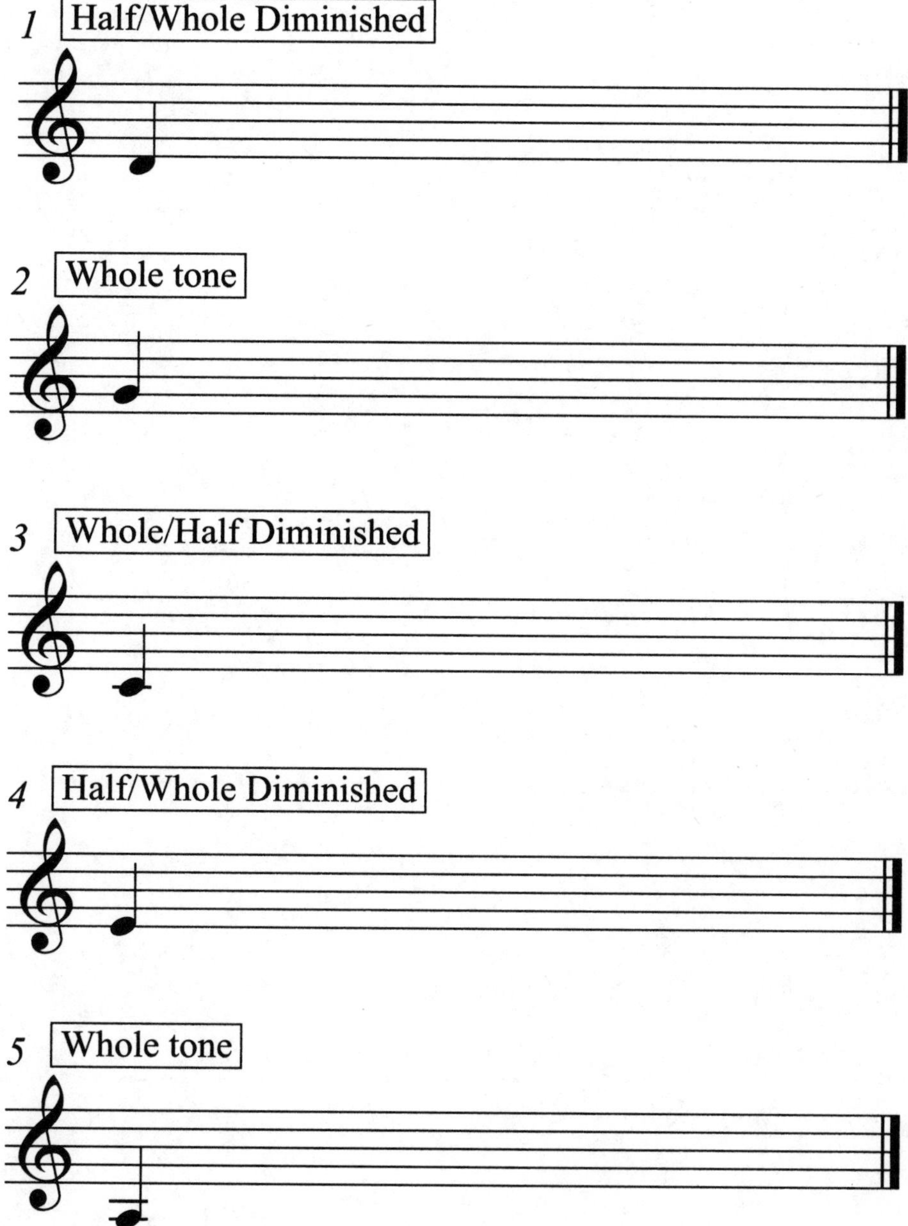

CHAPTER 7

Chords

Thus far, you have dealt with, at maximum, two notes at a time, when working with intervals. You have learned all about scales and key signatures, which give you all the possible arrangements of notes in a line. The next step is to look at chords and the basic foundations of harmony. Intervals combine into chords, and harmonies emerge from those chords, providing the foundation of tonality, which is the language spoken by the music you hear.

What Is a Chord?

What's a chord? Essentially, a chord is three or more notes sounded simultaneously. Chords can, of course, be more than three notes, so a few things need to be clarified. First, the simplest kind of chord is a triad, which begins with the prefix *tri,* meaning "three." A triad is a three-note chord, and the intervals between the notes (as you will learn soon) are always thirds apart—yet another use of the prefix *tri.*

Just like intervals, chords come in different qualities. The quality refers to the type of chord it is, which is always based on some sort of construction rule. The basic chord qualities for triads are major, minor, augmented, and diminished. Those are the same qualities that the intervals had (excluding perfect). So to recap, a chord, at its simplest, is a three-note triad with intervals that are thirds apart and notes that ring together. Before you go any further, look at **FIGURE 7.1** to see a simple C major triad.

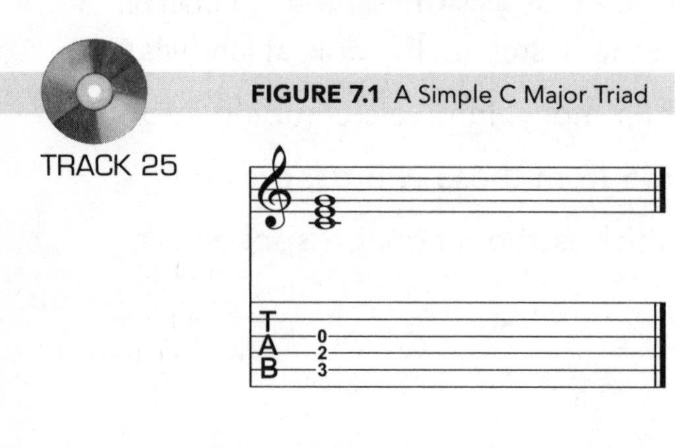

FIGURE 7.1 A Simple C Major Triad

That is the simplest way to look at a chord, essentially the model or prototype voicing, but rarely do you see chords in such clear order. You should think of triads as model chords. They are the simplest way to spell a chord. Unfortunately, rarely do you ever see such models of perfection in music. What you do see are chord voicings. A voicing is a rearrangement of the notes of the triad without adding or taking away from the essential ingredients (in the case of C major: C–E–G).

FIGURE 7.2 A Guitarist's Version of C Major

FIGURE 7.2 shows what a guitarist plays when asked to play a C major chord.

If you compare this chord with the pure triad in **FIGURE 7.1**, you can see that while they appear visually different on the page, in fact, they contain the same elements. Both chords contain the principal notes C, E, and G, but the guitar voicing repeats the notes C and E to fill out the chord and makes it sound fuller. Either way, it's still C–E–G, no matter how you slice it. When you analyze a chord, you look for the basic notes that define it. Typically, They are not all in a pretty little row, in triadic order; many times you have to hunt around, but you can do that later on. Now you need to define exactly what makes each chord what it is.

The son of a schoolmaster, Franz Schubert was born in Vienna on January 31, 1797, and died in Vienna on November 19, 1828, at the age of thirty-one. Even as a child he showed an extraordinary aptitude for music and studied the violin as well as the piano. His fame increased markedly after his death, and today he is perhaps best known for his piano sonatas.

Building Chords

If you understand your intervals well, building chords is no big deal. Each of the four triad qualities (major, minor, diminished, and augmented) has its own distinct building patterns, much as all the scales did: Once you learn the triad structures, you'll realize that they're so different from one another that it's hard to confuse them. Start by detailing the structure of the four basic triads in music, beginning with major.

Major Triads/Chords

The formations of each chord and triad are going to be described differently than in the past. Previously, it was formula first and then application. This time, you know enough to look at a chord first and then deduce the formula (with a bit of guidance).

Start by looking at a plain C major triad. See **FIGURE 7.3**.

Here's what you know about triads: They are three-note chords built in thirds. So, look at the structure of the intervals (which you know are thirds) between the notes and figure out the pattern.

FIGURE 7.3 The C Major Triad

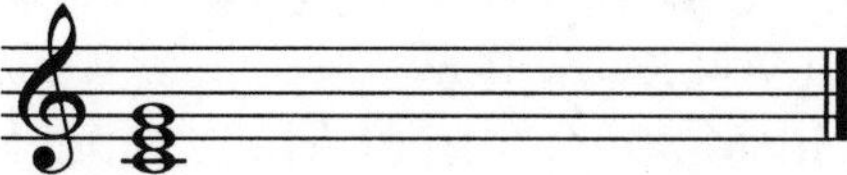

First up is the interval of C to E, which is a major third. Next is E to G, which is a minor third. You can now form formulas for major triads: Start with a root, any root you want, and add a major third from the root and a minor third from the resultant note. Think of it as major3/minor3 for short, knowing that with triads, you are always dealing with third intervals, and this will give you the fast way to spell this triad.

An Alternative View of Major Triads

Besides looking at the intervals in thirds, it is helpful to see a few other relationships that are present in the simple C major triad. First, look at C to E, which is clearly a major third interval. Now look at the interval from C to G. Intervals measure distance, and while the chord is composed of thirds, you're looking at the relationship only from one note to its adjacent note in the triad. What if you measured each interval from the root of the chord? Well, you would need to look at the distance from the first note (C) to the last note (G). The interval from C to G is a perfect fifth. To construct triads solely from the root, follow these steps:

1. Form a major third interval from the root of the chord.
2. Form a perfect fifth interval from the root of the chord.

It's important to know both ways to form triads. It's also beneficial to learn intervals from the root because you will realize something new: Triads have roots, thirds, and fifths!

Just like scales have to have seven notes and those seven notes have to use one letter from the musical alphabet each time they are spelled, triads must contain a root, a third, and a fifth. All of the basic triads from C will contain some form of C–E–G (with different accidentals, of course), but *all* C triads will have C–E–G. Knowing this fact makes spelling triads much faster—especially when you learn the derivative approach to forming triads from each other (which you will get to very soon).

The other thing to know about major triads is that they also have the root third and fifth from the major scale that they come from. For example, if you're spelling a D major chord, just take the first, third, and fifth notes from the D major scale (which you know how to spell so well now)—D–F♯–A—and bingo, you have an instant major triad. There's much more to triad formation, of course, and you will get into the whole range of what you can do with scales and their relations to chords in the section on diatonic chords later in this chapter. Now, it's on to minor chords.

Minor Triads/Chords

To help the derivative approach take root in your mind, look at all the chords in the chapter from a C root. This way, you can look at each possible variant and learn the differences among them. Sometimes, learning what stays the same and what changes can help you acquire knowledge faster. Start with a C minor triad in **FIGURE 7.4**.

Based on what you know about intervals, look at the distance between each of the third intervals to deduce a formula for this triad. Start with C to E♭, which is an interval of a minor third. E♭ to G is an interval of a major third. So the formula would be a minor third, major third. If you compare this formula with the formula for a major triad (major third, minor third), you see that both the major triad and the minor triad contain a major third and a minor third. What's unique is that both triads contain one of each quality of third, but they are backward. The major triad is major third, minor third, whereas the minor triad is minor third, major third.

TRACK 26

FIGURE 7.4 C Minor Triad

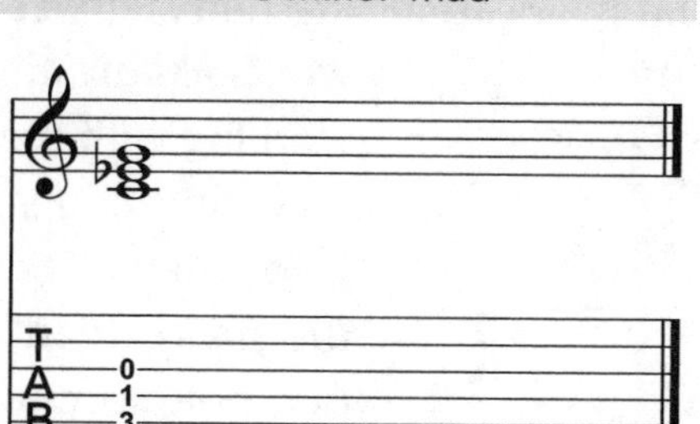

Here's a great way to remember the order of thirds in simple major and minor triads: The name of the triad will tell you the quality of the first third. Major triads start with major thirds, and minor triads start with minor thirds. Both triads conclude with the opposite interval; that is, major triads start with major thirds but conclude with minor thirds, and minor triads start with minor thirds but conclude with major thirds. Memorize this!

An Alternative View of Minor Triads

You can also look at the minor triads in a few other ways to aid your understanding. First, look at all the intervals from the root of C.

- The interval from C to E♭ is a minor third.
- The interval from C to G is a perfect fifth.

Remember that the major triad also had a perfect fifth. This characteristic is yet another reason that it is called a perfect interval. Since the fifths don't change, you have to look at the thirds to find the differences between the major and minor triads. Major triads have major thirds, and minor triads have minor thirds, and both have perfect fifths from their roots. It's amazing that the difference between a C major triad and a C minor triad is just one note, yet they sound so different. Use **FIGURE 7.5** as a sound example—change one note and the whole game changes.

Here's another look at the derivative approach to music: If you can spell any major triad, all you have to do to make it into a minor triad is to lower the third of the major triad one half step. It's a trick that always works. Many times, your speed at working with theory can come from changing things you already know. If you memorize the major scale and the major triad early on, changing one note to make either one major or minor isn't such a big deal. With music theory, you have to be very quick, and these tricks enhance your speed.

TRACK 27

FIGURE 7.5 C Major Versus C Minor: *A Sound Battle*

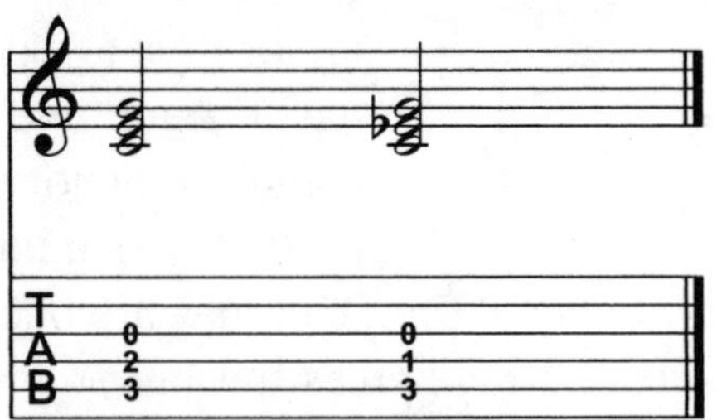

IN TIME

The major scale has been the basis for music theory. Many formulas and the entire idea of a derivative approach to theory exist because theorists are constantly deriving method and relationships from the major scale. As you will see, just about everything is some form of an altered major scale, or in the case of this chapter, a major chord.

The third way to look at a minor triad is to relate it to its corresponding minor scale. Remember, the major triad took the first, third, and fifth note from the C major scale. The C minor triad does the same thing, just from its corresponding minor scale. To spell a C minor triad, spell the C minor scale and select its first, third, and fifth notes: C–E♭–G. This may or may not be the fastest way for you to work.

Diminished Triads

Next up on your look at triads is the diminished triad. **FIGURE 7.6** shows a C diminished triad.

Break down the intervals in the C diminished chord. Start with the interval from C to E♭, which is a minor third. The next interval, from E♭ to G♭, is also a minor third. The intervallic pattern of this triad is minor third, minor third. This is important to note, because both intervals are minor thirds. Both the major and minor triads contain one of each third (one major third, one minor third), albeit each triad had the thirds in different order. The diminished triad has the same thirds (both minor). Think of it this way: Each triad contains two thirds, and there are only major and minor thirds to choose from. You can have two triads that use one major third and one minor third (in reverse order), and that gives you two possible triads (major and minor). If you use the same third twice, you can get two more triads. In the case of using two minor thirds, you get a diminished triad. You will see shortly what happens when you use two major thirds.

TRACK 28

FIGURE 7.6 C Diminished Triad

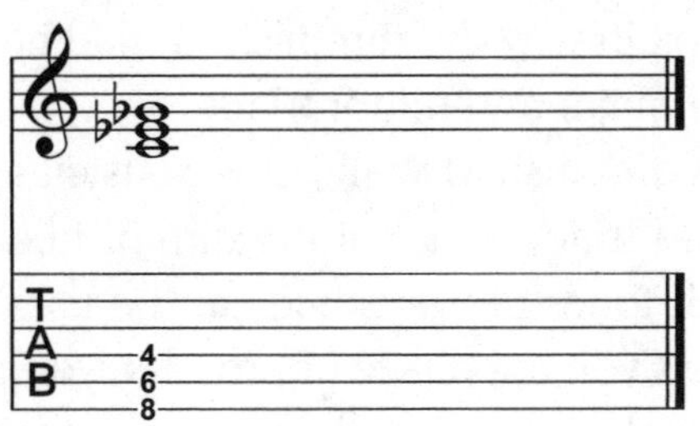

IN TIME

The diminished triad is used more in classical music than in popular music, although it is found in certain popular songs. A great example is "Michelle" by the Beatles, which uses a diminished chord in its harmony. Check out the sheet music to see where it is.

The naturally occurring scales are the major and minor scales. The other scales have been either created or are outgrowths of the major scale. Chords can be constructed solely on intervals, or they can be related to scales. As you will see shortly, they also can be derived from scales. The three triads you have explored thus far—major, minor, and diminished—occur naturally in music because of their relationship to scales. The final triad, augmented, is not a naturally occurring triad from any major or minor scale.

An Alternative View for Diminished Triads

Start off by looking at all the intervals in the C diminished triad, all measured from C.

- The interval from C to E♭ is a minor third.
- The interval from C to G♭ is a diminished fifth.

The diminished triad is the first time you see a fifth in a chord that isn't perfect. That could explain why the diminished triad has an unusual sound when compared to the major and minor triads.

Although there is a diminished scale, most musicians don't correlate the spelling of a diminished triad to that of the diminished scale, even though the first, third, and fifth tones of that scale can be used to form the chord. The reality is that unless you are a jazz improviser, you probably won't deal with the diminished scale except in theoretical understanding. For most of us, the derivative approach makes the most sense. If a C major triad is C–E–G and a C diminished chord is spelled C–E♭–G♭, then you can derive the following rule: To turn any major triad into a diminished triad, lower the third and fifth one half step.

You could alternatively derive the answer from the minor triad (1, ♭3, 5): To turn any minor triad into a diminished triad, lower the fifth one half step.

Augmented Triads

The last triad to examine is the augmented triad. At this point, you have seen triads formed from almost every possible combination of thirds; you're only missing one combination. A quick look at **FIGURE 7.7** will show you the intervallic formula of a C augmented triad.

FIGURE 7.7 C Augmented Triad

If you break down the chord by its third intervals, from C to E is a major third interval, and from E to G♯ is a major third. At last, you have every possible combination of thirds. The table below will explain what you can do with three notes and two thirds.

▼ **TABLE OF TRIAD FORMULAS**

Triad	Formula
Major	Major third, minor third
Minor	Minor third, major third
Diminished	Minor third, minor third
Augmented	Major third, major third

As you can see, these are all the possible combinations of major and minor thirds in a triad; these combinations yield the four triads that music uses.

Symmetry relates to intervals being consistent throughout a musical idea or form. Diminished and whole-tone scales are considered symmetrical because they contain either the same intervals (whole tone) or the same repeating interval pattern (diminished). With the introduction of diminished and augmented triads, your understanding of symmetry reaches the world of triads. Since diminished triads are composed solely of minor third intervals, they are symmetric triads. Also, since the augmented triad is composed solely of major thirds, it is also considered a symmetric triad.

POINT TO CONSIDER

If diminished triads are rare in popular music, then augmented triads are even more sparsely used. As always, learn as much as you can, and you may be the one to use an augmented triad in popular music. (Pink Floyd uses an augmented triad in "Us and Them.")

An Alternative View of Augmented Triads

Take another look at the augmented triad. This time look at all the intervals from the root of C.

The interval from C to E is a major third. The interval from C to G♯ is an augmented fifth. This is the second triad that has a nonperfect fifth (the other was diminished). It's also not a coincidence that the fifth is an augmented fifth, and the triad is called an augmented triad (the same with the diminished chords, diminished fifth interval).

Using the derivative approach for forming augmented triads, if you start with the C major triad (C–E–G) and compare it with the C augmented triad (C–E–G♯), you come to the following conclusion: To make any major triad into an augmented triad, simply raise the fifth note one half step.

Now, here's a recap of the derivative approach for all of the triads so you can become a triad speller in no time.

The Full Derivative Approach for Forming Triads

The derivative approach presupposes an ability to spell a major triad with ease. If you can't spell a major triad easily, work hard on major scales because much of the theory remaining in this book will derive from the major scale in some way; it's simply an excellent base.

The first slight change is that now you are only going to use numbers. So, instead of talking about the root, third, and fifth, you will simply say 1–3–5.

Here is the full listing of all the triads and how they derive from the major triad:

- Major 1–3–5
- Minor 1–♭3–5
- Diminished 1–♭3–♭5
- Augmented 1–3–♯5

Since this is a music book, look at all the triads side by side in **FIGURE 7.8** so you can see what's happening musically.

FIGURE 7.8 All Triads

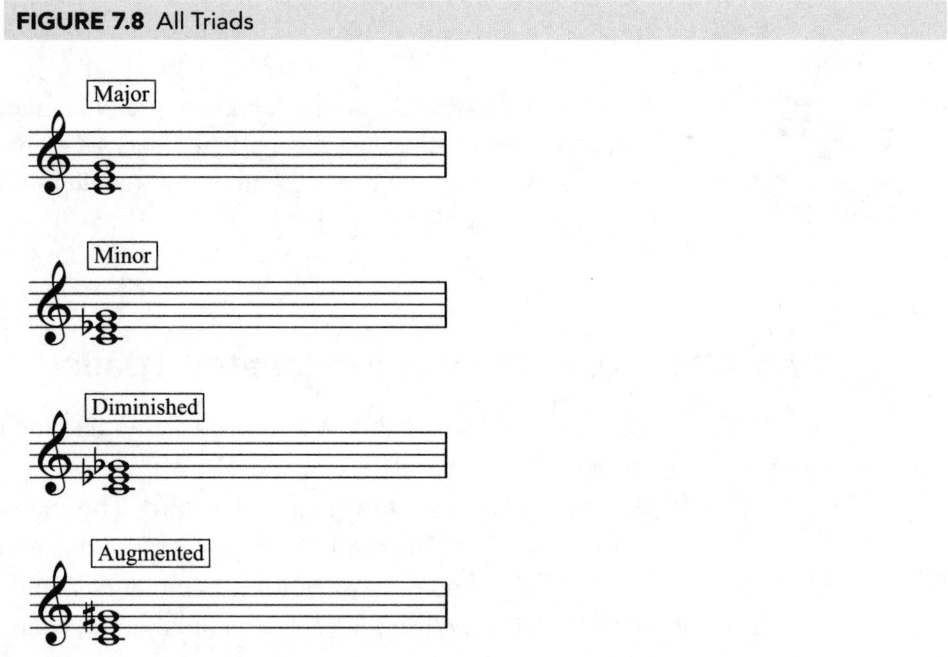

Knowing how to build triads on pure interval, from intervals from the root, and by deriving them from the basic major triad are all approaches that should be familiar to you.

Chords in Scales

Scales are very important. They are musical DNA—an essential building block. Now, it's time to revisit the C major triad. Look at **FIGURE 7.9**.

This triad can be constructed in a few different ways. First, take the first, third, and fifth notes of the C major scale and stack them together to build a quick C major triad. This trick works in every major and minor scale, so in theory, you could build any major or minor chord you need. Since chords are built from third intervals, it would make sense that you could do more than just stack the first, third, and fifth notes. There are many possible third combinations in a scale if you start on each note in the scale and build triads. What would happen if you stacked these different combinations from each note? You'd get a lot of different chords, seven to be exact—one from each degree of the scale.

FIGURE 7.9 Your Old Friend: *The C Major Triad*

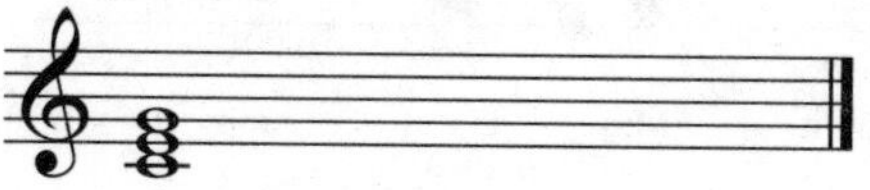

To learn how to make triads from every note in a C major scale, start with a C major scale and simply add triads (roots, thirds, and fifths) from each note in the scale. What you've just done is created all of the basic harmonies (and chords) in the key of C major by creating triads off each note. See **FIGURE 7.10**.

TRACK 30

FIGURE 7.10 Harmonizing the C Major Scale

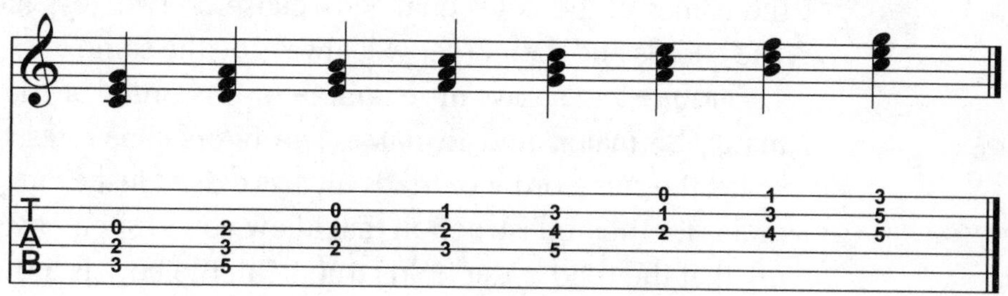

Don't downplay the significance of this accomplishment. You've just learned the basis for understanding harmony and chord progressions. Contained within those triads are seven different chords and endless possibilities for creating music. When you create triads from a scale and use only those notes to do so, you use a technique called diatonic harmony. *Diatonic* means using the notes from only one scale/key to make chords.

Diatonic Chords

In the last section, you added triads to each note in the C major scale, creating seven diatonic triads in that key. Now look at exactly what chords are created from making these triads (**FIGURE 7.11**).

FIGURE 7.11 Name Those Triads

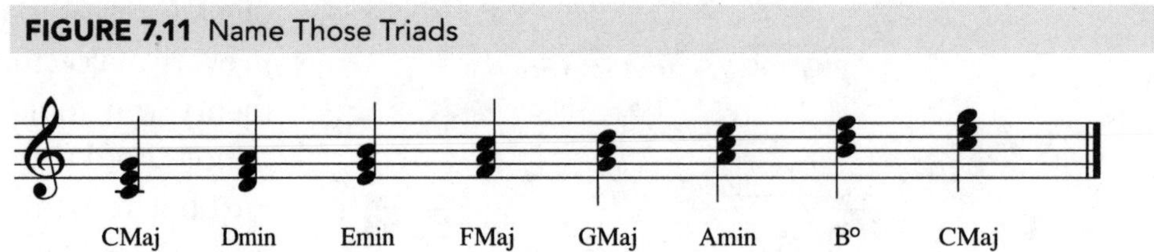

You can see from the example that a variety of triads are created. There is a major chord, minor chords, and a diminished chord. Strangely, augmented triads are missing.

The Order of Triads

The order of triads in the scale is important. In a major scale/key, the triads always progress in this order: major, minor, minor, major, major, minor, and diminished. Memorize this order; it's going to serve you quite well—and the best part is that what you've just done in the key of C major holds true in every major key. Since all major scales are constructed in the same fashion, with the same intervals, when you stack triads in any major scale, you always get the same order of triads/chords. This is a huge time-saver! Only the names of the notes change because no two keys have the same pitch. The chords and their order will always be the same.

FIGURE 7.12 shows an example of this order of triads in the key of D major, B♭ major, and E major. The figure illustrates that no matter the scale, the same order of triads always exists. Just as major scales have formulas for their construction that allow you to spell any scale easily, knowing that the triad order holds true to all the keys is a dependable element in music theory.

Notice that the notes in the scales are in different keys, but the order of chords (major, minor, minor, major, major, minor, and diminished) stays the same. This holds true for every major scale/key.

FIGURE 7.12 Different Keys, Same Triad Order

DMaj Emin F♯min GMaj AMaj Bmin C♯° DMaj

B♭Maj Cmin Dmin E♭Maj FMaj Gmin A° B♭Maj

EMaj F♯min G♯min AMaj BMaj C♯min D♯° EMaj

Roman Numerals

To music theorists, there isn't any real difference between any major key. Unless you have perfect pitch, so you can name a note just by listening to it, you won't be able to hear a difference between C major and D major scales. Since there is such equality in the keys, music theory has a system of naming chords relative to the note of the scale from which they are built. If you were to number the notes and their corresponding triads from the G major scale, you'd end up with the image in **FIGURE 7.13**.

FIGURE 7.13 Numerals with Triads

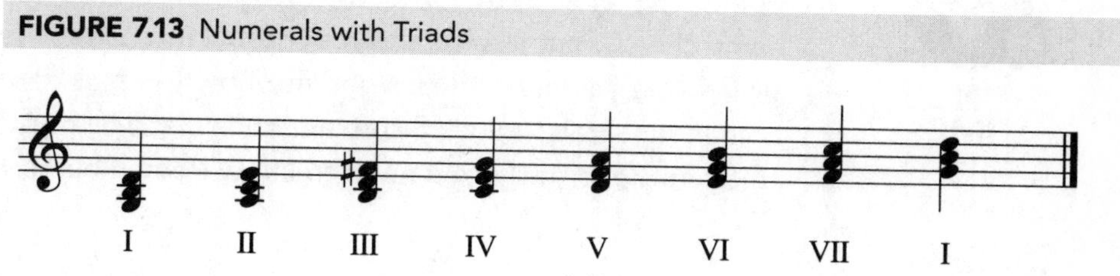

Since triads are built off the notes, they can be referred to by a number and/or Roman numeral. For example, a one chord in the key of C major is the chord built off the first note in the scale, which is C major. Since every major scale starts with a major triad, the one chord in any major key is major.

In Chapter 3, you learned the names of the scale degrees. When discussing chords, the scale degree names are used as well. I (one) chords are referred to as tonic chords, while V (five) chords are referred to as dominant chords. This corresponds with the information in Chapter 3 on the proper names for scale degrees.

The only limitation is that there is no way to convey whether that chord is major or minor simply by using the number 1, 2, or 3. Musicians use Roman numerals instead of Arabic numbers for this very reason. You may remember from math class that Roman numerals have lowercase equivalents. By using uppercase Roman numerals for major chords and lowercase Roman numerals for minor chords, musicians have created a system that makes sense in every key and conveys a lot of information about a chord.

FIGURE 7.14 shows the harmonized major scale with the corresponding Roman numerals. Notice that the diminished chord is denoted by a lowercase Roman numeral and a small degree symbol next to it. That's the standard way to indicate diminished chords.

FIGURE 7.14 Major Scale with Roman Numerals to Indicate Chord Quality

Roman numerals are a standard way for music theorists not only to name chords, but also to analyze choral structures in pre-existing music in order to gain some insight into how the music was constructed. Roman numerals are still a convention in classical music. If you plan to study music formally, you need to know Roman numerals.

Minor Scale Harmony

The minor scale has a few peculiarities. Although the minor scale has the same notes as the relative major scale/key signature it's derived from and should have the exact same resulting chords, in a different order, the minor scale has some quirks when it comes to harmony. Recall the harmonic minor scale, a minor scale with a raised seventh tone, from Chapter 4. The harmonic minor scale exists solely to correct the harmony of the minor scale and make it more useful. Look at the normal minor scale harmonized with triads in **FIGURE 7.15**.

TRACK 31

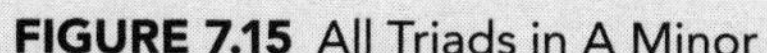

FIGURE 7.15 All Triads in A Minor

By harmonizing the A natural minor scale, you get the same chords as you did in C major, just in a different order. There is nothing wrong with the natural minor scale. However, in tonal music, that minor scale is not harmonized, because it's lacking what is known as a proper dominant chord. Chapter 9 examines functional chord progressions to show you how the minor scale is actually used in practice.

Hearing Chords

Just as we discussed in Chapter 2, you can use relative pitch to identify chord quality completely by ear. Rather than use individual songs, however, you can use musical perception. Here are some examples to get you started as well as songs/situations where those chords have been used.

- **Major chords:** Many musicians associate major chords with bright, happy times. This perception is further reinforced by movies and popular music. Love songs are often in major keys. Watch a movie and listen to the soundtrack. Whenever the good guy wins, you can bet that a major key/chord is being utilized.
- **Minor chords:** Minor chords have long been associated with sadness and melancholy. Whenever Darth Vader (or any of the Empire) is around in *Star Wars*, you can bet that John Williams opted for minor chords/keys. Beethoven's beautiful "Moonlight Sonata" starts out in a minor key/chord.
- **Diminished chords:** Diminished chords are a bit harder to identify, since they are less common and we don't hear music in diminished keys. Diminished chords often appear in the soundtrack during

suspenseful situations. Got a girl tied to the railroad tracks and the train is approaching? Use a diminished chord; most cartoons, old movies, and soap operas do.

- **Augmented chords:** Augmented chords are also difficult to talk about because they are also fairly rare. While diminished chords are suspenseful, augmented chords often sound dissonant. Although they can be quite beautiful in context, they are rarely consonant on their own.

Listen to each of these chords; get to know their sounds. It will help you as a music theorist and as a musician.

ETUDES

ETUDE 7.1 Etude One

Write major triads from the following notes

ETUDE 7.2 Etude Two

Write minor triads from the following notes

ETUDE 7.3 Etude Three

Write diminished triads from the following notes

ETUDE 7.4 Etude Four

Write augmented triads from the following notes

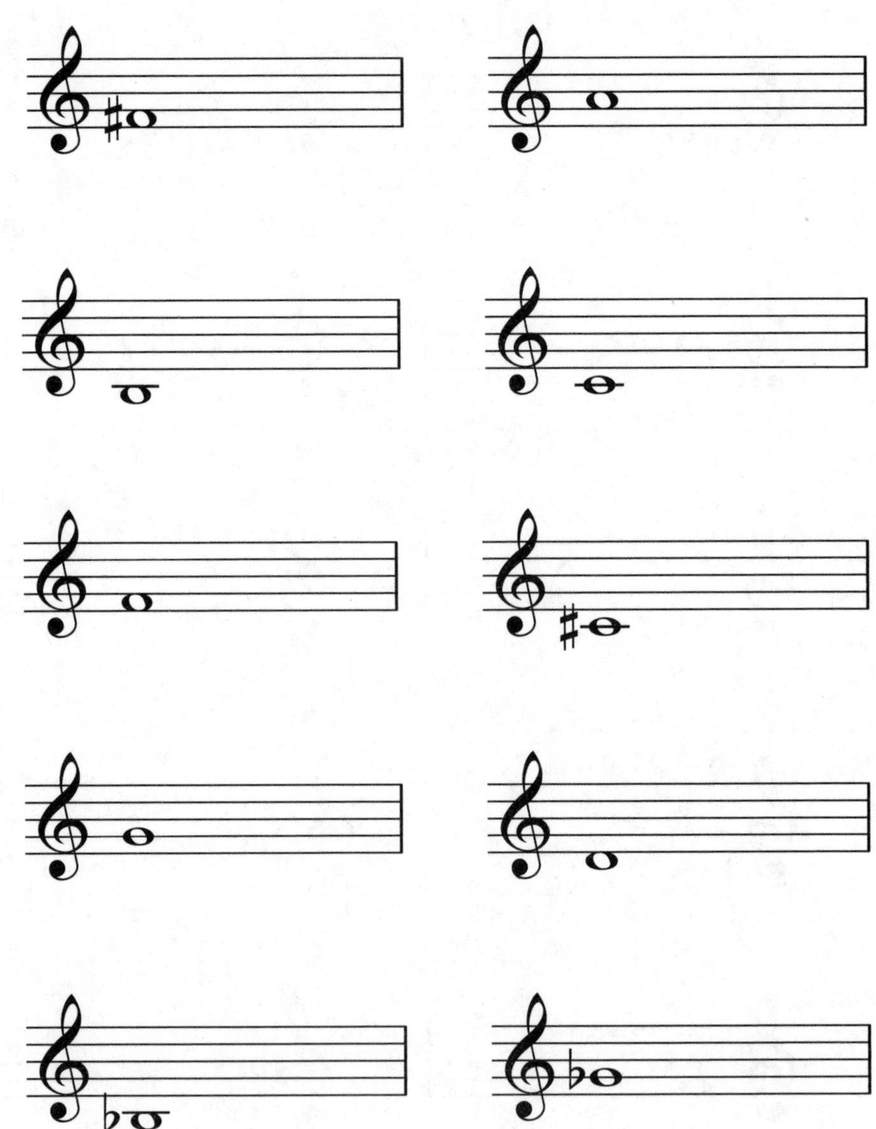

ETUDE 7.5 Etude Five

Write major scales from the following notes, harmonize with triads and name the chords.

CHAPTER 8

Seventh Chords and Chord Inversions

Chords are more than just a collection of intervals! You know from Chapter 7 that chords have their origins in scales and melodies. To understand chords in their entirety, however, you need to look at two more aspects: seventh chords and chord inversions. Used extensively in music throughout the ages, seventh chords are the next logical step after you understand triads. Inversions allow chords to move smoothly and efficiently from one chord to the next; this is the foundation for voice leading.

Seventh Chords

A triad is a three-note chord. Triads take care of most of the basic harmony, but not all of it. You build all chords in thirds. When you derived diatonic harmony from major and minor scales, you stacked thirds from each root and came up with seven triads—all built in thirds. Your knowledge of intervals allowed you to decode what the triads were and what order they appear in. See **FIGURE 8.1**.

FIGURE 8.1 Diatonic Triads in F Major

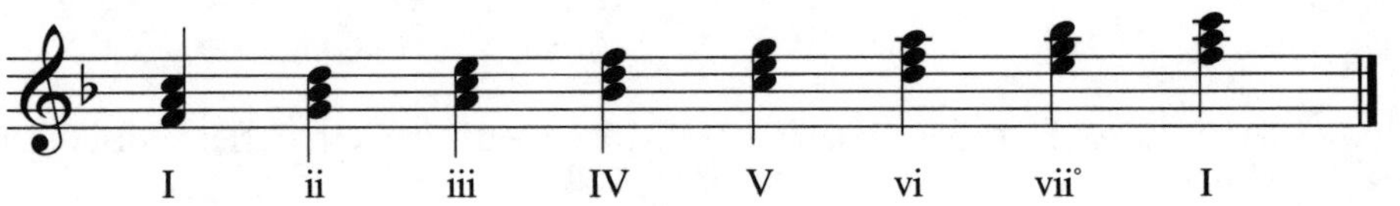

Now, what would happen if you added another third to your triads? Well, simply, you'd form seventh chords, which are so named because the last interval added is seven notes away from the root. You could call them quadads, but it doesn't have the same ring to it as seventh chord does—plus it sounds like a form of sit-ups.

The majority of the harmony you deal with is built in intervals of thirds. This type of harmony is called tertian harmony and is the basis for common practice or tonal harmony that is studied and still utilized today.

Diatonic Seventh Chords

Remember the term *diatonic*? It means "from the key." You first learned about diatonic when you formed simple triads within a scale. Do it again in F major.

Now, to make these diatonic triads into seventh chords, add another third on top of each triad, adding an interval of a seventh if you measure from the root. Remember to use only the notes from the F scale (F–G–A–B♭–C–D–E–F) when adding your thirds to keep this example diatonic. Doing so will leave you with these seventh chords (see **FIGURE 8.2**).

TRACK 32

FIGURE 8.2 Diatonic Seventh Chords in F Major

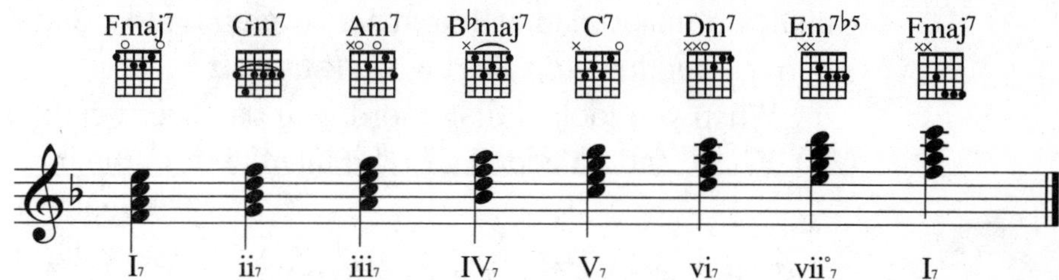

In this list, there are four different types of seventh chords: major seventh, minor seventh, dominant seventh, and half diminished seventh.

Notice that in **FIGURE 8.2**, the Roman numerals used to analyze the chords did not identify which kind of seventh chord it was. They simply added 7 next to each Roman numeral. The answer had to be spelled out. So you need to understand what makes a major seventh different from a dominant seventh, even though both use uppercase Roman numerals (signifying major chords) with sevenths attached to them.

POINT TO CONSIDER

Typically, even if your experience with theory is limited, you've come across, played, or heard about a G7 chord (or any other root). This is one kind of seventh chord (as you will learn about). This book uses the term *seventh chord* as a broad category. Seventh chords come in many different types, and G7 is simply one type.

Diatonic seventh chords are definitely useful, and in Chapter 9, you will see just how useful they are, when the focus is on chord progressions. For now, you need to understand the structure of seventh chords, because modern music uses more than just the four diatonic seventh chords.

Seventh Chord Construction

Here, you will explore all the available seventh chords. You should begin to think like this: A seventh chord is nothing more than a triad with an added seventh interval (when measured from the root). This gives you at least eight seventh chords (four possible triads and two sevenths), although there is one more that breaks the rules. Go through these chords one by one to see how they are put together and how they are named.

Major Triads with Sevenths

To make a major triad into a seventh chord, there are only two possibilities: a major triad with a major seventh on top, and a major triad with a minor seventh on top. Start with **FIGURE 8.3**.

When you look at that chord, you can see two things: a major triad, D (D–F♯–A), and an added C♯. The interval from the root of the chord to the seventh (D to C♯) is a major seventh. Call this chord a major/major seventh chord for a second because it tells you exactly what you have: a major triad with a major seventh interval added. Now, the rest of the world calls this chord a major seventh, as in D major seventh, or Dmaj7 for short. Many theorists use major/major seventh to be more specific, but if you say D major seventh, you're saying exactly the same thing. The major seventh chord is found on the first (tonic) and fourth (subdominant) degrees of a harmonized major scale.

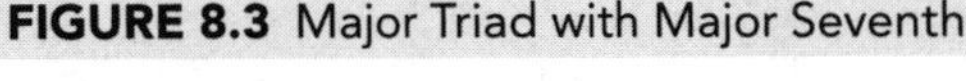

FIGURE 8.3 Major Triad with Major Seventh

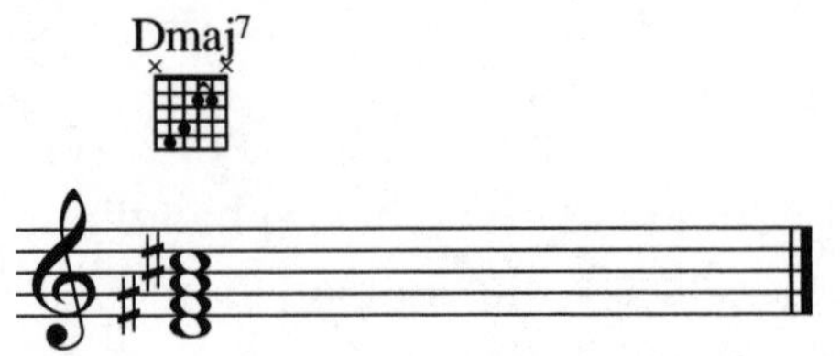

You could think of the formula for a major seventh chord as being: 1, 3, 5, 7. (This is if you take the scale degrees from a major scale.)

The major seventh chord is interesting for two reasons: First, you can spell it simply by choosing the first, third, fifth, and seventh notes from any major scale. This is because a major seventh chord is the tonic seventh chord in a major key. Second, its proper name of major/major seventh shortens to simply major seventh.

The next possible seventh chord would be **FIGURE 8.4**. Looking at this chord, you see another D major triad (D–F♯–A) and an added seventh of C. The interval between D and C is a minor seventh. This chord is fully called a major/minor seventh chord. When it's shortened, it's simply called a seventh chord, as in G7, or D7 in this case. The term *seventh chord* is far too general for music theory. Theorists and

FIGURE 8.4 Major Triad with Minor Seventh

many musicians call this chord a dominant seventh chord because, as illustrated in **FIGURE 8.1**, this chord occurs only on the fifth scale degree, which has the proper name of the dominant scale degree. Whichever you call it, G7 or G dominant seventh, both are acceptable and correct.

The formula for a dominant seventh chord is: 1, 3, 5, ♭7 (if you take the scale degrees from the major scale). Dominant seventh chords are really important. It's awfully hard to have harmony without dominant (V) chords.

Minor Triads with Sevenths

Minor triads with sevenths also have two varieties. Start with **FIGURE 8.5**.

Start with a C minor triad (C–E♭–G) and add a B♭. The interval from C to B♭ is a minor seventh, so this chord is called a C minor / minor seventh chord. It's shortened to simply C minor seventh or Cm7 or C-7. This is the basic minor seventh chord that is found on the second, third, and sixth scale degrees of a harmonized major scale. Again, just as the major seventh, when both the triad and the seventh are the same (both minor), the name of the chord is simply minor seventh. You can form the minor seventh chord by taking the first, third, fifth, and seventh notes from a pure minor scale (Aeolian). If you wanted to relate the scale to major, its formula would be: 1, ♭3, 5, ♭7 (relating the scale degrees to the major scale).

TRACK 35

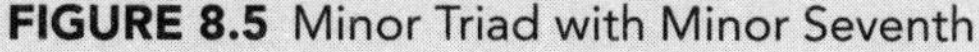
FIGURE 8.5 Minor Triad with Minor Seventh

The next seventh chord is the first unnatural seventh chord; it's not formed in the diatonic major or minor scales. Take a look at **FIGURE 8.6**.

This C minor triad with an added B natural gives a very unusual sound—unnatural, even. The interval from C to B is a major seventh, so the full name for this chord would be a C minor / major seventh chord. There is no other name for this chord; it is always referred to as a minor/major seventh chord. The only shorthand you may see is in the chord symbols in popular music: Cm(maj7), C-(maj7), or Cmin(maj7). While these chords have an unusual sound, they can be quite striking and beautiful when used in the proper context. Again, this triad does not occur anywhere in the natural major or minor scales.

TRACK 36

FIGURE 8.6 Minor Triad with Major Seventh

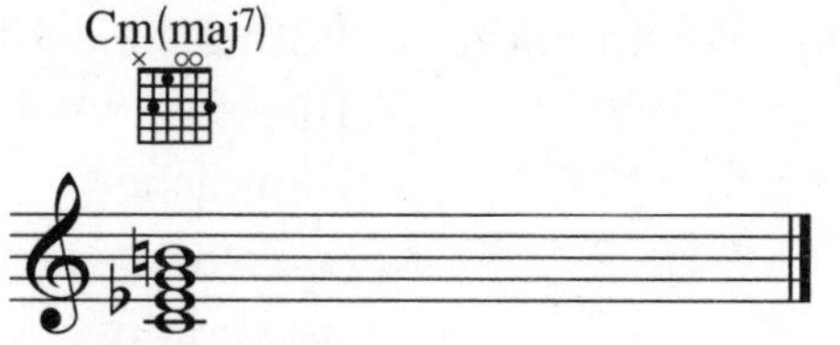

POINT TO CONSIDER

To harmonize the harmonic or melodic minor scales, you would spell a minor/major seventh from the tonic scale degree. This is where modern theorists see the chord originating. Others think that it is simply the natural extension of trying a minor triad with a major seventh interval added to it. Either way, it exists in jazz and popular music, most famously in "Us and Them" by Pink Floyd, on their legendary *Dark Side of the Moon* album.

A formula for a minor/major seventh chord would appear as follows: 1, ♭3, 5, 7 (if you take the scales degrees from the major scale).

That's all you can do to minor triads and sevenths. That brings your grand total up to four seventh chords, and you're through only major and minor. Next up: diminished.

Diminished Triads with Sevenths

Diminished chords are a bit tricky, especially when it comes to naming them. Start with the diatonic diminished seventh chord (see **FIGURE 8.7**), built from the leading tone of a major scale.

What you have is a B diminished triad with an added A. The interval from B to A is a minor seventh, so the full name for this chord is a diminished/minor seventh. However, here's where it gets tricky. This chord is called a half diminished chord. Half diminished chords use the symbol B$^{\varnothing}$7.

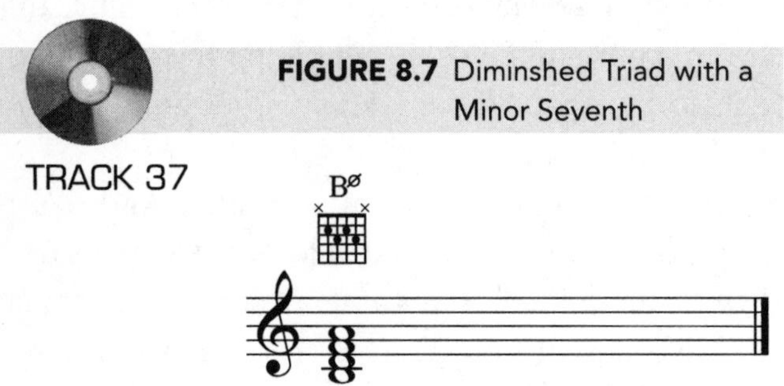

FIGURE 8.7 Diminshed Triad with a Minor Seventh

TRACK 37

A formula for the half diminished seventh chord would look like this: 1, ♭3, ♭5, ♭7 (if you take these from the major scale degrees).

This chord, while it may be the diatonic chord, is not the typical diminished seventh chord. Look at another diminished seventh chord in **FIGURE 8.8**, which will explain why that particular chord is called half diminished.

FIGURE 8.8 Diminshed Triad with a Diminshed Seventh

TRACK 38

Start with a diminished triad and add an A♭. The interval from B to A♭ is a diminished seventh. The full name for this chord would be a diminished/diminished seventh.

Just like major and minor seventh chords that share the same name and type of seventh, this is the diminished seventh chord. It's also called a fully diminished seventh chord, but for most people, diminished seventh will do. The symbol for a fully diminished seventh chord is B°7.

A formula for the diminished seventh chord would look like this: 1, ♭3, ♭5, 𝄫7 (if you take these from major scale degrees). *Note:* This is the first time you've seen a double flat in a chord formula. Fully diminished seventh chords don't occur in major or minor scales naturally; they are the result of stacking minor third intervals. You can also derive this chord if you harmonize the harmonic minor scale at the leading tone degree.

Half and Whole Diminished

It's a bit confusing—why is one diminished chord half diminished and another whole diminished? Well, for starters, it's a name. But there's more to it than that. The diminished triad is a symmetric chord in that it uses all minor third intervals. When you spell a diminished seventh chord, you actually use all minor thirds again (B–D–F–A♭). It is called fully diminished because it follows the pattern of all minor thirds and becomes perfectly symmetrical at that point. A half diminished chord (B–D–F–A) has a major third between the fifth and the seventh and isn't fully diminished because it loses the pattern of all minor thirds. That's where the difference comes from. Ninety percent of the time when you see diminished chords with sevenths, they are fully diminished seventh chords. Half diminished chords are used mostly in jazz but sometimes in classical and popular music as well.

Since the diminished chord comes in two flavors—half and full diminished—modern musicians, especially jazz musicians, help differentiate these two chords. They simply do not call a half diminished chord a half diminished. Look at a half diminished chord as a minor seventh chord with a ♭5. To avoid confusion, most modern music uses min7b5 instead of the half diminished symbol (ø). This way, when you see a diminished symbol (°), you can infer that it's a fully diminished chord.

Augmented Triads with Sevenths

Augmented triads are weird chords. They have a particular sound that isn't used very much. Nonetheless, modern music, especially jazz, uses augmented seventh chords, which come in two varieties. Start with **FIGURE 8.9**.

Start with the G augmented triad of (G–B–D♯) and add an F♯. The interval from G to F♯ is a major seventh, so this chord would be called an augmented major seventh. For short, the symbol G+(maj7) or Gaug(maj7) is used. A formula for this chord would look like this: 1, 3, ♯5, 7 (if you derive this from the degrees of a major scale).

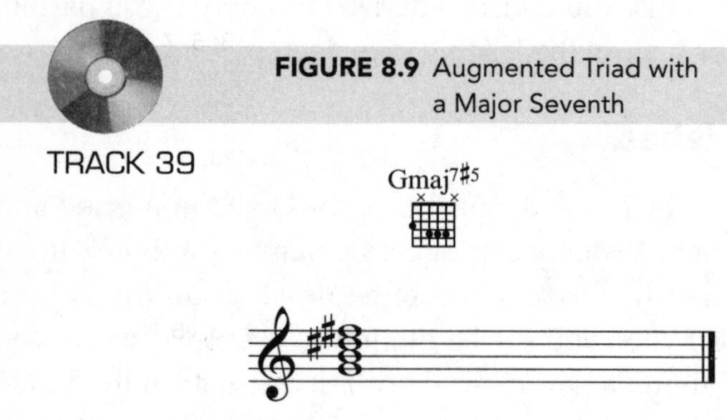

FIGURE 8.9 Augmented Triad with a Major Seventh

This chord does not occur in natural major or minor scales, but it is on the third degree (submedian) of the harmonized harmonic and melodic minor scales. It's a very strong musical sound and is used in modern jazz quite a bit as well as late romantic and twentieth-century music.

The other augmented chord is shown in **FIGURE 8.10**.

Start again with the G augmented triad and add an F. The interval from G to F is a minor seventh, so the full name for this chord would be an augmented minor seventh. Typically, this is shortened to G+7, Gaug7, or G7♯5—all are synonymous. The G+7 chord is closely related to a G7 chord. The augmented nature of the raised fifth is simply seen as an alteration. Typically, this chord functions much the same way as a dominant V chord does. You'll learn more in the next chapters on usage.

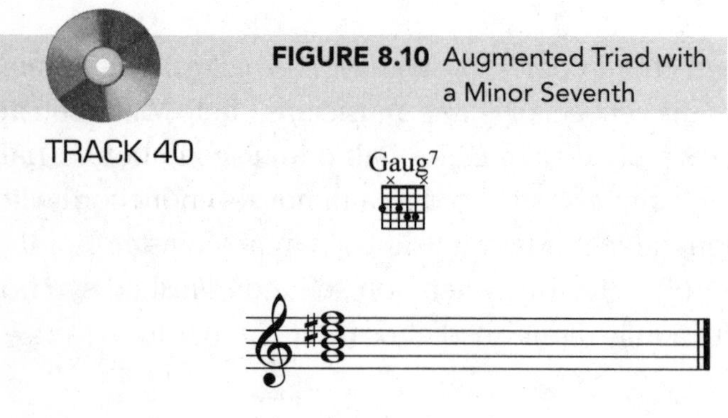

FIGURE 8.10 Augmented Triad with a Minor Seventh

The formula for this chord would look like this: 1, 3, ♯5, ♭7 (if you derive the formula from major scale degrees).

Well, as far as seventh chords go, that's it. As you will see from the music later in the book, four or five out of the eight chords appear in everyday usage, but if you want to know about chords and how they are formed, then you'll want to understand how to form them from their intervallic relationships.

Seventh Chord Recap

You just spent a fair amount of time going over all eight seventh chords. The following table contains all that information in one place as it displays all the formulas side by side.

▼ **FORMULAS DERIVED FROM A MAJOR SCALE**

Name	Symbol	Intervals
Major seventh	Cmaj7	1, 3, 5, 7
Dominant seventh	C7	1, 3, 5, ♭7
Minor seventh	Cmin7	1, ♭3, 5, ♭7
Minor/Major seventh	Cmin(maj7)	1, ♭3, 5, 7
Half diminished seventh	CØ7	1, ♭3, ♭5, ♭7
Fully diminished seventh	C°7	1, ♭3, ♭5, 𝄫7
Augmented major seventh	C+(maj7)	1, 3, ♯5, 7
Augmented seventh	C+7	1, 3, ♯5, ♭7

You have almost completed your study of chords. Now, you will learn about chord inversions.

Inverted Chords

When you think of the word *inverted,* what comes to mind? Most people think of *upside down* or *backward.* When it comes to inverted chords, this is actually not too far from the truth. Every triad and seventh chord you have seen in this book has been in "root" position. Root position means that the root of the chord (the tone its name is derived from) is the lowest note in the chord. Although there are a lot of times when chords appear in root position, it's not the only way that they function. Any other note in the chord can take the lowest voice, and that is exactly what an inversion is: when the third, fifth, or seventh note (if present) is in the bass voice.

Inversions can make chords a bit harder to spot on paper because that wonderful third order disappears. Regardless, inverted chords are found in all styles of music throughout almost the entire history of written music, so you should know a lot about them. With inverted chords comes a new set of symbols. Start with triads and their inversions and then move on to seventh chords, as they are treated a bit differently.

Inverted Triads

Okay, start off with your friend, the root position C major triad (**FIGURE 8.11**). By now, you should be able to identify this chord quickly as a root position C triad. Go a step further and analyze it with a Roman numeral. The answer is Roman numeral I, because in the key of C, C is the tonic or I chord.

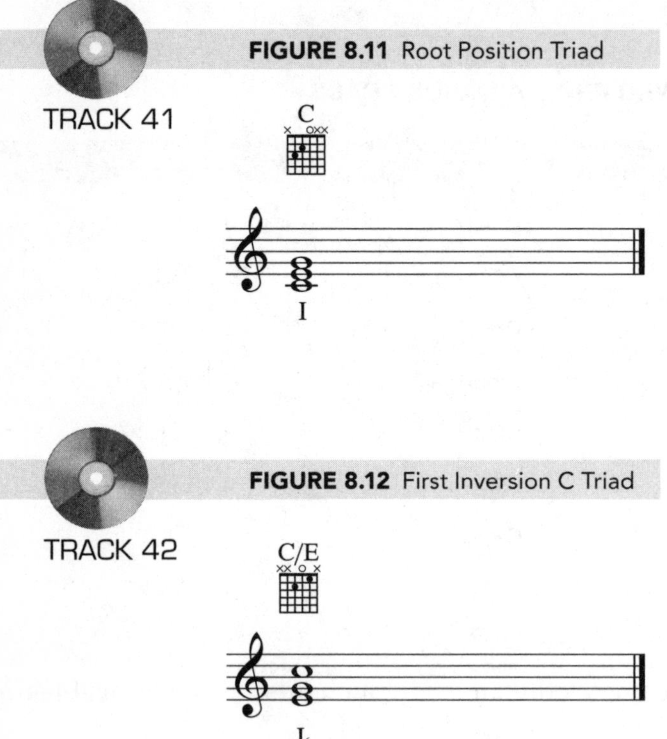

FIGURE 8.11 Root Position Triad

FIGURE 8.12 First Inversion C Triad

Now, to start inverting this triad, raise the bass note (which is C) one octave. The result is **FIGURE 8.12**.

With the C raised an octave, the third of the chord (E) becomes the lowest-sounding note in the chord. Whenever the third of the chord is in the bass (the lowest-sounding) voice, that triad is said to be in first inversion. Now, there are two ways to name this chord: the classical way and the modern way. You will be given both.

The classical way of naming this triad would be to call it a I_6. Why is it called a I_6? If you look at the interval between the lowest note in the chord (E) to the C, it is a sixth; that's where the six comes from. The interval from the E to the G is disregarded because it's a third and it's accepted that it would be a third. That is just the way it has evolved.

When analyzing this chord in classical style, every first inversion chord will have a small subscript 6 next to its Roman numeral. This is true no matter what kind of triad it is; major, minor, diminished, and augmented in first inversion are all 6 chords. It also doesn't matter which Roman numeral they are functioning as. All seven chords in the harmonized scale can be in first inversion with the marking of a subscript 6.

Now, as to the modern notation, this one is easy: The triad is simply called C/E, which translates to C chord with an E in the bass. The slash (/) is commonly referred to as *over*, as in triad over bass note. Regardless of which is easier, it's good to know both—if you want to learn traditional theory at some point, you'll need to know these figured bass symbols.

Remember how the first inversion was made? You simply took the lowest note and popped it up one octave. Well, to get to a second inversion, you are going to do exactly the same thing. This time, you start with a first inversion

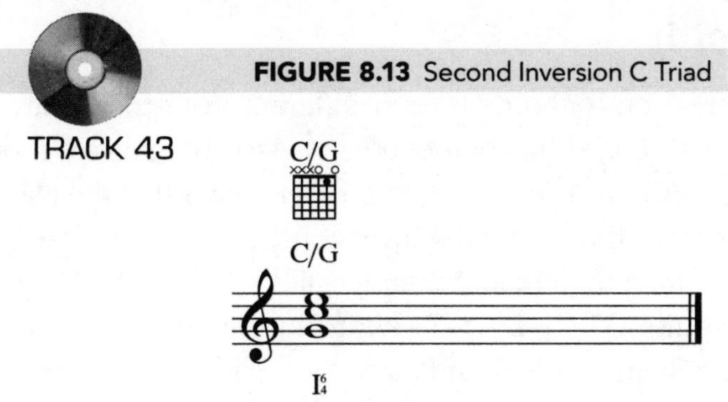

FIGURE 8.13 Second Inversion C Triad

triad and move the E up an octave. The result is shown in **FIGURE 8.13**.

That wasn't so hard to do, was it? So, to summarize what you have now: You still have a C triad and the notes C–E–G; those elements never change. What has changed is that the lowest note in the chord is now the fifth of the chord (G). Whenever the fifth of the chord is in the bass of any triad, it becomes a second inversion triad.

The classical way of naming this triad would be to call it I $^6_4$. It's a I $^6_4$ triad because the intervals from the lowest note (G) are as follows: G to E is a sixth and G to C is a fourth, so that's where $^6_4$ comes from.

In baroque times, harpsichordists read inverted chords written as figured bass. Figured bass was basically a bass note and a bunch of numbers under the notes. Based on the numbers present, the player would know what chord to play and in what inversion, very much like the modern jazz guitarist or pianist who reads off a lead sheet.

A modern musician would see that chord as C/G, which is defined as a C triad with G as its lowest note.

Since triads have only three notes, you are all out of inversions. Here's what you've learned about inversions:

- If a chord is in root position, no further action is necessary.
- If a chord is in first inversion (the third of the chord is in the bass), it is called I_6 or C/E (depending on the triad; C is just an example).
- If a chord is in second inversion (the fifth of the chord is in the bass), it is called I $^6_4$ or C/G (if C triads are used as examples).
- Any triad, regardless of its type—major, minor, augmented, or diminished—can be inverted.
- Every chord in the harmonized scale can be inverted, so every Roman numeral from I to VII can be inverted using the figured bass symbols for first and second inversion.
- If you see a Roman numeral with nothing after it, it is in root position.

Now, on to seventh chords, which invert the same way, except they have one more note and that changes how they are named.

Inverted Seventh Chords

In theory, inverted seventh chords are no different from triadic inversions. However, a seventh chord has one extra note, so you get one more possible inversion: the third inversion. The other difference is that the classical music theory figurations that name the inversions are completely different for seventh chords. Other than that, the same rules apply.

You're going to use the G7 (G–B–D–F) chord in the key of C, so this chord functions as a dominant, or V, chord.

In root position, nothing changes, so there's nothing to show, it's simply G7 or V.

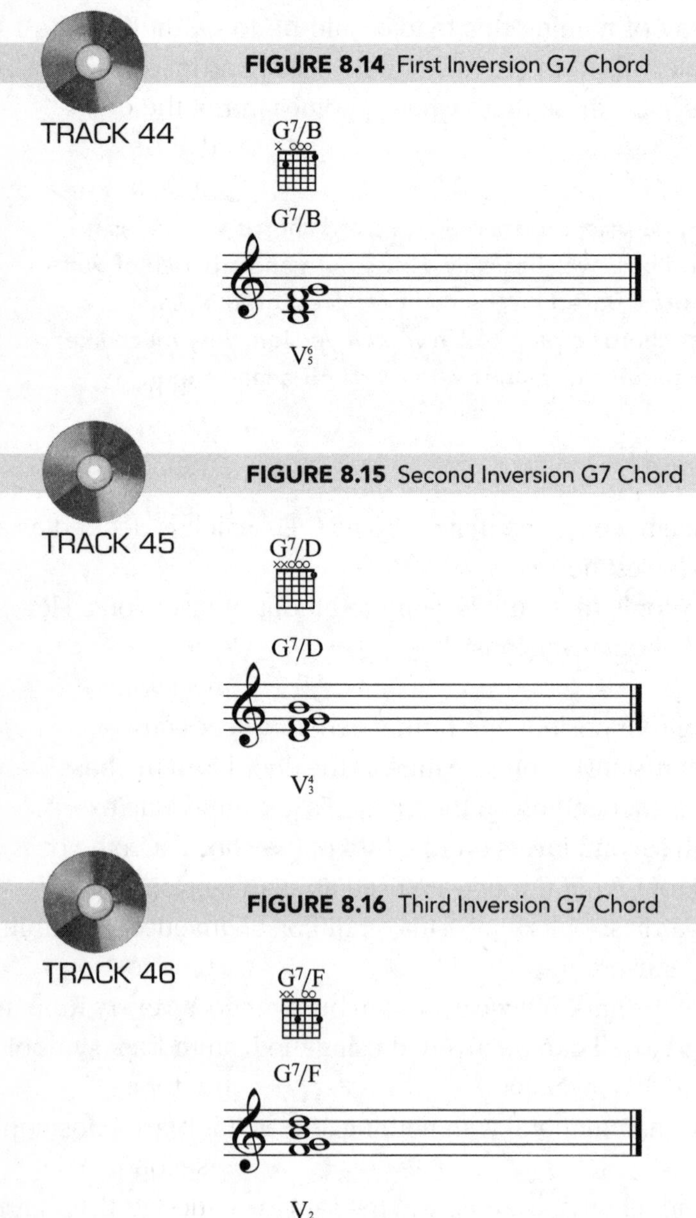

FIGURE 8.14 First Inversion G7 Chord

FIGURE 8.15 Second Inversion G7 Chord

FIGURE 8.16 Third Inversion G7 Chord

The first inversion of a G7 chord moves the G up an octave, placing the B in the lowest voice (see **FIGURE 8.14**). This inversion is specified with the symbol V^{6}_{5}. You could also call this chord G7/B, or G seventh with B in the bass.

The $^{6}_{5}$ may seem confusing, but it's not really. There is a sixth from B to G and a fifth from B to F.

The second inversion puts the B up an octave, leaving the D as the note in the bass (see **FIGURE 8.15**). The inversion is specified as a V^{4}_{3} chord. The fourth is from D to G and the third from D to F. This chord could also be called G7/D, or G seventh with D in the bass.

The third inversion of a G7 chord places the D up an octave, leaving the seventh of the chord, F, in the bass (see **FIGURE 8.16**). The figuration of this chord is called a V_2 chord. The 2 is there because the interval from F to G is a second (since everything else in the chord is thirds, you don't need to list them).

This chord could also be called G7/F, or simply G seventh with F in the bass.

Here's an easy way to remember the inversion figurations of a seventh chord. Start with $^{6}_{5}$ for a first inversion, $^{4}_{3}$ for a second inversion, and 2 for the third inversion. The numbers descend from 6: 65–43–2. That's easy to remember, right?

Here's a recap on seventh chords:

- If a seventh chord is in root position, no further action is necessary.
- If a seventh chord is in first inversion (the third of the chord is in the bass), it would be called a V$^{6}_{5}$ or G/B (depending on the chord; G is just an example).
- If a seventh chord is in second inversion (the fifth of the chord is in the bass), it would be called a V$^{4}_{3}$ or G/D (if G is used as an example).
- Any seventh chord, regardless of its type—major, minor, augmented, or diminished—can be inverted.
- Every seventh chord in the harmonized scale can be inverted, so every Roman numeral from I to vii can be inverted using the figured bass symbols for first, second, and third inversion.
- If you see a Roman numeral with nothing after it, it is in root position.

See, that wasn't so bad, was it? You're essentially through the basic chords now. Now you'll learn about why composers use inversions, and then take a look at an example from J. S. Bach to see how a master uses inversion.

Why Invert?

Inverted chords make music more interesting. Using inversion can help chords move from one to another more smoothly; this is called voice leading. Inversion can also help keep bass lines smooth and musical. Root position triads tend to bounce around the musical staff in a jagged fashion. Take a look at an example from Bach to see inversions in action.

Just a quick note for those of you who aren't studying traditional theory: in the modern music world, especially the guitar-driven rock world, inversion can be rare, although inversions come up from time to time. The Beatles' "While My Guitar Gently Weeps" is a great example of inversion in modern music. The first four chords are simply a tonic minor chord with a descending bass note. Each chord is an inversion of the tonic chord in some way. Leave it to the Beatles to keep things interesting. If you look hard enough, you can find many other examples, such as the second chord of Lynyrd Skynyrd's "Freebird." Keep looking for inversions and what the end result is. In modern music, it's almost always to connect chords and their bass notes in a smoother way. On to Bach!

Quick Study: Bach Prelude in C

Few will dispute Bach's genius and the impact he had on music. In the baroque era, he wrote a set of pieces for solo piano called *The Well-Tempered Clavier*, which included a prelude and a corresponding fugue in every possible key on the piano. Most of you will recognize his Prelude in C Major. In **FIGURE 8.17**, you're going to look at the first few chords of this piece (even though the rest of the prelude is full of inversions). Even in the few first measures, you'll be able to see what inversions are all about—especially seventh chord inversions.

Just the first few measures contain a bevy of chords, most of them in inversion! Each measure is simply an arpeggiated chord spread across the piano, so you'll have to take inventory of the notes that happen in each measure to follow along. Look at a blow-by-blow recap of what you see.

- **Measure One:** C major chord (I), root position. No big surprise here.
- **Measure Two:** D minor chord (ii), third inversion. Not a shocking chord, but the inversion allows the C to stay in the bass from the first measure—very smooth.
- **Measure Three:** G7 chord (V) in first inversion. The first inversion allows a B to take the lowest voice. That's only a half step down from the preceding C in the measure before. Again, look how he's connecting these chords.
- **Measure Four:** C major chord (I), root position. The B from the last measure has come back to C. In four measures, with four chords, the bass note has either stayed the same or moved down only one half step.
- **Measure Five:** A minor chord (vi), first inversion. The C stays in the bass because of the inversion.
- **Measure Six:** D7 chord (II—in all fairness, you haven't learned about major II chords, but this one is too good to pass up, major II chords happen from time to time), third inversion. The third inversion keeps the C in the bass yet again.
- **Measure Seven:** G chord (V), first inversion. The C from the preceding three measures has finally moved, but only down to B, one half step.
- **Measure Eight:** C major seventh chord (I), third inversion. The B from the last measure will stay in the bass because of the third inversion of the C major seventh chord. (Give Bach some props here for using a jazz chord 200 years before jazz came into existence.)

FIGURE 8.17 Prelude in C Excerpt

Prelude in C

From *The Well Tempered Clavier*

J.S. Bach

That's a good place to stop and take inventory. There are a bunch of different chords: C, C major seventh, D minor seventh, D7th, G7th, and A minor. In eight measures, you went through six different chords, and most, if not all, were in inversions. What's the result? The result is an abundance of musically interesting chords that move so smoothly from one to another that it almost sounds as if they're molten lava flowing from voice to voice. In those eight measures, the bass note started at C and never went below B. That's only a half step down. Amazing.

Check out the rest of the piece. The book stops here because things start to get theoretically complex and Bach introduces chords and concepts you haven't learned yet. By the end of this book, though, you should be able to analyze the rest of the piece with ease. And it's worth looking at—many theorists rely on this piece as a perfect example of common practice harmony in action.

Next you'll learn how chords progress from one to another.

ETUDES

ETUDE 8.1 Etude One

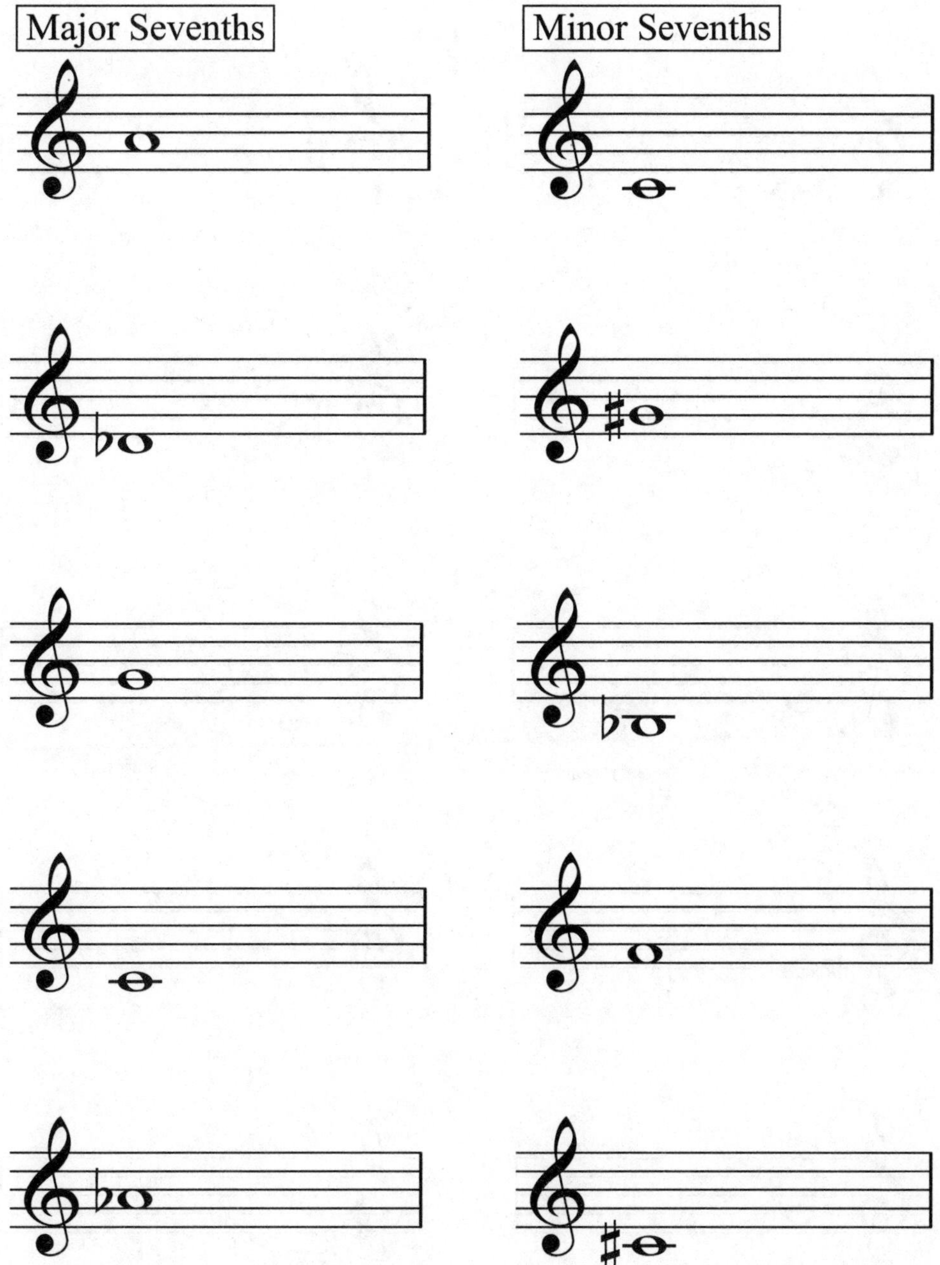

ETUDE 8.2 Etude Two

Create dominant seventh chords from the following notes

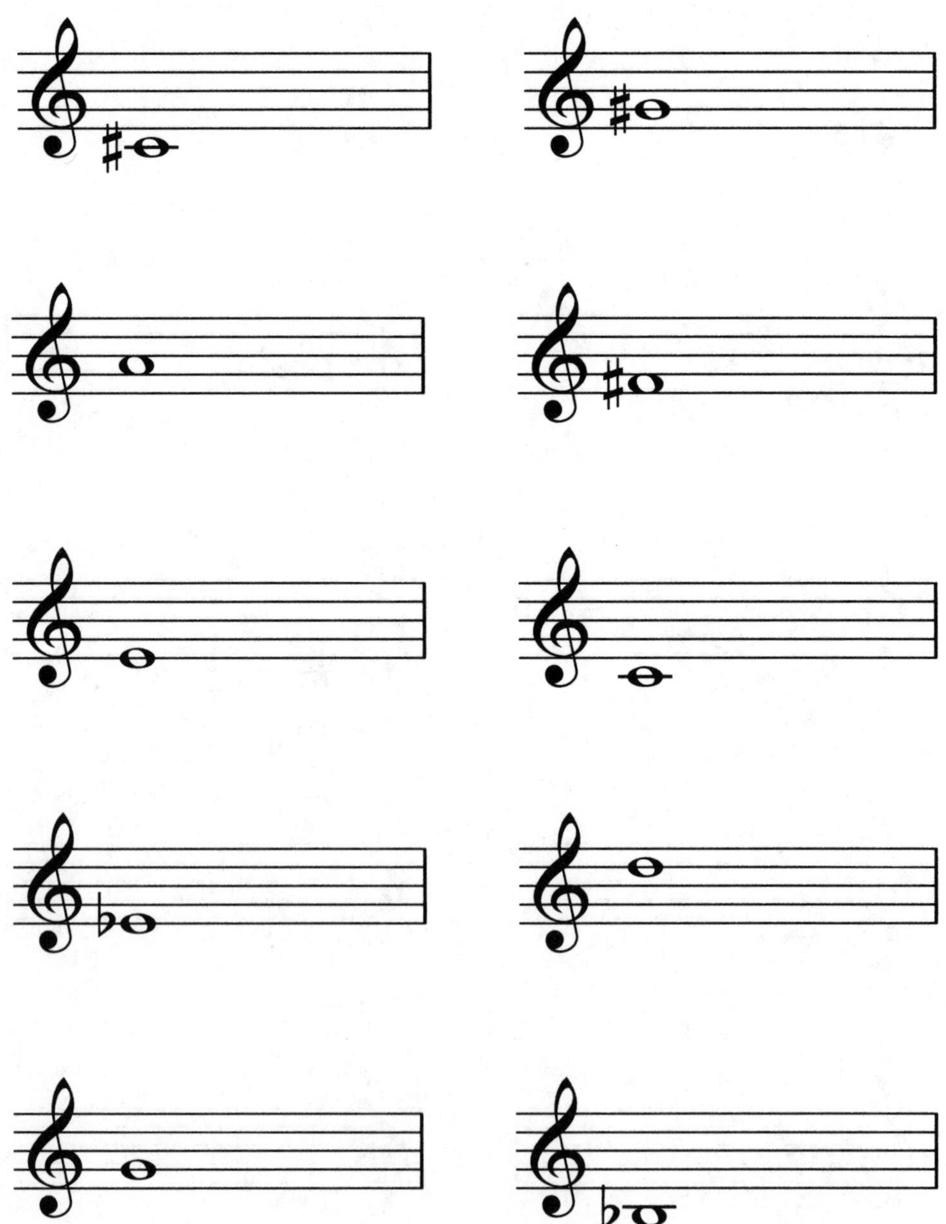

ETUDE 8.3 Etude Three

Create half and fully diminished seventh chords from the following notes

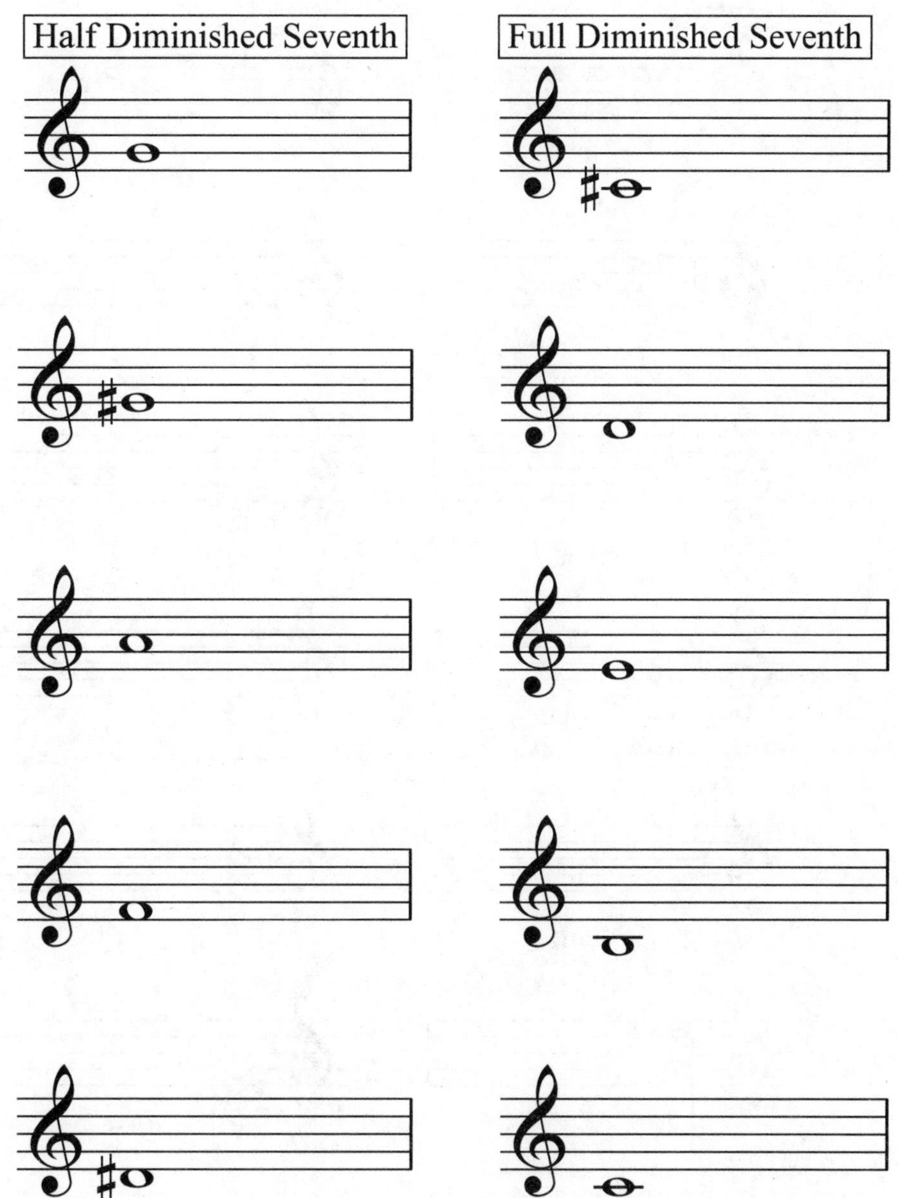

ETUDE 8.4 Etude Four

Transform the root position triads to inverted triads from the following chords

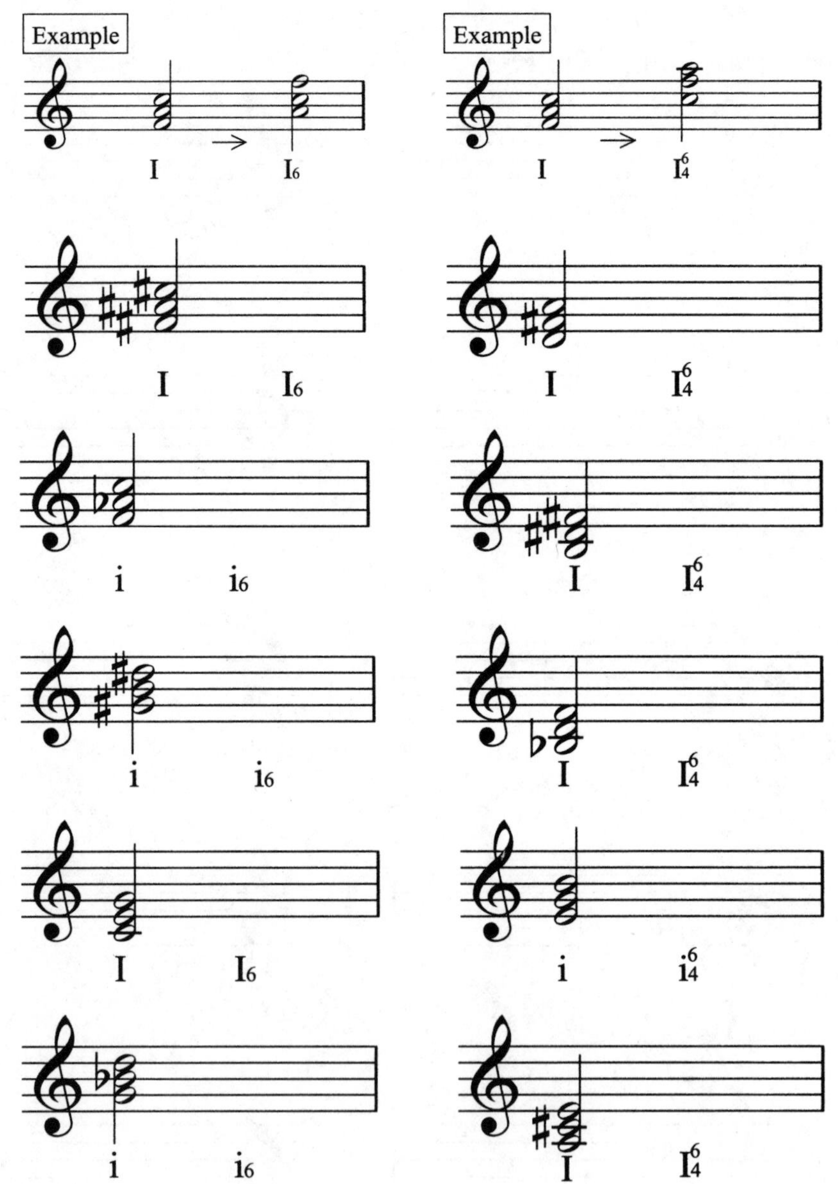

ETUDE 8.5 Etude Five

Transform the root position dominant seventh chords to inverted seventh chords from the following chords

CHAPTER 9

Movements: Chord Progressions

Understanding chords and how they are spelled is only the first step. Once you can look at a chord and give it a name, you need to look for context. What chord preceded this one and what comes after? Are there patterns to observe? This chapter contains the answers to all these questions as you study how chords move from one to another.

What Is a Chord Progression?

Simply put, a chord progression is a movement of chords from one point to another. If you've ever heard a blues song, you've heard a progression of chords. All the pop music from the last 100 years is loaded with chord progressions. If you play guitar or piano, you know all about chord progressions. The trick now is to figure out what they are, why you need to know them, and, more important, how this information is going to help you.

Chord Stacks

When you studied how to make chords, you looked at the chords a few ways. First, you stacked diatonic notes from the scales and ended up with seven different chords. You also dissected the intervallic properties of every triad and seventh chord in existence. This is one way of looking at chords. But there is another angle. When you talk about chords as vertical stacks of notes, you essentially are adopting a philosophy that chords are objects.

POINT TO CONSIDER

Chords and melodies are tied together very tightly. When you play a melody, you can almost imagine what harmony is present with that melody. As a result, it's possible to think melodically and harmonically at the same time. Beyond the theoretical underpinnings of what melody notes fit with which chords, when you listen to a melody, that melody has a way of telling you what chord it wants to have accompany it—all you have to do is listen.

The Chicken or the Egg?

The concept of vertical stacks works pretty well in studying a single chord. Looking back through the development of music shows that chords, although they are vertical stacks of notes, are closer to being vertical collisions of voices. What does this mean? Well, imagine that you are not playing guitar or piano; you are in a choir. There are soprano, alto, tenor, and bass voices. At the simplest level, there is one singer per part. Is a person in the bass section singing one note at a time, singing chords? No, she's singing a line—a melody, to be more specific. Since one voice can't make a chord, you have to look at the net result of what the choir is singing. There are four melodies going on at once. Each part is different. Now, if you freeze any single slice of vertical time, you could look at all the notes that are sung on the first beat of the first bar and come up with a chord. That would make sense because music should sound rich and consonant, and chords and harmony allow this. Now ask yourself which came first: the individual lines of music or the chords, and the voices simply fleshed out the chords as they went along?

The answer is complicated. It's hard to say for sure because most of the composers are dead. However, throughout the development of music, especially classical music, lines ruled and chords were afterthoughts.

Put simply: Composers wrote lines of melodies that summed together as chords when musicians looked up at them (vertical thinking). Since music theory has a wonderful ability to look back at composed music, it's easy to forget that lines were dominant.

How about Now?

Is music any different now? Depends who you ask. Do singer/songwriters write in lines? Sure, they sing a melody line, but do the chords they play on their guitar or piano come from that same thinking (linear)? Nowadays, especially in pop music, chords and chord progressions are units that have little to do with the old model. That's not to say that they can't, and that popular music has no voice leading in it, but the largest amount of popular music is conceived with chords as blocks of information, and melodies are layered on top of the chords. Now, all musicians—old school and new school—can learn from each other. Look at history and see what happened.

Progressions in Time

Using the tools of music theory, you can look back at any piece of music, new or old, and figure out what chords are used and why. The better question to ask is why. Why did anything happen the way it did? Why did Bach use certain chords and not others? Why did Beethoven and Mozart use similar chords? Were they working from some sort of rule book, so to speak? The answer is no. Harmony developed. It's as simple as that. Diatonic harmony was a long time in the making. It started with one voice, then a second was added, and so on, and then eventually triads and harmony fell into place. It wasn't until the baroque era that harmony started to solidify into something recognizable. This wasn't because Bach and his buddies had a handbook. The music evolved because musicians listened and studied what had come before. They took what they liked and moved forward.

Theorists look back and try to fit all the music into a set of rules. But this is not always in your best interest. It is worth noting that a certain sequence of chords happens over and over and over again, but trying to figure out why will drive you crazy.

To help you tackle this issue, this book is going to do about 300 years' worth of homework, sorting through the massive amounts of music and arriving at some conclusions. In the end, you'll understand that there are sounds associated with feelings, moods, and other things that cannot be quantified with theory. "Amen" can be summarized by playing a IV chord followed by a I chord. Much of music can be summarized in this way, but which chord to use and when is up to you. After you've studied a few examples of some common progressions, the rest of music and composition is up to you to explore. Beyond the basic tools, there are no rules. Some of the coolest modern music breaks every rule there is, yet it sounds beautiful. Remember: music first, theory second. In this chapter, you're going to get a bunch of theory; it's up to you to turn the theory into music in the next chapters. It's a good challenge worthy of anyone who loves music enough to study it.

Diatonic Progressions and Solar Harmony

The logical place to begin is with progressions that are purely diatonic (coming from the major or minor scales). Just using the chords from the diatonic major scale can make a lot of music. **FIGURE 9.1** illustrates the key of D major and its chords.

FIGURE 9.1 Diatonic Chords in D

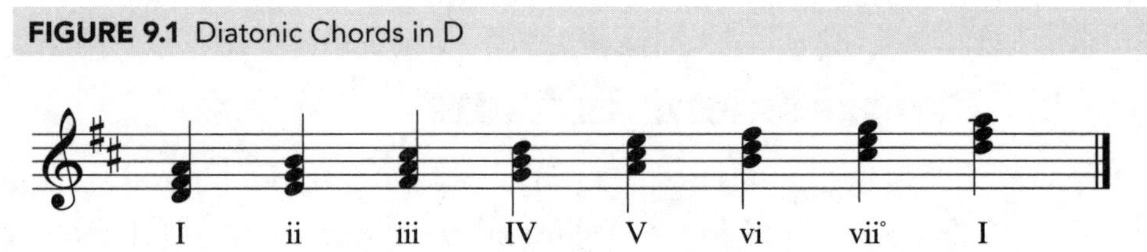

In the key of D, any of these chords are acceptable for use, since they are made exclusively from notes in the D major scale (just stacked together).

Now, you're looking at seven different chords—some major, some minor, and one diminished. Which ones do you choose and why? Well, first start out with a concept, and then explore the chords you see most often.

In any musical key, the tonic, whether it's a note or a chord, carries the most weight and importance. So, you could say that the "one" chord is the center of your universe, and you'd be right. In harmony, especially traditional tonal harmony, the tonic is a point of resolution. Music typically, if not always, comes back to that one chord.

The analogy about the tonic chord being at the center of your universe is going to serve your musical imagination very well. Imagine that the one chord is at the center of the solar system; it's the sun. All the other chords rotate around that central chord with different degrees of pull (more on that later). This concept is called "solar" harmony and it's an accepted way to look at chords. The tonic chord is really important, just like the sun.

Primary Chords

In a major key, there are three primary chords, which are the basic chords used to spell out and harmonize the key. The primary chords in any major key are I, IV, and V.

Not coincidentally, all three of the primary chords are major. Now, what can you do with just primary chords? The majority of folk music, sacred music, all of blues, and a good chunk of rock are based on primary chords. Ever heard the phrase *three-chord rock*? Well, those are the three chords. For an illustration, look at a song most people know, "Amazing Grace."

FIGURE 9.2 is an example of a lead sheet. For ease of reading, this song was kept in D major. The melody is on top and the chords are listed only by symbol. For the benefit of the guitar players, chord grids were put in. A piano player would have to realize the chord voicings on his or her own, but this does not change the fact that this simple folk melody is properly harmonized with the three primary chords from its home key.

This is the first step to analysis. The key signature tells you D major or B minor, but the existence of D, G, and A chords tells you that you are in the key of D major because those chords—I, IV, and V—are the primary chords for D major.

The primary chords can go a lot further; they are not relegated to pop and folk music. Classical music makes heavy use of primary chords—all tonal music does.

Three chords will get you only so far, so you need to look a bit deeper into the scale to see what else you can find to use.

FIGURE 9.2 Primary Chord Study: *Amazing Grace*

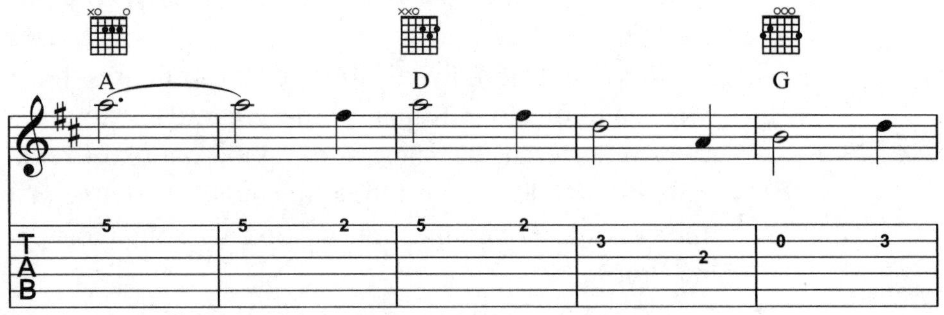

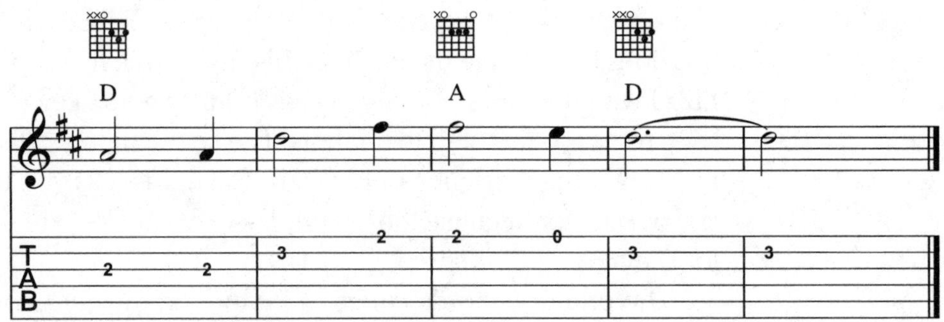

Secondary Chords

In addition to the I, IV, and V chords, you have the secondary chords in the key. The secondary chords are the ii, iii, and vi chords in any major key.

As you can see from the lowercase Roman numerals, all three chords are minor. Once you know what chords are diatonic to a key, just remember that the primary chords are the major ones and the secondary chords are the minor ones.

But what about the diminished chord? The diminished chord is special and needs to be treated with some care. In general, it occurs more in jazz and classical pieces than in pop, although it does exist in all styles of music. To learn about the diminished chord, look at the solar harmony universe and the chord ladder to see when diminished chords are actually used.

Is music written with only secondary chords? Not often, although there are almost always some rule breakers. The secondary chords embellish the primary chords and give chord progressions variety. Here is an example of a simple chord progression with no melody (**FIGURE 9.3**), which contains voicings for piano and guitar using both primary and secondary chords in the key of A major.

FIGURE 9.3 Primary and Secondary Chord Progressions

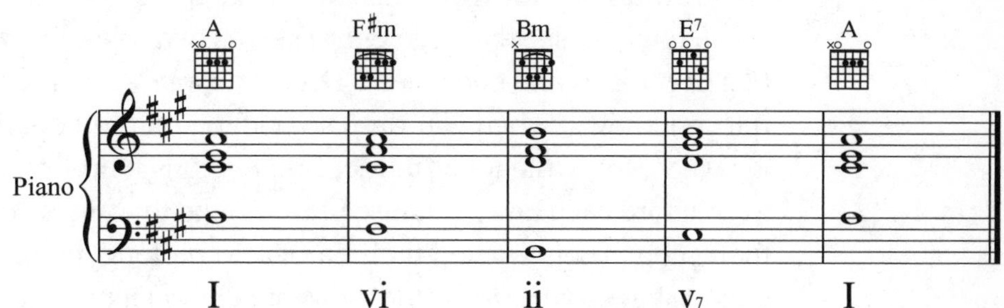

As you can see in the example and hear from the recording, this progression flows well. This example uses only chords that are diatonic to the key of A major and while the result may not rock the world of music, it's a nice-sounding chord progression.

The key point here is that chords aren't chosen at random. There are some very nicely established norms when using chords. The first step is to understand how to use diatonic chords and how to write with them. Afterward, you can explore, through analysis of other music (music you like), exactly how far outside the lines you can color, so to speak.

Now, here are some typical ways that chords progress from one to another. You're going to study solar harmony and the almighty chord ladder.

Look at the two examples of chord progressions in this chapter. Notice anything? Well, to start, each progression starts and ends on the tonic chord. The penultimate (second-to-last) chord was a V chord in each case. Is this merely an accident, or do V chords precede I chords at the end of a progression (also called a cadence)? You'll just have to read on to find out for sure.

Solar Harmony and the Chord Ladder

Although there are seven diatonic chords available, there is no steadfast rule about which one to use and why. No one can tell you how to compose! However, it is possible to study the evolution of music and see some trends that are worth investigating, even if you choose to go off in your own direction and look at chords differently.

Earlier, this book touched briefly on solar harmony by stating that the tonic chord is the most important chord in any key and that the other chords circle around it. Now you'll discover what this actually means.

In tonal music, the tonic chord serves two roles: the start and the end. It begins phrases and ends them. The term *gravity* is hard to explain on paper, but you know it when you drop something on the floor. With musical gravity, when you write tonal music, progressions tend to gravitate back to the tonic chord each time. Because phrases tend to want to come to rest and end there, composers worked their hardest to prolong the inevitable moment of coming back to the strong tonic. Eventually, tonality in classical music fell out of favor because too many composers found the strong tonic chord increasingly difficult to use in new ways. Amazingly enough, to this day, tonal music thrives, and harmonic gravity gives music its power and beauty.

FIGURE 9.4 gives a good example of tonal gravity. Listen or play this example on an instrument right now.

TRACK 49

FIGURE 9.4 An Unfinished Example

Isn't that brutal? Doesn't that F♯ want to pull up to the G more than you can express? Why does it do that? No one knows for sure, but you have hit on exactly what makes melodies and chord progressions move: the inevitable pull back to the tonic note. You saw it with a simple melody; it appears in **FIGURE 9.5** with a single chord voicing.

FIGURE 9.5 More Musical Torture

TRACK 50

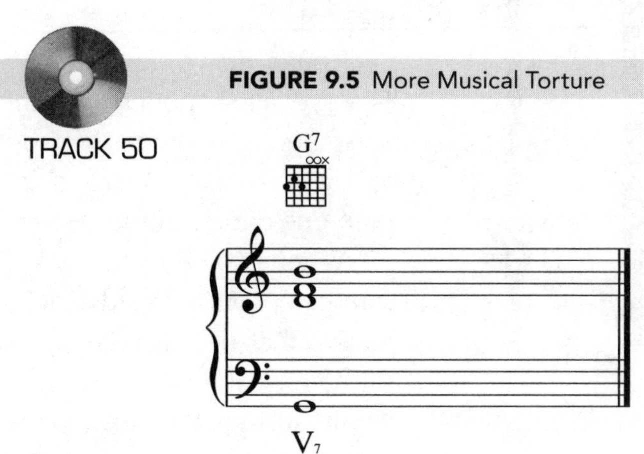

Why is it that this chord refuses to sit still? This chord, a G7 chord, is diatonic to the key of C major. It is the V chord, or dominant chord. In this example, it is a seventh chord. So, why does this chord want to go someplace else? Harmonic gravity. It's not the tonic chord, it's actually one step removed from it; it's the closest chord to tonic (more on that soon), and it wants to go to tonic. So, here's how it resolves in **FIGURE 9.6**.

FIGURE 9.6 Resolution!

TRACK 51

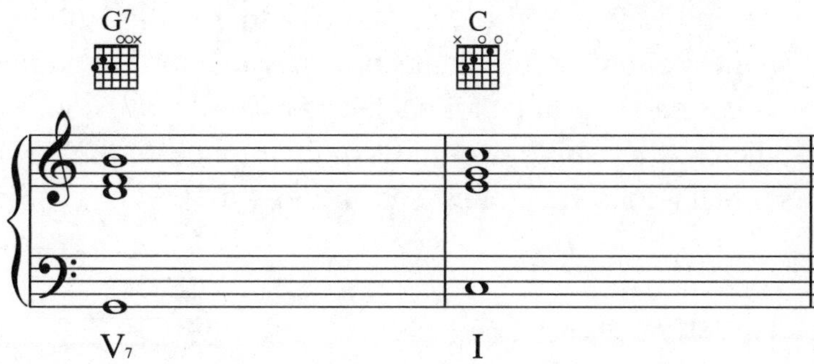

You came back to the tonic, back to the center of the musical system, and finally you have resolution. Tension and release are what make this whole game work.

You've heard about two chords: I and V. Now, look at the rest of the chords and how they align with the tonic chord by looking at the chord ladder.

The Chord Ladder

The chord ladder is a neat little device that shows the relationships among all the diatonic chords in a key. Take a look at the ladder in **FIGURE 9.7**, and then you'll learn more about exactly what it's showing you.

FIGURE 9.7 The Almighty Chord Ladder

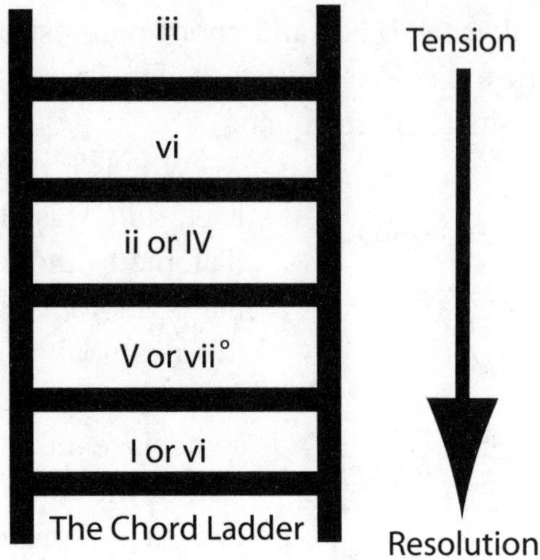

It's a ladder with chords on it. Basically, this ladder is a reference to the "harmonic" gravity mentioned earlier. All the chords in some way fall to the I chord at the end.

There are a few things to observe. First, notice that there are different steps on the ladder, and occasionally, there is more than one chord on those steps.

When two chords occupy the same step on a chord ladder, it means that the chords can substitute for each other. Before you go any further, you need to know what makes a chord substitute for another chord.

Chord Substitutions

On the first step of the chord ladder is the I (tonic) chord and a very small vi chord on the final step. They occupy the same step because both chords can substitute for each other. They share common tones; more specifically, they share two-thirds of their tones. In the key of C major, I and vi share the following tones (see **FIGURE 9.8**).

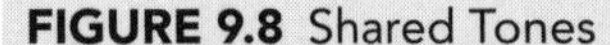

FIGURE 9.8 Shared Tones

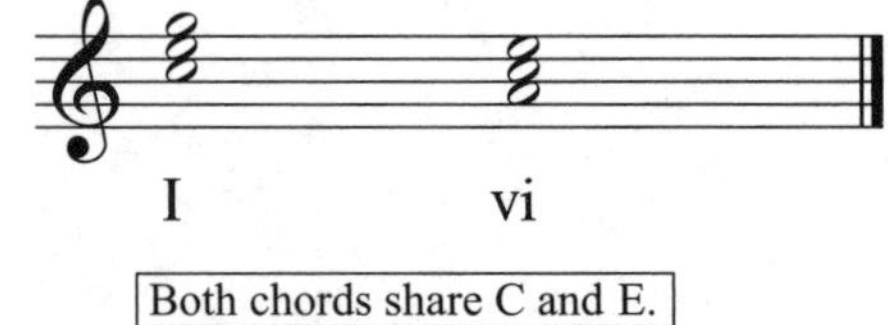

On every step of the ladder, when you find two chords occupying the same place, it's because they can substitute for each other due to sharing of tones.

Ladder of Fifths

Remember the circle of fifths, here's a ladder of fifths. Many, many chord progressions are based on movements of fifths. So, now look at the chord ladder without the extra chords and view it as strictly fifth-based movements from the tonic chord up (see **FIGURE 9.9**).

FIGURE 9.9 The Chord Ladder in Fifths

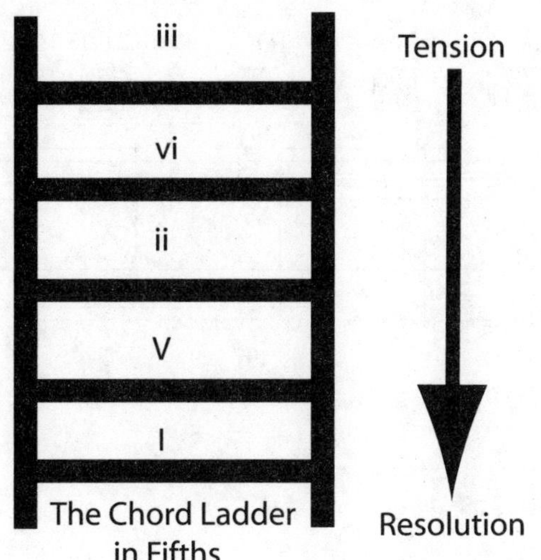

You end up with a progression of iii, vi, ii, V, I. Look at that for piano and guitar in **FIGURE 9.10**.

TRACK 52

FIGURE 9.10 Full Fifths Progressions

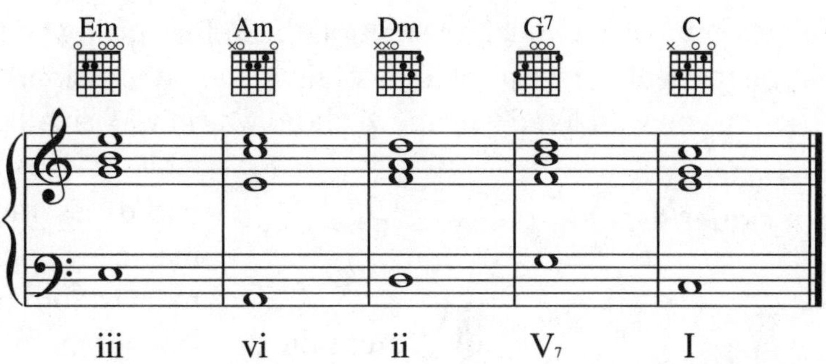

This example sounds fine, doesn't it? Sure it does!

Now start to throw in some of the substitute chords, as in **FIGURE 9.11**. See what replacing the ii with a IV and the V with a vii° chord look and sound like.

You get a nice-sounding progression. Unfortunately, no matter how you slice any of these progressions and no matter how crafty you are, when you get to the V (or its substitute, the vii° chord), you pull back to I. Or do you? Remember the small vi chord next to I on the chord ladder.

FIGURE 9.11 Use Some Substitute Chords

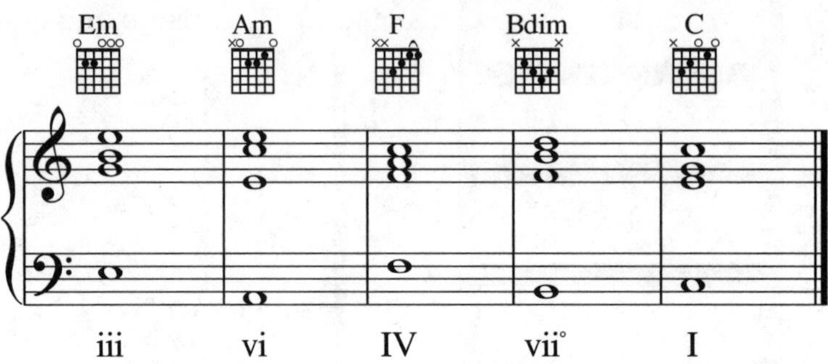

Deceptive Resolutions

The small vi chord is there as a deceptive resolution to the I chord. Essentially, you break the pattern that V has to resolve to I by allowing V to resolve to vi. It's called a deceptive cadence.

Here's what so neat about the progression: Just when you think you're going to cadence back to I and essentially end the progression, the music pulls a fake out and gives you a vi chord. It prolongs the progression as it sets you back a bunch of steps on the ladder, giving you more time to keep the musical phrase alive and continue the progression.

If you wondered why the vi chord was in very small print, that's because while it substitutes for the tonic chord, it's more of a transport, magically linking you back to the real vi chord on the chord ladder. Maybe the ladder should have looked like **FIGURE 9.12**.

FIGURE 9.12 Chord Ladder Warp!

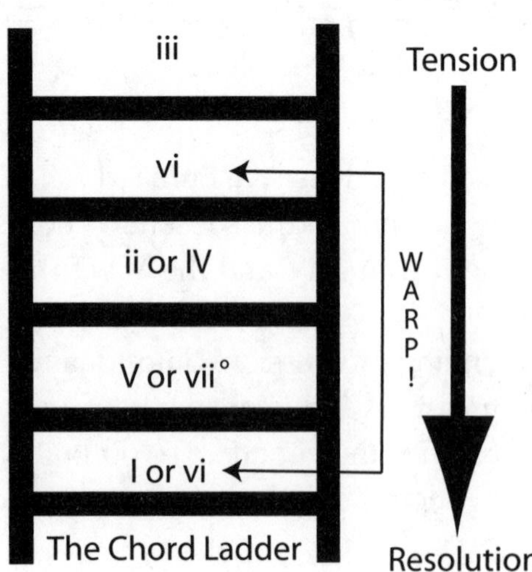

The chord ladder does not dictate what you should or should not use when writing music. It simply presents a number of choices that will work well together. The ladder illustrates how chords typically progress in diatonic situations. Feel free to use it as a starting point and go your own way from there.

ETUDES

ETUDE 9.1 Etude One

Circle the primary chords and name the chord progression with Roman numerals

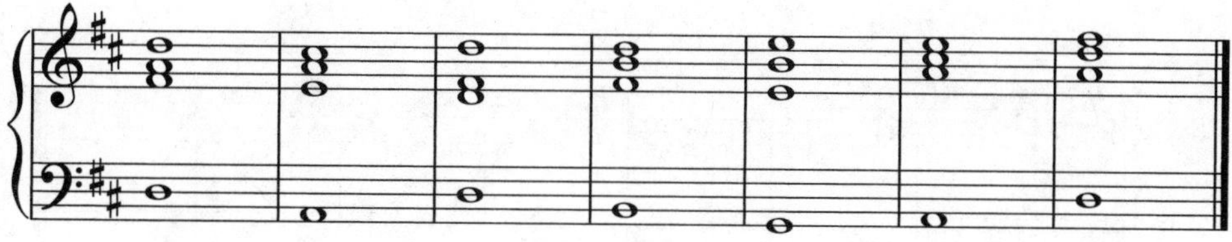

ETUDE 9.2 Etude Two

Circle the secondary chords and name the chord progression with Roman numerals

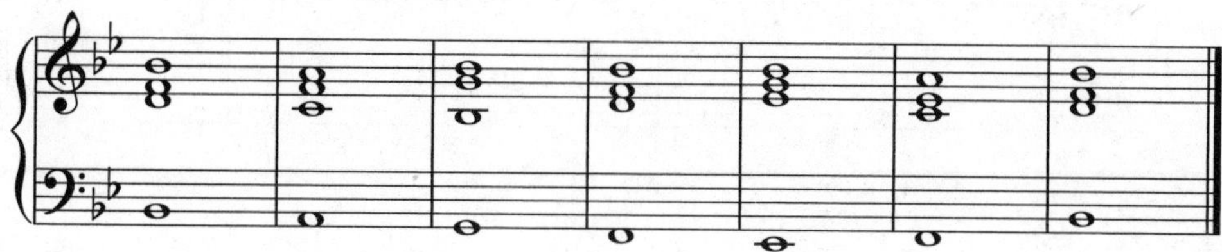

ETUDE 9.3 Etude Three

Using the chord ladder, find a substitute chord for the ii chord and insert it in the progression below

ETUDE 9.4 Etude Four

Circle the chord that breaks the progression from moving completely in fifths

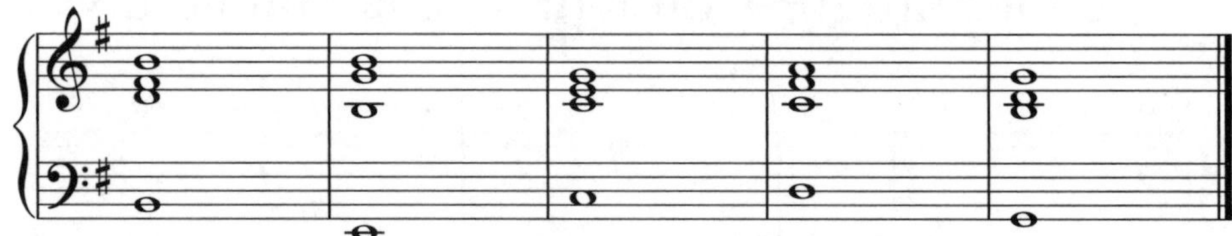

ETUDE 9.5 Etude Five

Circle the deceptive resolution in the following chord progression

CHAPTER 10

More Chord Progressions

The next task is to spell out some very common progressions, look at how the minor scale differs from the major scale, and once and for all explain exactly why V pulls to the I chord so heavily each time it comes around. Now you will look at the norms and figure out creative ways to go beyond them. Chord progressions and harmony comprise a vast subject, and you have only started to scratch the surface. Other chords and scales exist and yield great possibilities for analysis and composition.

Tonic and Dominant Relationships

Before delving into other chords or any other information, the first thing to do is to strengthen your understanding of chord progressions. You need to study the relationship between tonic and dominant chords, especially the dominant seventh and the diminished chord that often substitutes for it.

In the last chapter you saw how strong a pull the leading tone could have by playing a scale and stopping on the leading tone, leaving the scale yearning to resolve. You also played a single dominant seventh chord and let it hang out to dry, so to speak. Both the leading tone and the dominant seventh chord felt unresolved. In the case of the leading tone, you achieved resolution by completing the scale, playing the full scale, and concluding on the tonic note. Resolving the chord required playing another chord after it. The fact that the dominant seventh chord was acting as a V7 chord was solidified by its resolution to a I, or tonic, chord.

Harmonically speaking, the existence of a V7 and I (or i) chord indicates that you are in the key of the tonic chord. That's all you need when it comes to harmony to define what a key is.

It has always been a challenge to define a key clearly. In tonal music, and especially in the common practice period that music theory so often studied, the tonic dominant relationship will identify exactly what key you are in. Now, look at what makes a dominant chord pull so strongly to the tonic chord.

Voices in Motion

The relationship between V and I is all about tension and release—yin and yang and balance. V chords, especially when they have sevenths and even more when they are substituted by vii (diminished) chords, are extremely tense. The tension lies in the chord itself. Look at the V7 chord in **FIGURE 10.1** and see what you have.

Stay in the key of C major to keep it simple. The G7 chord shown in **FIGURE 10.1** contains the following tones: G, B, D, and F. Now, remember what you learned about leading tones. Remember how strong they are? In the key of C, the leading tone is the seventh degree of the scale, which happens to be a B. The G7 chord has that note in it. Within the C scale

FIGURE 10.1 Dominant Seventh Chord Exposed!

TRACK 54

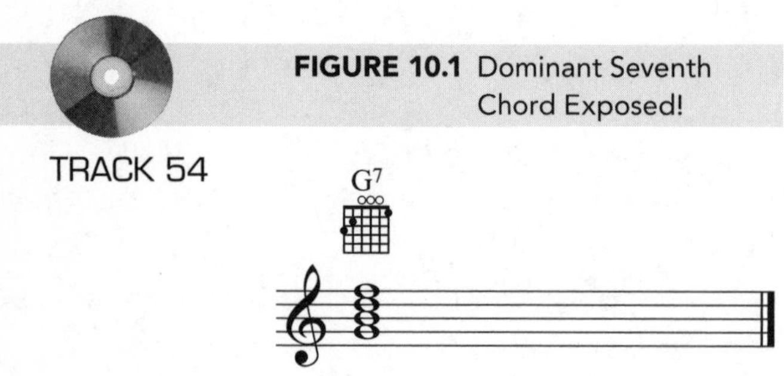

is another leading tone of sorts. Between the fourth and third degree is another half step. When you stop on the fourth degree of the scale (F), it pulls down to E fairly heavily. It's nowhere near as dramatic as the pull from B to C, but it is there. Check it out in **FIGURE 10.2**.

FIGURE 10.2 The Pull from 4 to 3

In that example, you heard a full scale, which went up to the fourth above the octave (which still counts as the fourth). Again, the note does not want to stay there; it has gravity of its own and pulls back to the third of the scale. In a V7 chord, you have the other leading tone (F). So, in one chord, two unstable tones are played together at the same time—no wonder it sounds tense! But wait, there's more. You can go another step deeper into this chord. Since B and F have been identified as tension notes within the dominant chord, look at the interval that they produce (see **FIGURE 10.3**).

TRACK 56

FIGURE 10.3 B and F

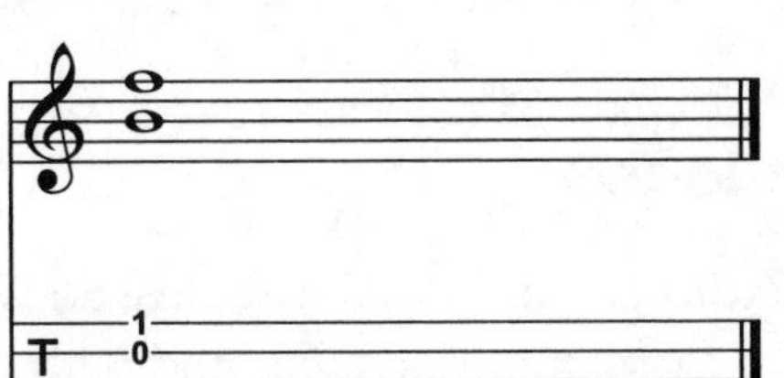

By taking these notes out of the chord and playing them together, you can get an even better sense of what's going on. The interval from B to F is a tritone, the most unstable and dissonant interval you would deal with on most normal days. Not only does the V7 chord contain both leading tones (the fourth and seventh of the scale), but the interval created between those tones is a tritone (another unstable sound). This chord is clearly waiting to do something.

The B and the F need to resolve. The B wants to go up to C. The F wants to move down to E. You already have a G, in the G7 chord, so it doesn't need to move. Right there, you spelled the resolution of V7 to I (see **FIGURE 10.4**). The D in the G7 chord can resolve to either C or E in the C chord. Either way you slice it, the third of the G7 chord must go up and the seventh of the G7 chord must go down.

TRACK 57

FIGURE 10.4 A Good Resolution

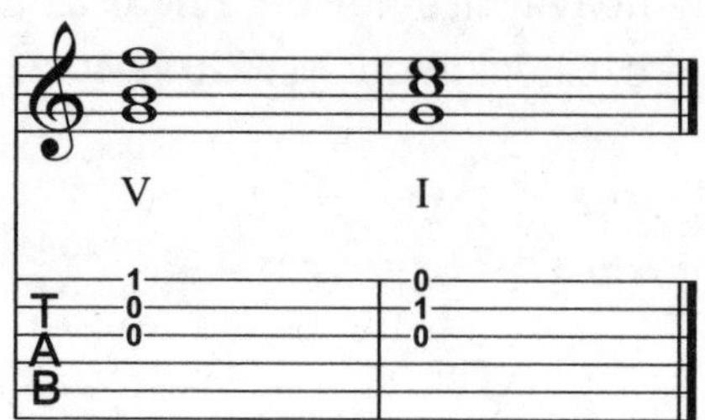

That's it, folks. If you can grab on to this, you will understand tonality. The relationship between V and I is the cornerstone of tonal harmony. Sure, there is music that doesn't make heavy use of it, but you'll see more dominant to tonic chords than you will know what to do with once you learn to see them.

The diminished chord in the major scale (vii°) often substitutes for V. It has a dominant function because it also pulls very strongly to I. The vii° chord contains both the leading tones discussed earlier and, if spelled as a fully diminished seventh, it adds an additional leading tone (the lowered sixth of the scale), which pulls down to a note in the tonic chord. This is why V and vii° can substitute for each other.

Now it's time to talk about minor keys and their chord progressions.

One of the reasons that the relationship between dominant and tonic chords is so important is that if you inventory the tones between both chords, you essentially spell the entire scale out (well, almost entirely). The C and G7 chords combine to give C–D–E–F–G–B–C (a C major scale, excluding A). That's exactly why two chords can tell you what key you're in; they spell it out for you with their tones.

Minor Chord Progressions

Minor scales come directly from major scales. So when you create diatonic triads, you'll have the same triads you had with the major scale; the only difference is that the Roman numerals will change position.

Look at a diatonic B minor scale, harmonized into triads, in **FIGURE 10.5**.

FIGURE 10.5 Diatonic B Minor Triads

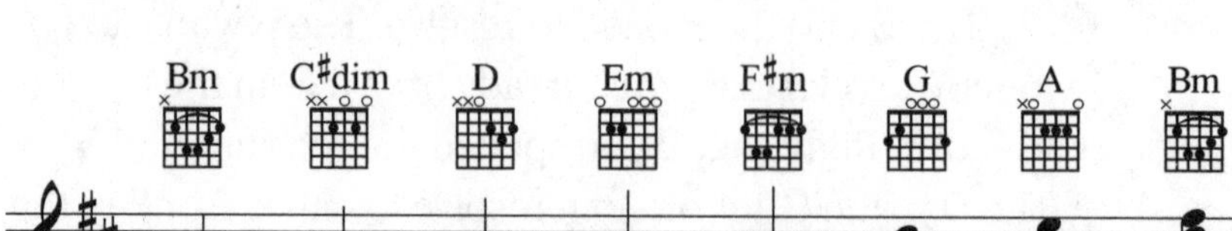

Compare this with the related major key of D major in **FIGURE 10.6**. You will see the same triads, just in a different order.

FIGURE 10.6 Diatonic D Major Triads

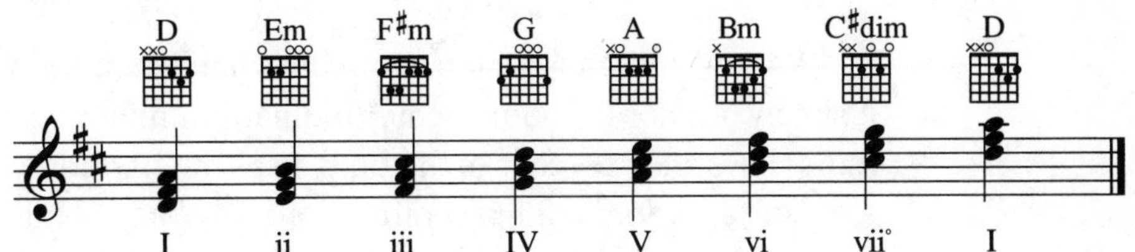

When it comes to the chord ladder, the minor key doesn't look all that different from the major version of the chord ladder. **FIGURE 10.7** presents the minor chord ladder.

FIGURE 10.7 Minor Chord Ladder

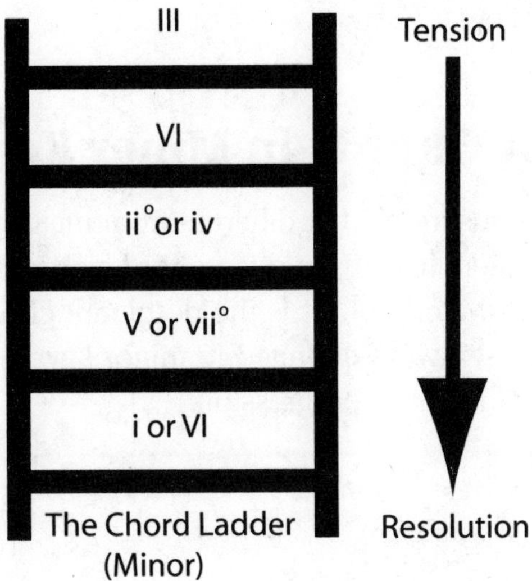

You will notice a few things:

- The ladder progresses in movements of fifths, just like the major chord ladder.
- The substitute chords always share two notes in common with their possible substitutions.

- The V and vii° chords look funny. Compare them to the diatonic triads in **FIGURE 10.5** to see two main differences:
- The V chord has been changed from a minor triad to a major triad.
- The vii° chord has not only changed from a major triad to a diminished triad, but its root has also moved up one half step.

What would cause such dramatic changes in the minor scale? To put it simply, it's not the same scale (the natural minor scale). Harmonizing in minor keys, 99.9 percent of the time, uses the harmonic minor scale to give a major (and dominant seventh) chord on V and a fully diminished chord on vii° (which creates a diminished chord on the leading tone and substitutes for V7).

The importance of the relationship between V and I was discussed at the beginning of this chapter. The relationship is just as important in the minor scale. The natural minor scale does not have the proper V chord (diatonically, it's minor), and the ♭VII chord does not substitute or pull up to the tonic either. So add a raised leading tone to the scale (raised seventh tone), which affects the V and vii° chords, making them both true dominant chords. Look at the effect of these new chords on some sample chord progressions in minor keys.

Using Dominant Chords in Minor Keys

Minor key progressions aren't that different from major progressions. There is still a lot of movement in fifths and the chord ladder is definitely in effect, but the one thing to watch out for is the dominant chord functions. V and vii° chords are almost always changed in minor keys. **FIGURE 10.8** shows a simple progression: the i–iv–v progression.

TRACK 58

FIGURE 10.8 i–iv–v–i Progression

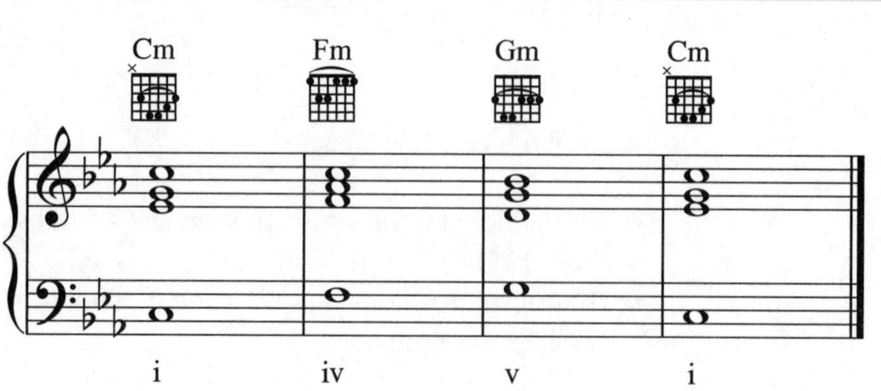

What's wrong here? Listen to it. What's missing? There is a common progression, the i–iv–v, and it works on the chord ladder, but something sounds off. The quality of the v chord didn't change. Because it's a minor chord, it simply doesn't have the gravity expected from the V chord (which should be about as strong a chord as is). Changing the V to a major chord (see **FIGURE 10.9**) makes it sound a whole lot better; just listen.

TRACK 59

FIGURE 10.9 i–iv–V–i Progression

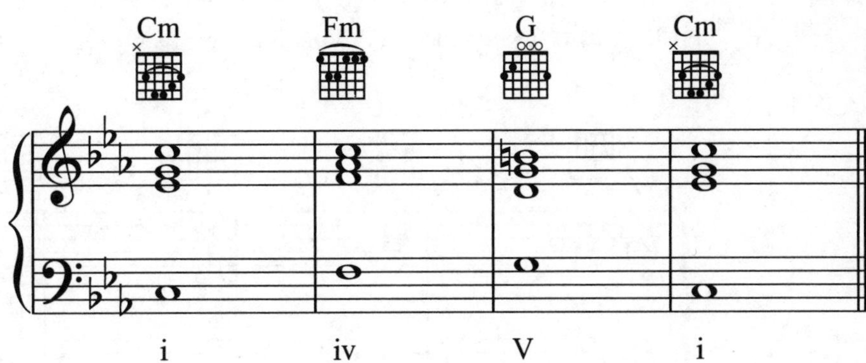

Now it sounds better. There is always the option of adding a seventh to the V chord for even more pull, as in **FIGURE 10.10**.

TRACK 60

FIGURE 10.10 i–iv–V7–i Progression

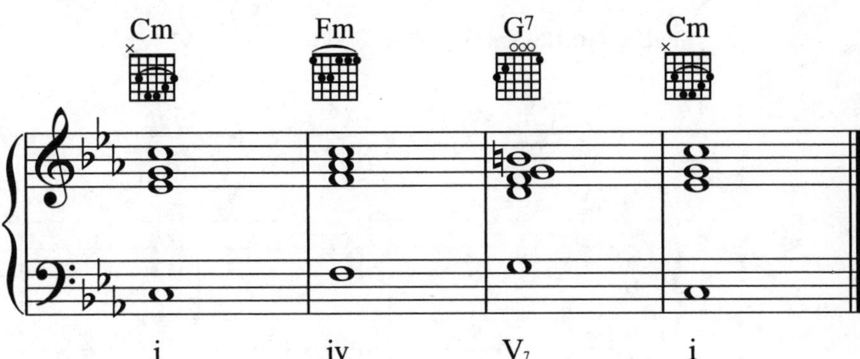

Functionally, both progressions work, but the added seventh makes things resolve a touch stronger.

Any of the chord progressions from the major key will work well, and as long as you mind your dominant chords, all will be fine.

So, what changes? Although the chord ladder may look similar, minor keys sound completely different because the function of each chord is different than in a major key. All of a sudden, iv chords are minor and VI chords are major in the minor key. Also, the distance from note to note is different in the minor key because the minor key has a different interval pattern from the root and, thus, sounds different. Take a parallel progression in major and minor to compare just how different they sound. **FIGURE 10.11** shows a I, vi, IV, V progression in C major.

TRACK 61

FIGURE 10.11 Diatonic Major Progression: I, vi, IV, V

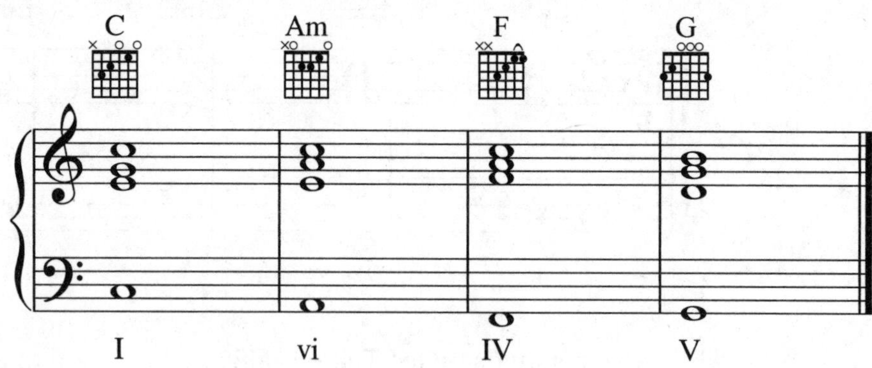

Now, transfer this directly to C minor, as in **FIGURE 10.12**. Now look at and listen to how much things change.

TRACK 62

FIGURE 10.12 Diatonic Minor Progression: i, ♭VI, iv, V

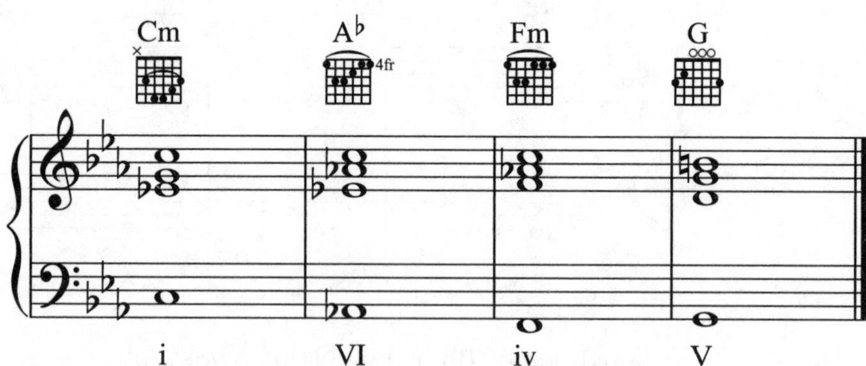

What's the lesson here? To start with, listen to everything. The Roman numerals begin to look the same after a while. Theory can't exist solely on paper; it has to come alive.

For the rest of the progressions, start mixing and matching chords as appropriate in the keys. Use the accepted ladder of chords as a starting point, but remember that it is by no means a set of rules—far from it! The ladder of chords is a common starting ground. As you start to analyze music on your own, which you will have to do since you are not going to get any more examples of chord progressions right now (the music you already have and know holds plenty of information), you will see a great deal of music that uses the chord ladder. File that music away by how it sounds. Do you like the way it sounds when the scales are used diatonically? It's an agreeable sound.

You will find some music that does not go through the expected set of chords. You may see some huge "rules" broken. You may see chords that simply "don't belong." File that away, too, because in the end, no one approach will win. Ask yourself if you like the sound of what you're hearing. No matter your answer, analyze it and figure out what makes it work. If you love it, see if you can adopt some of those movements into your chord progressions. If you hate something, see what to avoid in your writing. Either way, you will learn the most by looking at as much music as you can. You have a very good set of tools now, and you will continue to strengthen them, especially in the etude section at the end of the chapter, where you will analyze and create some music of your own based on what you have learned.

Harmonic Rhythm

Another concept worth discussing separately is harmonic rhythm. Studying chords and chord progressions is actually looking at slices of time in an abstract fashion. Certain styles of music simply move quickly from chord to chord, back and forth, repeating as it goes. In other styles of music, chords progress very slowly. The pace at which this happens is called harmonic rhythm.

The harmonic rhythm of jazz is typically very fast. Usually, there is at least one chord per measure in most jazz standards. Because chords are improvisational milestones, they tend to change rapidly. A good counterexample of this is the modal jazz of Miles Davis's famous *Kind of Blue* album, which features exactly the opposite: chords that rarely change.

The chord progressions thus far have had absolutely no rhythm attached because they are examples devoid of music: They are just the raw data. Real music moves in rhythm and so do the chords. So, before dismissing a simple progression, play around with the duration of each chord. Also pay great attention to the music you like and see how often the chords move from one to another. In general, classical music can go either way, either long or drawn out, or very fast. Pop music tends to move at a fairly good clip. It's very hard to generalize; again, look at what you like.

Voice Leading

The term *voice leading* comes up often in discussion of music theory, especially when you talk about chords and chord progressions. Voice leading has two definitions:

1. The art of connecting chord to chord in the smoothest manner possible
2. A particular practice in music theory that teaches a set of rules for exactly how voices should move from chord to chord, which is almost always taught in four-part writing

Now, you can concern yourself with the first definition. Voice leading in the traditional sense is an academic practice that is taught when you study music theory deeply in high school or college. It's valuable for some things, especially when you consider that all the rules are taken almost exclusively from Bach's writing style. Because Bach was a genius, it's not a bad thing to study. But too many students get bogged down with the rules and believe that music has to adhere to them.

Go back to the last example in Chapter 8 (Bach's Prelude in C) and look at the voice leading from chord to chord, especially the inversions. Better yet, go through the Roman numeral analysis and play them as block chords and listen to how they sound. Good voice leading can take a simple chord sequence and transform it into a masterpiece.

The challenge is teaching voice leading in a way that makes sense to everyone. The academics can teach voice leading in their own way; here, you will experience a different approach.

Practical Voice Leading

How can you get practical about this? Well, for starters, chords rarely appear in tightly voiced triads as shown in **FIGURE 10.13**.

FIGURE 10.13 A Compact Chord

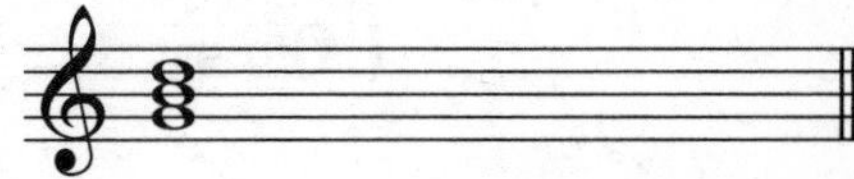

FIGURE 10.14 Typical Guitar Voicing

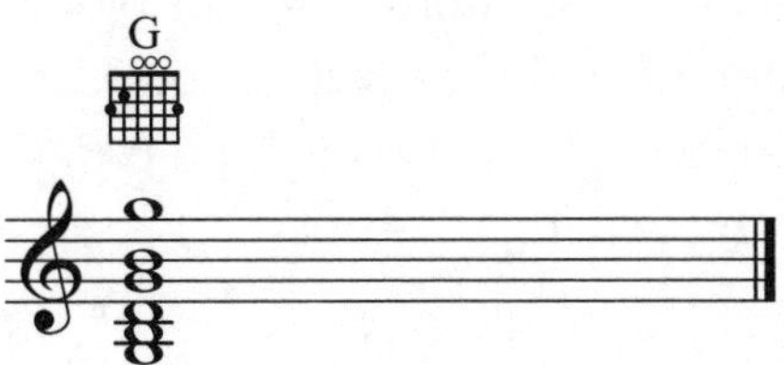

Take the standard guitar chord shown in **FIGURE 10.14**.

All the voices are fairly spread out. The object of voice leading is to try to smooth the transitions from chord to chord as much as possible.

Here is a simple way of looking at voice leading. In **FIGURE 10.15**, voice leading is intentionally omitted through a ii–V–I progression.

FIGURE 10.15 Bad Voice Leading: Block Chords

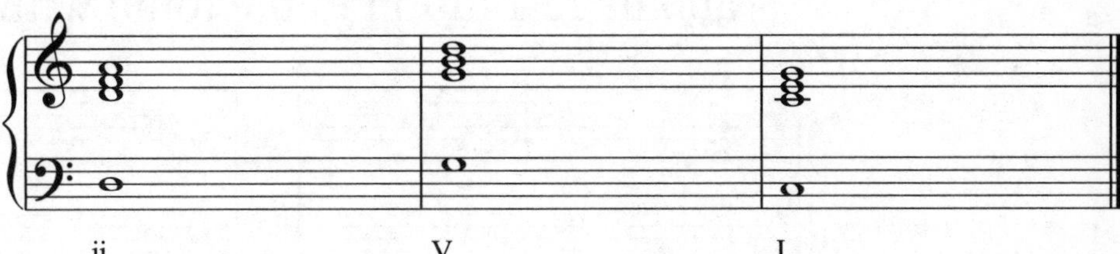

See how all the block chords in the treble staff bounce from one to another? It looks bad and sounds even worse. Take the following as a mantra and you'll be amazed at the difference in the sound: Wherever you are, get to the closest note in the next chord. **FIGURE 10.16** illustrates the same progression with better voice leading.

TRACK 64

FIGURE 10.16 Better Voice Leading

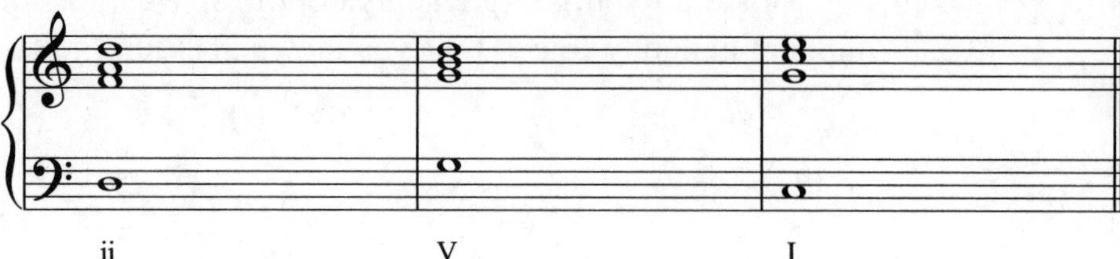

Not only does it look better, it sounds better. The chords have more of a flow than in the previous example. Always try to connect the chords when you write them. Remember that chords are not blocks of information but voices that come together. Keep the individual voices moving as smoothly as possible. As you keep studying how to use chord progressions with inverted chords, your voice leading will improve.

ETUDES

ETUDE 10.1 Etude One

In the following examples, indicate the leading tone and its resolution to the tonic with an arrow

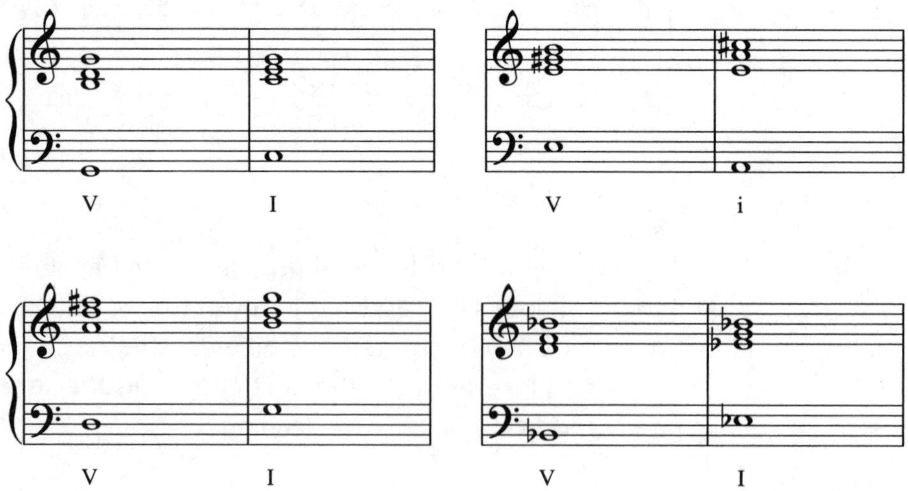

ETUDE 10.2 Etude Two

Using arrows, indicate the proper resolution of the tritone in the following V7 chord

ETUDE 10.3 Etude Three

The following minor chord progression has a mistake in it. Can you find it and correct it?

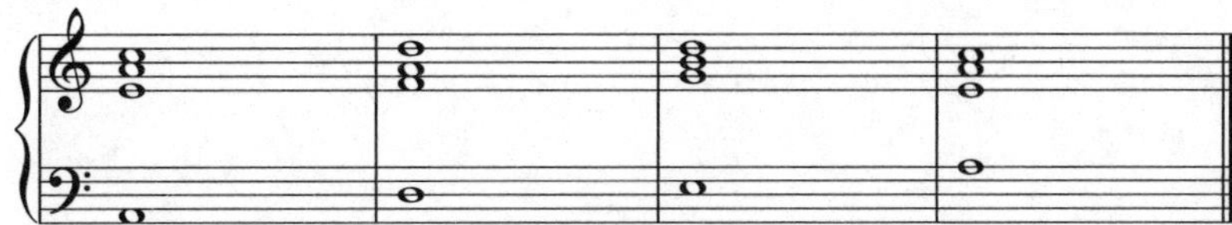

ETUDE 10.4 Etude Four

Transpose the example progression from major to the parallel minor, altering the notes as needed

ETUDE 10.5 Etude Five

Using the Roman numerals and the provided bass notes, realize the chord progression below

CHAPTER 11

Melodic Harmonization

The past few chapters dealt with chords; now it's time to learn about melody. Understanding how chords and melody are related will complete your knowledge of harmony. Chords never exist alone and melodies can't survive without chords to support them. You have learned about scales and how they make melodies. You have learned about chords and their origins. You have studied how chords progress from one to another, but it's time to learn how melody and harmony relate to each other.

What Is Melody?

You have studied so many elements of music in this book, and yet you have never asked this simple question: What is a melody? Certainly, melody is a very important aspect of music! You have learned about scales, which can lead to melodies, but never what a melody is.

Well, there is a good reason for not broaching this question—it's really hard to answer. At its simplest, a melody is the tune of a song. Sing "Happy Birthday" to yourself. You just sang the melody. That was easy because that particular song is practically all melody. What does *all melody* mean? Well, in the case of "Happy Birthday," while there may be some chords behind it, they're not necessary; the tune stands on its own with or without chords. The melody is the memorable part, not the chord progression. Now, for some contrast, listen to a Beethoven symphony and try to sing the melody. That's going to be harder because a symphony is not as clear-cut! There are multiple melodies going on at once. So, why go to all this trouble? The relationship between melody and harmony is crucial to the study of music theory. No matter how well you understand scales and chords, if you don't understand how they relate to one another, your knowledge will be incomplete.

Supportive Chords

Let's use a simple analogy to explore the relationship between melody and harmony. Chords are like ladders, supporting melodies. At its simplest, a single melodic tone can be harmonized with a chord as long as the chord has the melodic tone in it.

So, if you are in the key of C major, you have a melody note C, and you want to figure out what chord would work with that note, look to the key of C major and its harmonized chords. Then select a chord that had the note C in it. Now you have the three choices shown in **FIGURE 11.1**.

FIGURE 11.1 Harmony Choices

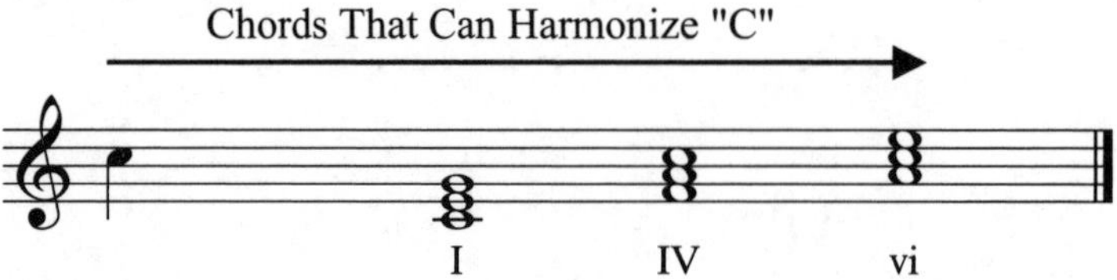

The chord you choose depends upon a few variables. You could listen to each chord and select the one you want. However, you're dealing with one moment in time, and you'd probably want to see the context that this note occurs in throughout the piece, taking into account chords that precede and follow it.

At the most basic level, a single note is supported by a chord that shares the same note. Chapter 12 will expand on this fact. If you've ever wondered why "insert any chord here" is being used at any moment, look to the melody; it always will be related in some way.

POINT TO CONSIDER

When harmonizing single notes, remember that the chord you choose will contain the melody note as either its root, third, or fifth. If you stick only with simple triads, you will always have three choices. Add a seventh chord and you have four choices for chords. It's nice to have choices.

Point for Point

As you start this process, learn how to harmonize a scale point for point, meaning that each note of the scale gets its own chord. Each melody note has at least three choices for chords, which leads to a staggering number of choices. Rather than list them all, here is an example (see **FIGURE 11.2**) that will work well here. Instead of choosing random chords, the chord ladder was the starting point, and the rest of the chords were selected by ear.

TRACK 65

FIGURE 11.2 Harmonizing a Scale Point to Point

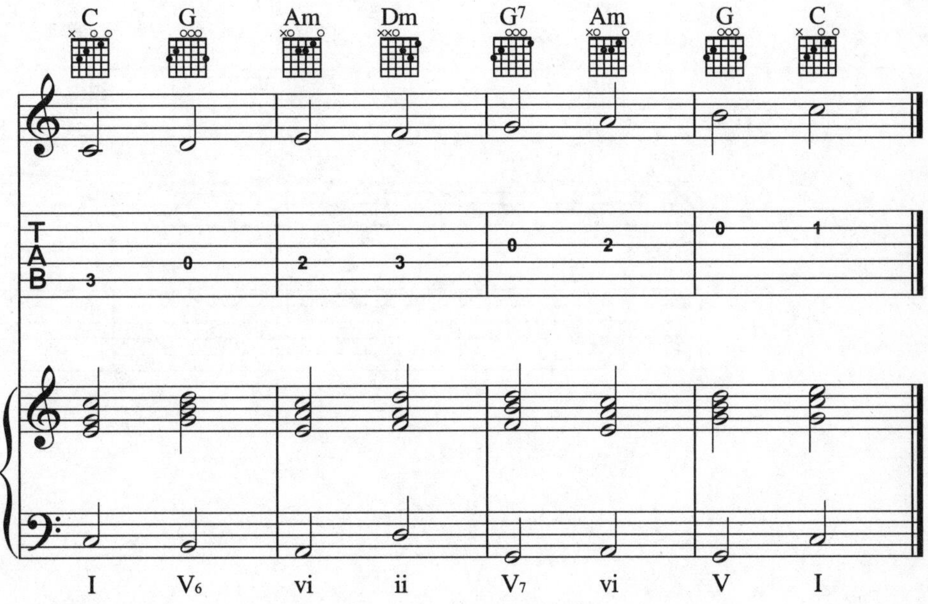

This illustration gives you an idea of how to choose chords for melodic tones—and dig that groovy flute playing the melody on the CD.

Does every melody note get its own chord? Not always. Remember the earlier example of "Amazing Grace." Here it is again in **FIGURE 11.3**.

FIGURE 11.3 "Amazing Grace"

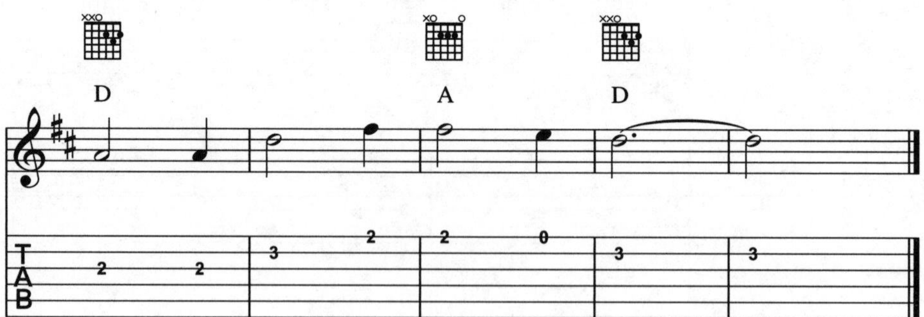

The harmonic rhythm (the pace at which the chords appear and change) has been slowed down considerably. The truth is that not every note in a melody needs to be harmonized with a chord of its very own—that would definitely be overkill.

Look at the sheet music to any pop song you like. You will see that 99.9 percent of the time, chords support several melody notes. There is almost never a new chord for each melody note unless the melody is very, very slow—at which point the harmony is keeping the song from sounding like a dirge.

Chord Tones and Passing Tones

The interaction of chords and melodies centers on one basic point: chord tones or passing (nonharmonic) tones. In **FIGURE 11.2**, each note of the major scale harmonized with its own chord. Since each melody note was found in each chord that supported it, only chord tones were used. **FIGURE 11.3**, "Amazing Grace," used more than just chord tones in the harmonization; it used passing tones as well. Now revisit that example and see what's really going on.

FIGURE 11.4 Chord and Nonchord Tones in "Amazing Grace"

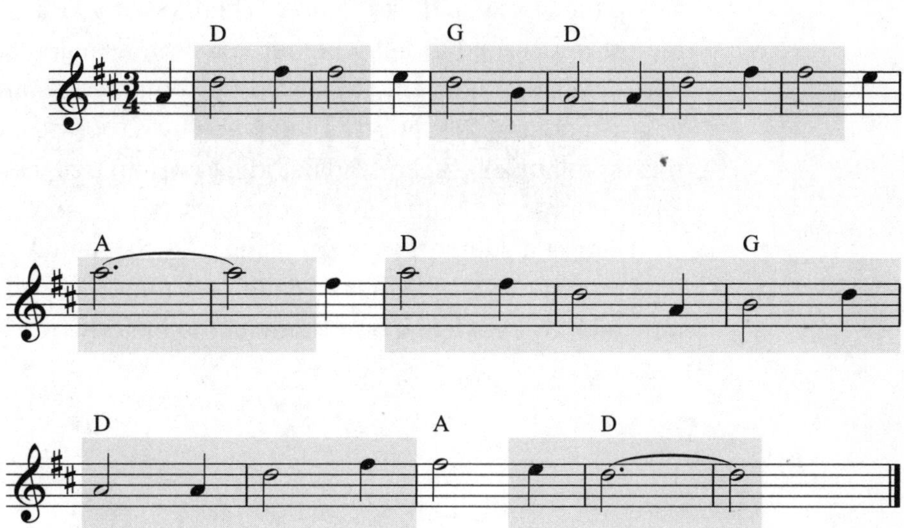

In the example in **FIGURE 11.4**, the chord tones are highlighted and the passing or nonchord tones are printed normally. Compare the harmony to the melody, and you will see many different points of similarity. In general, for a harmony to work for any given melody, the majority of the melodic tones should be contained in the chord that supports it. There is no steadfast rule of how many tones per bar, but for music to sound consonant, the melody needs to line up with the harmony enough times to make the listener feel as if they're in the same key. A passing tone does not necessarily have to move by step to and from a chord tone, but if you think of the odds, a triad has three notes and a scale has seven, you're most likely using a passing tone as the triad takes three-sevenths of the scale with it and leaves three of the other four tones as passing tones. Only one tone will exist as a true nonharmonic tone, but then again, it may sound just fine.

POINT TO CONSIDER

You're back to thinking vertically again, which is good. It's important to see the effect of harmony against melodies and vice versa. It's a bit of the chicken-or-the-egg question. Just don't forget to listen and play each example so that you can hear and not just think about the music. Certain things won't make much sense on paper but will work wonderfully as you listen.

Key Control

One of the nice things about melodic harmonization is your ability to set up the keys you'd like to use. When looking at a single-note melody, it's almost impossible to tell whether you're in a major or a minor key unless you have some harmony to support it. When you start with just a melody, you can control the mood of the piece by choosing either the major or the related minor key. Since any melodic tone can be taken by at least three different chords, you can control your keys very closely.

Here is a simple example, using a key signature of no sharps and no flats, which could be either C major or A minor. The example uses a whole-note melody over a few bars. Look at the melody by itself in **FIGURE 11.5**.

FIGURE 11.5 Basic Melody

TRACK 66

Although a melody could apply to either key that the key signature supports, there is one thing that could sway it to the minor key. Remember the leading tone? In the key of A minor, the G♯ is a telltale sign that the piece is in the key of A minor. The melody stayed away from that—completely on purpose—as that would have locked the music into that key.

Getting back to the example, since the G was avoided, look at **FIGURE 11.6** to see how this could become a C major melody.

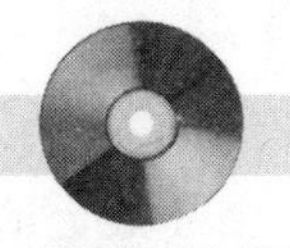

FIGURE 11.6 Basic Melody Harmonized in C

TRACK 67

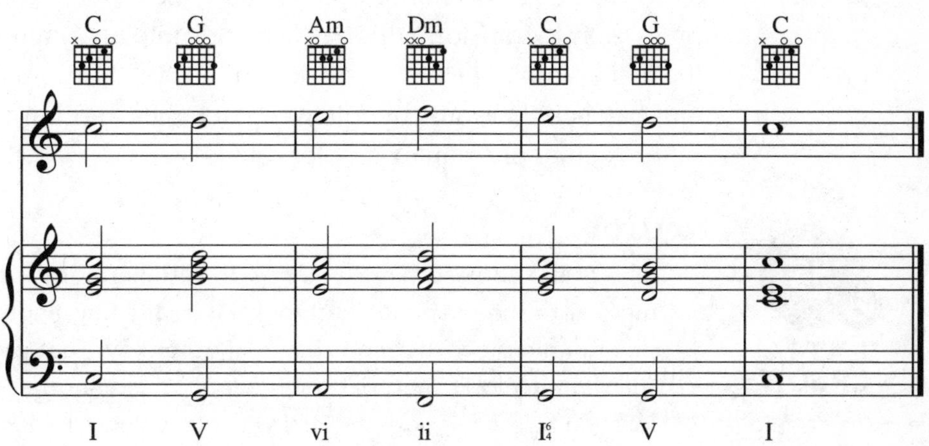

Simply by choosing chords from the key of C, making sure to throw the all-important dominant V chord in, establishes the key of C major. There might have been a chord ladder used, but it was more of a process of elimination at a piano or guitar to see what chords fit best with the notes written.

Now, to push the piece in the direction of A minor, just use chords from the key of A minor and make sure that it has its own dominant V chord—in this case, E7. **FIGURE 11.7** shows the result.

FIGURE 11.7 Same Basic Melody Harmonized in A Minor

TRACK 68

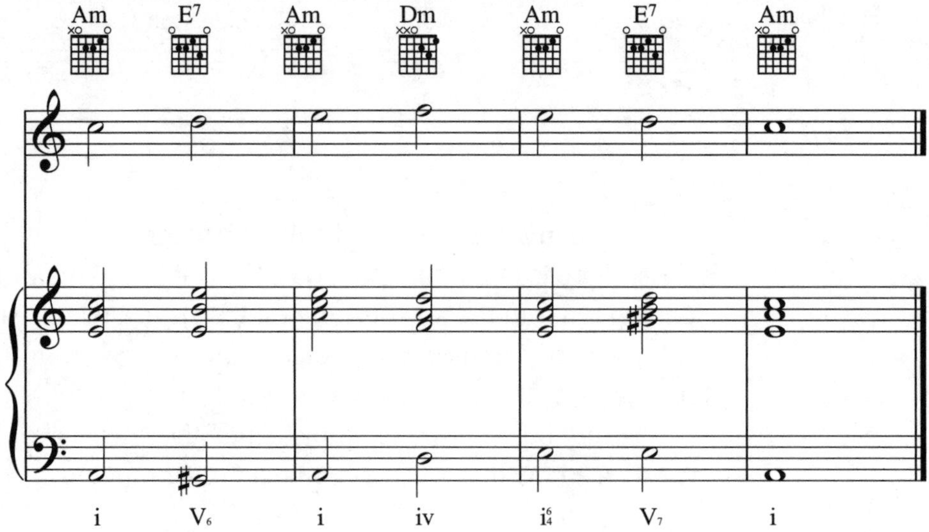

By sticking to A minor chords and typical progressions in that key, it is pretty easy to transform this basic melody into an A minor melody. It's amazing that a simple melody has to be defined by its chords, but this is the general balance that must be followed: Melodies and harmonies rely on each other. Neither one can exist solely on its own.

One of the coolest things you can do with harmony is take a phrase of music (like the example), harmonize it in one key, and then at some point in the piece, harmonize it in another key. That process will give the same melodic material some contrast and another flavor. It will allow you to reuse good material without making it sound stagnant.

True Melodic Harmonization

Let's move on to another aspect of melodic harmonization that doesn't have to do with harmony. Think of a few recent musical acts that use harmony: Simon and Garfunkel, the Indigo Girls, and the Beatles. These groups use true melodic harmony: notes that sound consonant with each other. You've no doubt heard some bad attempts at harmony, usually at holiday parties after a few glasses of spiked eggnog. Someone tries to sing a second part to "Silent Night" or some other tune. The result is usually less than desirable.

It's important to have a general idea of what notes work when harmonizing single-line melodies. This is how chords evolved. Gregorian chant started with a single line of music, called monophony. As time went on, a second voice was added. Limited intervals were allowed, usually fourths and fifths (hence they are called perfect). Over many hundreds of years, a system of harmony built on thirds evolved. This system, known as tertian harmony, has been the focus of this book because it is the basic formula for harmony. Since tertian has as its root tertiary or three, thirds are a great place to start.

One Third Fits All

The first place to look is thirds. Simply put, you can spot harmonize any melody by harmonizing a diatonic third above the original melody.

The diatonic part is key here. You can't just play any third (major or minor), you have to know what key the melody is in and play the notes that fit with it. **FIGURE 11.8** gives a very simple example in D major.

FIGURE 11.8 Melody Waiting to Be Harmonized

To harmonize this melody, start a second part, three notes up in the D major scale, and follow the contour of the original melody. The result is shown in **FIGURE 11.9**.

TRACK 69

FIGURE 11.9 Melody Harmonized in Thirds

The second line is harmonized a 3rd above.

Inverse

The inverse of a third is a sixth, and a sixth is another very nice way to harmonize a melody. Typically, you'd harmonize a sixth down, diatonically. This brings you to the same notes that you had when you went a third up. The difference is that the harmony is now below the original melody note. Both approaches work well. Check out the first example, this time with parallel diatonic sixth harmony, in **FIGURE 11.10**.

TRACK 70

FIGURE 11.10 Same Melody, Harmonized a Sixth Below

The second line is harmonized a 6th below.

Both sound quite nice.

Historically, when harmonizing notes, composers had to be especially careful with voice leading, moving notes in parallel with each other (where one voice follows the exact shape of the original melody). Thankfully, thirds are always nice when used in parallel motion.

Intervals You Can Use

When harmonizing, certain intervals work almost all the time, and others are very hard to use. Here is a list of the intervals by type. Remember that when you are harmonizing melodies in keys, think diatonically for the melody notes.

- **Unison/Octave.** Not really a harmony per se, but the effect of doubling a melody can be a nice way to add some textures.
- **Seconds.** Seconds verge on the edge of tension and dissonance and should be handled with care. They can work at certain points in a harmony for some color, but you'll rarely find more than one in a row; you can forget parallelism.

- **Thirds.** You can't go wrong with thirds. They just always sound nice. They work great in parallel, too.
- **Fourths.** Fourths can be nice, but not in parallel. Parallel fourths are one of the major no-no rules of voice leading. However, since there is a fourth interval from the fifth of a triad to the root, a fourth can be just the right interval.
- **Fifths.** Fifths are also consonant intervals that work well. You don't want them in parallels either as they break the other major rule of voice leading. Plus, if you harmonize with straight parallel fifths, it will sound like Gregorian chant.
- **Sixths.** Sixths are the inverse of thirds. Sixths also always sound very good all the time. They work in almost all situations, especially in parallel motion.
- **Sevenths.** They are another dissonant/tense interval. They may work at certain points, but in general, sevenths won't sound consonant. You're also rarely, if ever, going to see them in succession one after another.

In general, the tense intervals, the seconds and sevenths, are not something to avoid. A bit of tension and release is what music is built on, so using those intervals sparingly may add just the perfect color to your music.

If you want to study harmony in even more depth, you should check out counterpoint. Counterpoint is best exemplified in the fugues by Bach, Mozart, Beethoven, and Shostakovich. Theorist J. J. Fux's treatise on counterpoint still remains the quintessential work for learning about this subject. A highly recommended read if you're interested in learning more about how notes interact with one another.

Single-Line Harmony

Harmony has been the domain of chordal instruments throughout this book. Sure, a clarinet in an orchestra contributes to a sense of harmony in terms of the whole score, but how can all of the single-line instruments (ones that can play only one note at a time) get in on this party? (There are more single-line instruments than chordal instruments.)

Remember an arpeggio? Sure you do—an arpeggio is a chord played one note at a time. Play enough arpeggios and you end up with chords. They aren't chords in the vertical sense; as single-line instruments can't play that way, but they are harmony, more specifically, implied harmony.

The good news is that if you play a single-line instrument, you've probably already played harmony this way. Many of you didn't even know that you played implied harmony. **FIGURE 11.11** gives an example.

FIGURE 11.11 Single-Line Harmony

TRACK 71

Since the arpeggios are labeled and named with Roman numerals, you can clearly see that harmony is definitely going on here. It's simply moving across the page instead of up and down.

If you want to see single-line harmony, here are a few places to look: the solo cello suites by Bach (and his flute and violin solo works, too) and concertos by Vivaldi, Mozart, and Beethoven. Those are the well-known ones. Every instrument has some principal composers; for example, Rodolphe Kreutzer is known exclusively as a violin composer. You'll easily find etudes and pieces to play and study on your instrument.

Single-line harmony is an unavoidable part of playing tonal music. Think of it this way: Everything starts as scales. Scales combine to form chords, which, in turn, form harmony. It's almost impossible to write music without being aware of harmony and its implications. Music for single-line instruments would be boring without some sense of harmonic implications. The music would wander without purpose.

Take a good hard look at the content of any piece of music for a single-line instrument and you're going to find a lot more than just notes. The next etude will show you some examples, but search your own musical archives; you're sure to find more than enough to work with.

ETUDES

ETUDE 11.1 Etude One

In the key of B♭, indicate which chords harmonize with the note E♭

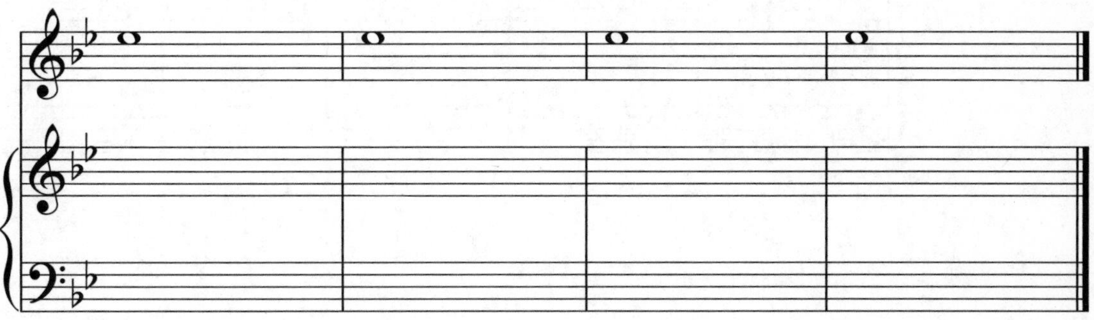

ETUDE 11.2 Etude Two

In the following harmonized melody, circle the chord tones

ETUDE 11.3 Etude Three

In the following harmonized melody, circle the non-chord tones

ETUDE 11.4 Etude Four

Harmonize this melody with diatonic 3rds and 6ths

ETUDE 11.5 Etude Five

Harmonize the following melody with only diatonic chords

Dealing with Accidentals

Here is a short but important question: How do you harmonize a note that is not diatonic to a scale? Say you're in the key of C major and you have a melody note of F♯. That note isn't in any of the diatonic chords, so what do you do? Read Chapter 12 and learn about advanced chord progressions, specifically how to deal with chromatic harmony (harmonizing notes outside the scale).

CHAPTER 12

Advanced Harmony

Diatonic harmony will get you only so far in understanding music. As music progressed, the variety and complexity of harmony also evolved. Composers augmented diatonic chords with other harmonies to expand the timbre and color of music. This chapter will introduce you to other ways to add color to your music, and introduce more issues you will encounter as you analyze music. You will also cover the important topic of changing keys and modulation.

Beyond Diatonic

As a student of music theory, it's only logical to start learning about diatonic harmony, both major and minor harmonies. As with any set of guidelines, however, composers found ways around the rules and started to add other chords to the canon of harmony to give greater variety.

Diatonic harmony supports diatonic melodic writing. How do you deal with melodies that contain notes outside the scales? Also, the chord ladder seems to be something you can't easily escape. How do you create interesting progressions that don't simply follow the ladder from end to end? You have already learned that the dominant chord is the basic end of the progression. When you reach that chord, your options are either to cadence and begin a new phrase or to resolve it in some deceptive way. Composers over the course of music history have sought ways to prolong the amount of time it takes to get to the dominant chord. With diatonic harmony, there is only so much that you can do. By providing some additional chords in extended harmony—more specifically, secondary chords—composers could keep the ball in the air a bit longer.

Secondary Chords

A secondary chord is a simple concept: Take any chord in the diatonic scale and precede it with a related chord that is outside the diatonic scale, adding a bit of color and an extra side step in the harmonic picture.

Secondary chords come in two flavors: dominant and diminished. Secondary chords can be used with fully diatonic melodies, adding more richness to already functional, melodic writing. Since dominant and diminished chords are essentially substitutes for each other, you should know why a secondary chord works in any setting.

Secondary Dominant Chords

Dominant chords are typically the V chord of a key and they have a very strong tendency to resolve up a perfect fourth or down a perfect fifth (you'll arrive at the same note) to a tonic I chord. You also know that they are so strong as to define keys by themselves. If you moved the V chord temporarily, to precede another chord in the key, would it work?

The answer is yes. A secondary dominant is a simple action that places a temporary dominant chord a fifth away from any chord in the key. Think of it as a harmonic detour.

Now set up an example. Use the IV chord as the target chord. You want to precede the IV chord with a dominant chord. In the key of C major, IV is F major, and F's dominant chord (a perfect fifth away) is C7. You can see the progression in **FIGURE 12.1**.

FIGURE 12.1 I–IV–V–I

TRACK 72

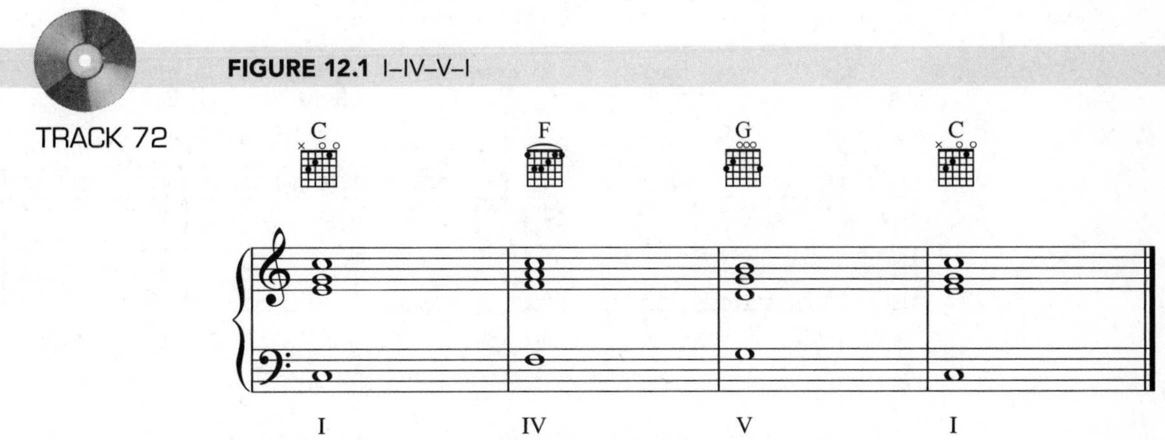

Now, add the secondary dominant to IV in the progression, and you get the progression in **FIGURE 12.2**.

FIGURE 12.2 I–?–IV–V–I

TRACK 73

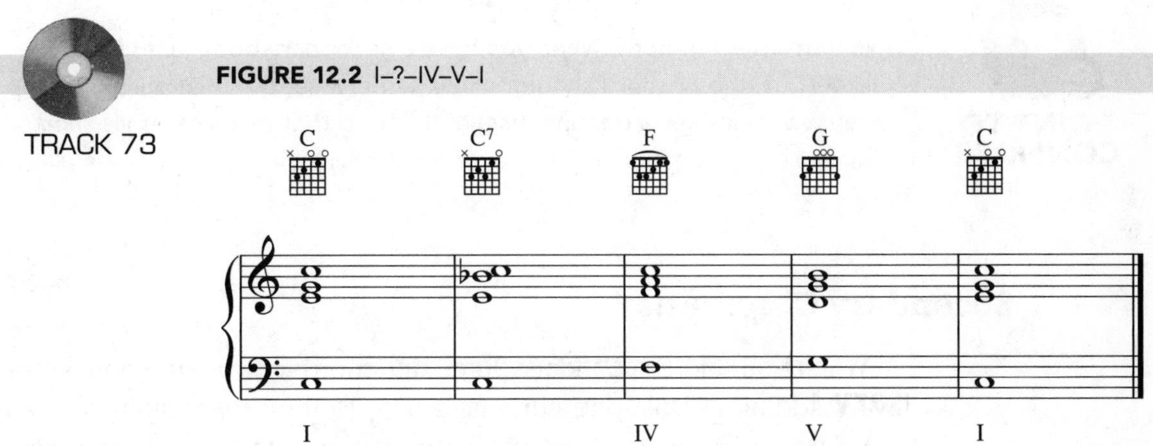

There are two things to discuss here. First, the additional dominant chord adds a great flavor to an otherwise "stock" progression. Think of the other chords that could have preceded IV; few have the flavor of the secondary dominant. Second, what do you call this chord? In the progression, there is a temporary question mark in place. The chord is C7, so you could call it a I_7 chord, but that would miss the relationship between the secondary chord and its destination. Instead, you would call that chord V_7/IV, or "five of four." The word *of* is depicted as a slash and shows clearly that you are adding a chord that is related to the IV chord, instantly resolving to the proper destination: IV.

FIGURE 12.3 shows the proper naming for the progression using Roman numerals.

TRACK 74

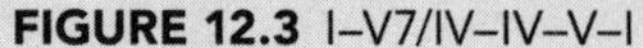

FIGURE 12.3 I–V7/IV–IV–V–I

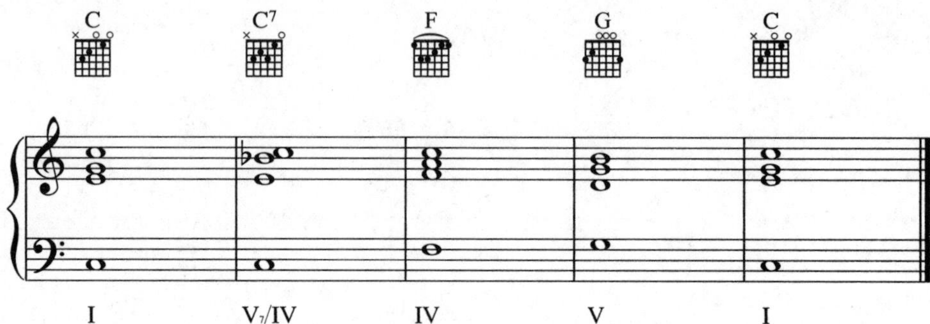

It is perfectly clear what the function of the nondiatonic C7 chord is in the progression. You could easily realize this progression (write one yourself) in another key simply using the Roman numerals.

POINT TO CONSIDER

In functional harmony, when you have a secondary dominant chord like V7/IV, the IV chord should follow. Otherwise, the relationship that you are creating—a dominant seventh chord that resolves—falls short because the dominant chord never resolves.

Secondary Chromatic

When you add a secondary dominant chord to a progression, you are always adding at least one chromatic note to the progression (V/iii adds two). Since these chords have notes that fall outside the diatonic key, you get a greater variety of tones. In the example, the B♭ would seem to smash our sacred leading tone in the key of C (B), but since it's part of a dominant chord, it sidesteps the key for a second and sets up an expected point of conclusion: IV. Once you resolve, it's business as usual and the actual V chord in the key restores the B♭ to a B natural and the key has function again.

Which Chords?

Which chords can have secondary dominant chords? In a diatonic progression, all chords except the vii° chord can have secondary dominants.

In all fairness, you can't count I either, since its dominant is not secondary but diatonic. So, here is a list of chords that can support secondary dominants:

- ii
- iii
- IV
- V
- vi

Exclude I and the vii° (diminished) chord, and you are all set. Now, you can't just throw these chords in whenever you feel like it. Well, you can, if you are writing chord progressions without melodies. But if you are harmonizing melodies, you need to be a bit more careful; certain conditions need to be met.

What Conditions?

Where exactly can you use these chords with a melody that you have already written? Well, a few things have to align for this to work. First, when you are talking about secondary dominant chords, you are actually talking about two chords: the secondary dominant and the chord it resolves to. Since both of these chords have to have connections to your melody, you need to have a situation where your melody supports both chords in succession. **FIGURE 12.4** gives an example where it works really well:

FIGURE 12.4 I–V7/ii–ii–V–I

TRACK 75

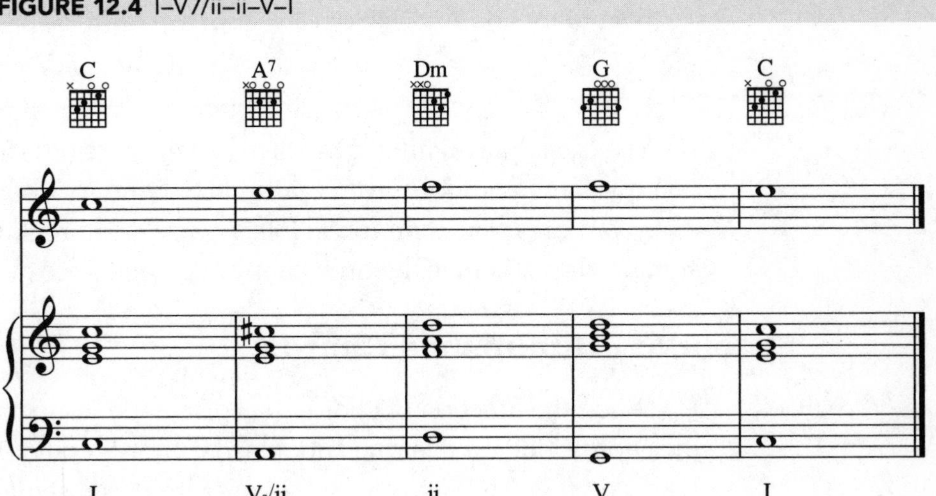

Using a simple whole-note melody, you can see that the second and third chords are your points where the secondary chords come into use. The melody in bars two and three use the notes E and F. Now, you could harmonize E and F lots of different ways. When this progression was being constructed, it was obvious that it would cadence with a ii–V–I; it just sounded right after a few tries at the piano. But what about the harmony under the E? There were several choices:

- A I_6 chord (C/E) could have been used to harmonize the E.
- A vi chord could have been used to harmonize the E.
- A iii chord could have been used to harmonize the E.

Theoretically, they all worked on paper. As sounds, there were some issues. The I_6 chord simply sounded funny going to ii; the voice leading of the bass line going from E to D just didn't sit right. The iii chord has never sounded that compelling in any diatonic progression (it's too far from I), so that was out. The vi sounded good and would have been a solid choice; however, the V7/ii, which is an A7 chord, was ultimately chosen. The vi chord is an A minor chord; the A7 has the same bass note and two-thirds of the chord tones are the same. No wonder it worked so well!

How do secondary dominant chords apply to minor keys? The same way they do in major keys. The key is not the crucial step here, only the chords themselves. A secondary dominant is a dominant chord that resolves to a chord in the key. It is not a key change, rather a temporary side step, which can happen in both major and minor keys.

The tricky part is finding spots to use these chords in music. Sometimes you use them and don't even realize it. Secondary dominant chords, especially V/V, are quite common in folk, country, and rock music. You may just stumble upon them in a grand, happy accident.

Secondary Diminished Chords

When the function of chords was discussed, especially when it came to the chord ladder, you learned about what chords could commonly substitute for each other. The V (dominant) chord can be substituted by the vii° chord. Both chords function as dominant chords in that they resolve back to tonic with strength and great pull. So, in the spirit of secondary dominant chords, what about secondary diminished chords? Yes, those exist, too. If the chords basically function the same way, you can use them the same way.

Secondary diminished chords have their own set of rules. Think about regular diminished chords. Typically, you see these chords as vii° chords, so you can infer some rules about their actions.

A secondary diminished chord will:

- Be either a diminished triad or a fully diminished seventh chord
- Be built a half step lower than the chord it is resolving to
- Always resolve up by a half step

As for their written symbols, instead of calling these chords V/something, call them vii°/something.

You see secondary diminished chords in classical and jazz much more than in pop music because the diminished sound is not as accepted and common as other chords.

Regardless, they are very nice chords because they have a very slippery sound to them. What does "slippery" have to do with music? It's all about the voice leading. **FIGURE 12.5** provides a demonstration in the same example you had before.

FIGURE 12.5 I–vii°/ii–ii–V–I

TRACK 76

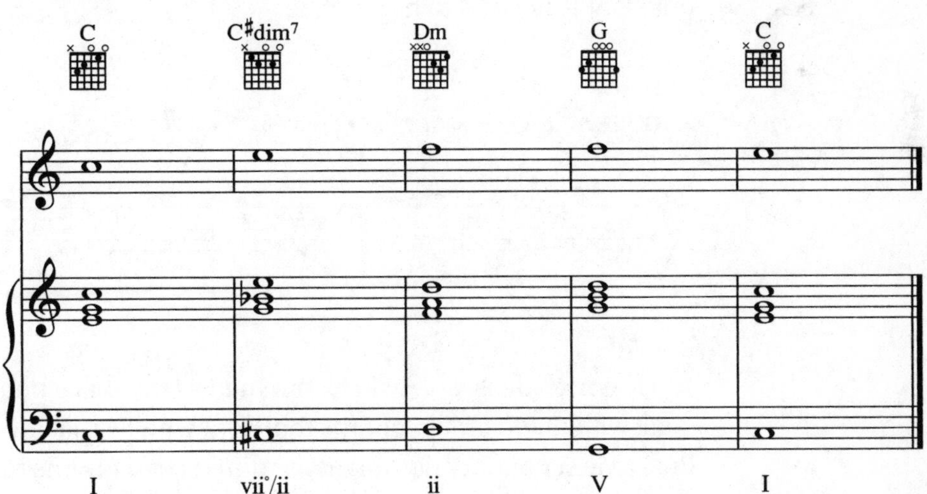

Here is the same melody as in **FIGURE 12.4**. The note that had to be harmonized was an E. Everything else was more or less set. In **FIGURE 12.4**, V/ii, an A7 chord, was chosen. In **FIGURE 12.5**, vii°/ii, a C♯ diminished chord, was selected. Since the chord was only a half step below the ii chord, the secondary diminished chord slid into the ii chord. Even the bass line from the beginning of the progression—C–C♯–D—was a very smooth, slippery movement of bass notes and harmonies.

Both A7 and C♯ diminished support the E as a melody note since they both have E in their chords. In addition, if you were to step outside the key of C for a second and think about A7 as a dominant chord, you would have to imagine the key of D (the key where A7 is V). The substitute dominant chord in the key of D is C♯ diminished. If you compare **FIGURE 12.4** and **FIGURE 12.5**, you'll see that all that happened was that a secondary chord was chosen for the ii chord, but each example simply substituted a dominant chord of some sort (either dominant or diminished) that resolved normally to the ii chord.

It provided a "temporary" V I (dominant tonic) relationship, on another chord besides the real tonic chord. That's why these chords work—they provide the pull, the tension and release that you need, but they do so at other points in the harmony. This may seem a bit hypothetical, but just put it to use and you will hear it for yourself.

Chromatic Harmony

The secondary chords come under the umbrella of chromatic harmony, meaning that they provide notes outside the key or they help to harmonize melodies that use notes outside the key. **FIGURE 12.6** provides a simple example of a chromatic melody that is basically in C major but adds a chromatic note that is needed to harmonize

FIGURE 12.6 Chromatic Melody

The melody is largely in C, but the F♯s that have been added need to be dealt with; there are no chords that deal with F♯ that are diatonic to C major. But some secondary dominants or diminished chords may be. Try to harmonize the rest of the chords and exclude the F♯ (or at least the measure that it's in). See **FIGURE 12.7**.

FIGURE 12.7 Chromatic Melody with Partial Chords

You are left with a fairly benign I–vi–?–V7–I progression.

To deal with the chord in ?, look to the chord after it, a V chord, G7 in this key.

What's the secondary dominant of that chord? V/V is D7, spelled D–F♯–A–C, so it works! Plug it in (**FIGURE 12.8**) and see how it sounds.

TRACK 77

FIGURE 12.8 Chromatic Melody, Full Harmonization

It works! Not only did you take care of the chromatic note in the melody, but you also generated a pretty interesting chord progression, one that any theory teacher would be proud to see.

Note: You could have also used vii°/V (F♯ diminished) as a good substitute chord for the D7 as both D7 and F♯ diminished. In this case, since there was a D in the melody and the diminished chord has an E♭, it's best to stick with D7. Functionally, it would have been okay, but to the ear it's not pretty.

Chromatic harmony is an interesting topic. Notice how composers deal with chromatic notes in their melodies and which chromatic chords they use.

IN TIME

There are two other chromatic chords that are often studied in high-level theory. One is called the Neapolitan sixth chord, and the other is a family of chords called augmented sixth chords. Both are important chords in the development of harmony but are a bit beyond the scope of this text. If you study further, you will no doubt encounter these chords from time to time.

Modal Mixture

What is a modal mixture? It's very common when you are in a major key to borrow aspects from other keys as you go along. The most common way is to borrow chords from the minor key with the same name (C major/C minor). These are called borrow chords, and they are a pretty neat way to spice up your harmony. Because the major and minor key are so close in some respects, you can interchange these chords for some cool sounds. Look at some examples and see what chords you can borrow.

Borrowed Chords from Major

Here, you are in a minor key (any one you choose) and you are going to borrow some chords from the major key. Look at the diatonic major and minor keys together to see what their harmonic differences are.

If you look at the chords, number by number, you can see differences; they are, in fact, different keys. Now, think about this: Discussions of minor keys typically include the addition of dominant chords on V and diminished chords on vii to make the keys function better. This is analogous to the discussion of the harmonic minor scale and its chords. In a sense, you have already borrowed the V and vii chords from the major key (see **FIGURE 12.9**). The other most common chord to borrow is the IV chord from the major key.

FIGURE 12.9 Parallel Major and Minor Harmony

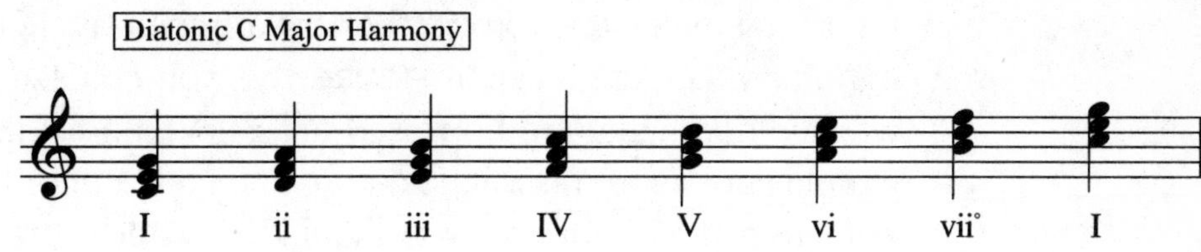

Diatonic C Minor Harmony

i ii° III iv v VI VII i

Here is an example in **FIGURE 12.10**, using a major IV chord in a minor key.

TRACK 78

FIGURE 12.10 Borrowed IV Chord in Minor

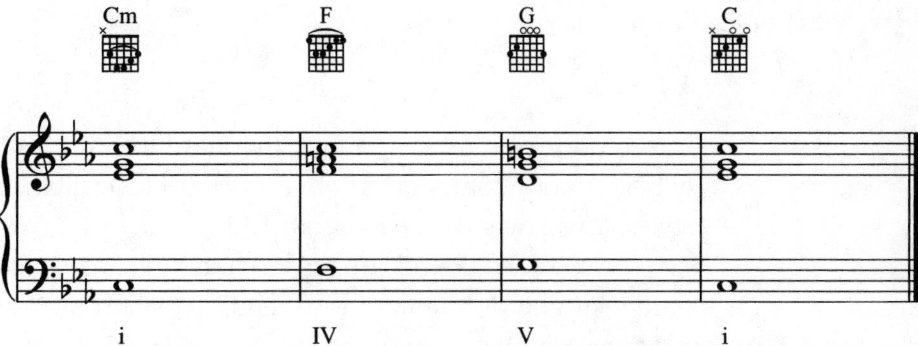

You could certainly take any chord from the major key, but if you count IV, V, and vii°, those are three typical chords that are often seen in minor keys. Add to that secondary dominant and diminished chords, and you have a pretty nice lineup of harmonic choices.

You could even think of a Picardy third (a raised third that forms a major triad in the final chord of a composition in a minor key) as a borrowed I chord. Since it happens only at the end of pieces, it's not a true borrowed chord.

When you start looking at borrowing from the minor key into major, there are a lot more choices.

Borrowed Chords from Minor

In any major key, you can borrow a bunch of chords from the parallel minor key. Looking back at **FIGURE 12.9**, you can see the differences. The typical chords that are borrowed are iv, ♭VI, and ♭VII. In the jazz chapter (coming up next), you will hear about one other chord that is used in modern music, the ii°. For now, you should know about the iv, ♭VI, and ♭VII. Start with iv. The iv chord is very commonly used in major keys and it's all over music of all genres and ages. It's in Mozart and the Beatles. **FIGURE 12.11** gives a nice example using a iv chord in a major key context.

FIGURE 12.11 Minor iv in Major

TRACK 79

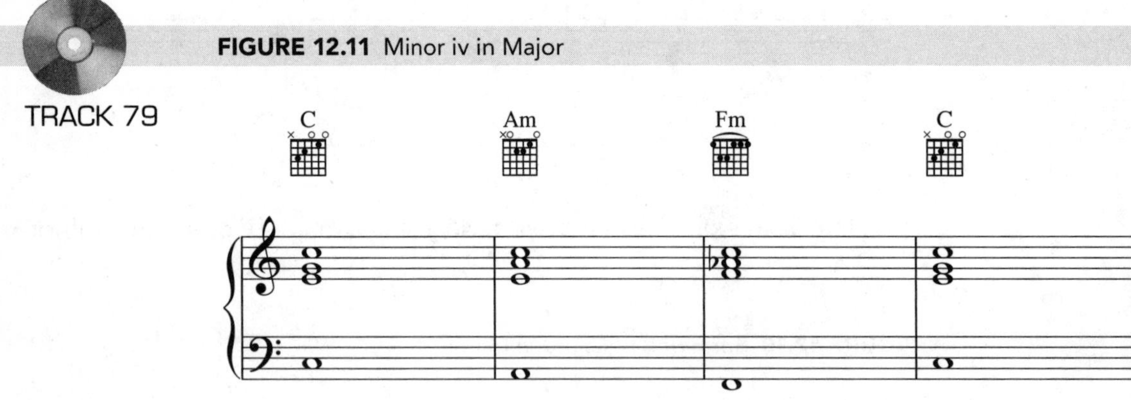

You don't even have to look that hard to find this borrowed chord. It's actually more common in folk and pop music than in common practice styles. It's all over the Beatles' music!

The next two chords are the ♭VI and ♭VII. In **FIGURE 12.12**, you see these particular chords, commonly ascending toward the I chord, typically coming between V and I as the example illustrates. There are other ways to use them, but this is by far the most common.

The reason to talk about borrowed chords at all (it's considered a fairly high-level subject) is that they occur often in all different styles of music, across genres and time periods. Most importantly, you see them in pop music, so this may eliminate some of the chords you've been trying to analyze that simply didn't seem to fit into the key.

FIGURE 12.12 Excuse Me, May I Borrow That ♭VI and ♭VII Chord, Please?

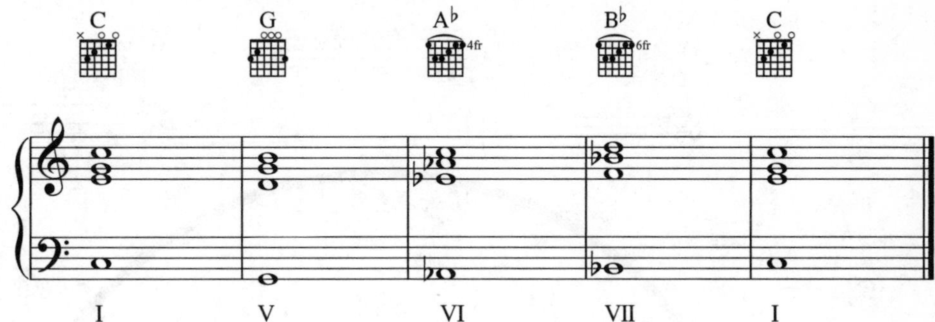

Modulation

How do you change keys? This topic is large enough for its own book, but the title *The Everything® Harmonic Modulation Book* just didn't seem to flow, so it will get a section here. Modulation is simply the art of shifting the tonal center to another key and staying there. What do you know about tonal centers? Essentially, they involve chords and melodies that define certain keys. Most importantly, dominant V chords and tonic I chords are the basic ingredients.

Secondary chords provide a temporary tonal shift. But if you simply held on to secondary chords for long enough, you could shift the tonal center to another key. You could finally modulate.

The simplest way to change keys is to go to a key that is spelled very closely to the key you are in. The rule of thumb is simple: The fewer notes you have to shift, the easier your job is. Start to look at the related keys.

Related Keys

Related keys share notes in common with one another. The more notes they share, the more closely related they are. Review the key circle in **FIGURE 12.13** for a second.

FIGURE 12.13 The Circle of Keys

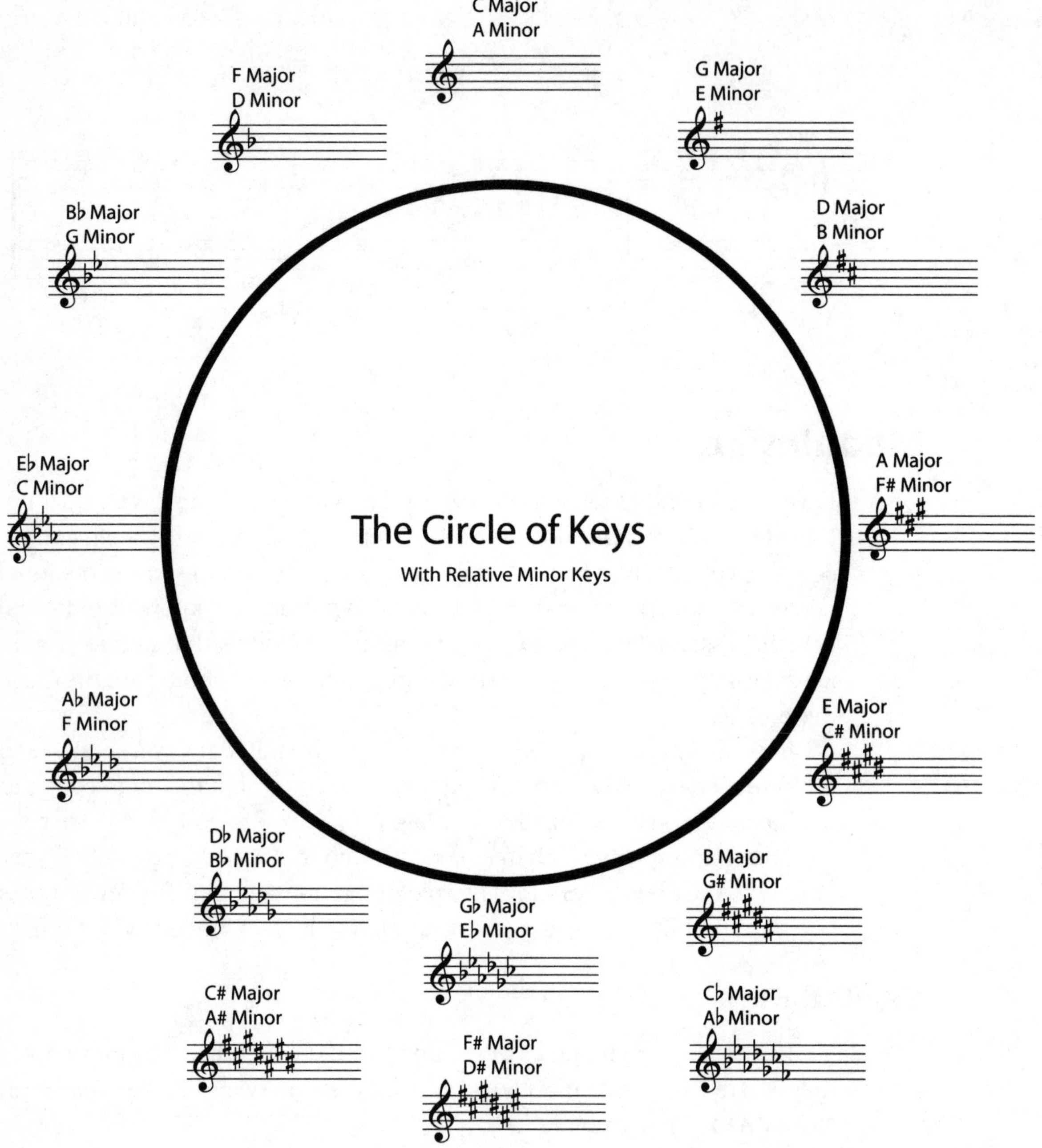

You are in C (an old favorite). The closest related key would be one key to the right or one key to the left, so G and F are keys that you can move into easily. As you start to lose notes in common, it becomes more difficult to slip into a new key. Nothing's impossible, but typically, movements are by fifths, either up to G or down to F, if you start in C.

New Dominants

When you throw in a secondary dominant, you alter a key's landscape by adding a chromatic tone. In these situations, that chromatic tone always goes away. What if you stuck with it? What if you had a section of music that you kept analyzing V/V, V and it never really came back to I? You may have just stumbled onto a modulation.

Here's an example shown in **FIGURE 12.14**. Start out in C and end up in G. This will be a fairly long progression because you want to set up the idea of the key change and establish the new tonic/dominant relationship so that it sticks.

FIGURE 12.14 Simple Harmonic Modulation

TRACK 81

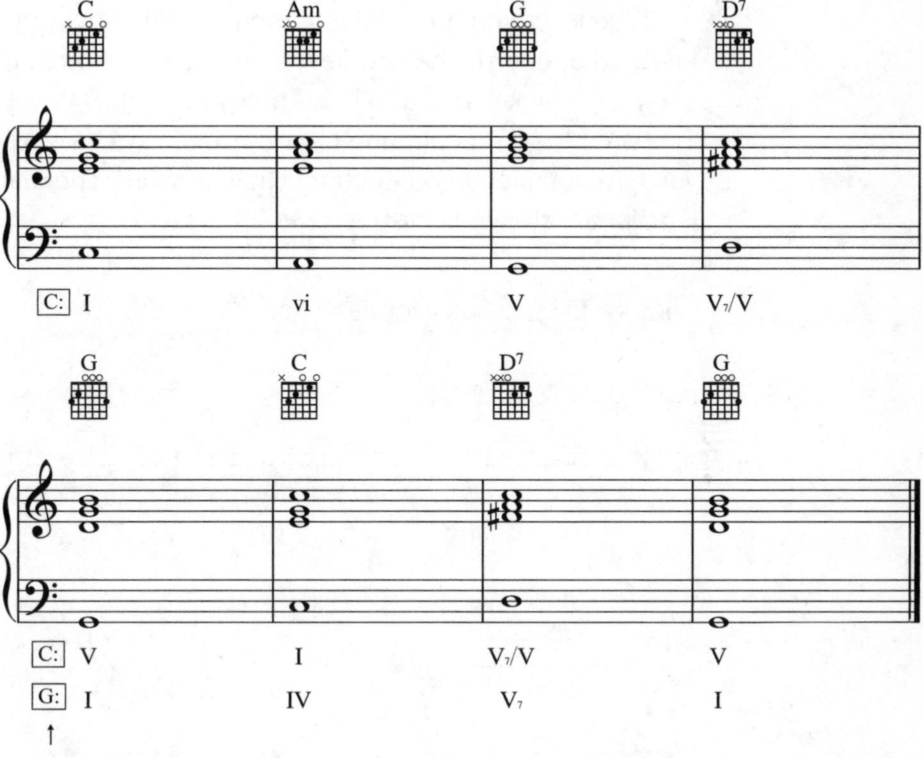

As you can see and hear, you started in one key and ended up in another. You achieved this with two devices. The first is a secondary dominant to the new key. Your goal was to move to the key of V (G major). To do so, V needs to be in the new key (V of G is D7), so you made sure to do that. The minute the V/V showed up, you had an F♯ in the key. The trick is not to let it go back to F♮, so you did the progression again to solidify the sound of the new key. The other way that this is accomplished is with common chords. For example, to change keys, you need to think in the new key for a second. A I–IV–V progression in any key is pretty strong. You can pull off that progression by using common chords. I–IV–V in the key of G is G–C–D. In the key of C, you have C and G chords already. The only addition is the D, which you get via the secondary dominant chord (V/V). The real trick is not making the G chord a G7. G7 would pull back to C; in **FIGURE 12.14**, it's kept a triad. Common chords can go further in helping you establish a new key. I–IV–V is not the only progression, as you already know. Look at other common chords. (Notice how you can analyze **FIGURE 12.14** in both keys? The analysis is provided for you in C and G. It makes much more sense to look at the second line in G.)

Common Chords

Whenever you are thinking about modulating to a new key, it's nice to know what chords the two keys share; these chords are easy to use effectively. Use the key of C and F this time and look at how you might modulate. The V/V is never a common chord; you always have to change the key, but you have a bunch of other chords that do work. The diatonic triads of C and F major are shown in **FIGURE 12.15**.

FIGURE 12.15 Chords in C and F

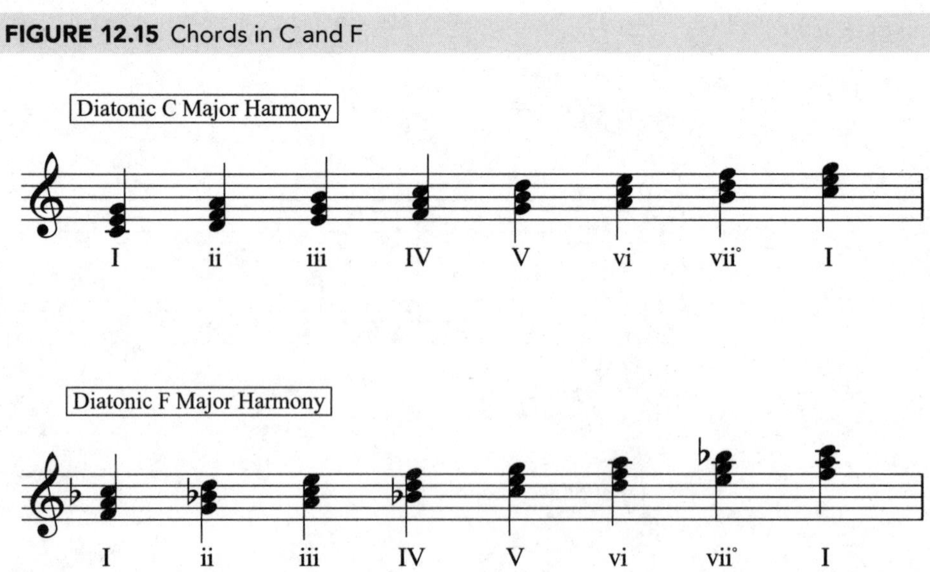

You see a bunch of chords in both keys—C, Dm, F, and Am. In the key of F, those chords are V, vi, I, and iii respectively. So, you do have a V/V chord in this case (it's just not a C7 chord), which you need to fix with a chromatic note. In the key of F, the vi chord is important. What you are missing is a pre-dominant chord, either ii or IV. Neither of those chords is common, but once you've done the whole secondary dominant (or diminished) thing, the next progression after the cadence can continue on as if it's in the new key. The G minor chord you're going to add won't sound odd, because you've already introduced the chromatic tone (B♭) to the key; it will actually sound as if it belongs to the key of F (see **FIGURE 12.16**).

FIGURE 12.16 Common Chord Modulation

TRACK 82

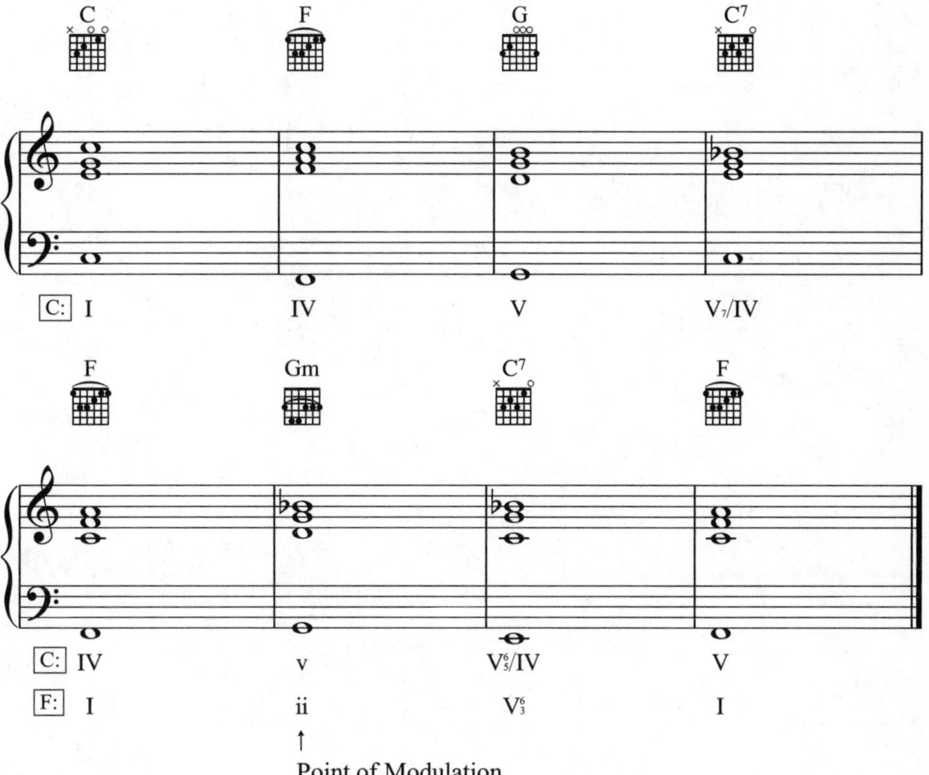

The way to make a secondary dominant not feel secondary is to not turn back to the old key at all, keep going in the key of F and use typical, diatonic progressions for that key. As you keep writing in the new key, the listener will forget about the key of C since you have tonic-sized the F chord so many times it sounds as though you have modulated, and you have.

Modulation is a big topic with some very simple rules. You know how harmony works, and you know that to move you have to shift the harmony to the new key. The trick is to analyze some music, especially classical music (because of the common modulations), to get used to seeing exactly how it's done.

Just a word of warning: Sometimes the hardest part about modulation is simply knowing a modulation when you see it. As soon as you see chords that don't make sense in the original key, that is a clear sign that you may not be in that key anymore. Look for patterns in other keys. If you can fit the mystery progression into another key, chances are that's exactly where you are. One last thing: You can't modulate without a chromatic note. On the other hand, chromatic notes do not always signal movement into other keys. They could be slight diversions and resolve. Either way, look for the signposts, and most of all, listen. If a chord sounds like a I, it probably is.

ETUDES

ETUDE 12.1 Etude One

Realize the secondary dominant chords from the key and Roman numerals below

ETUDE 12.2 Etude Two

Realize the secondary diminished chords from the key and Roman numerals below

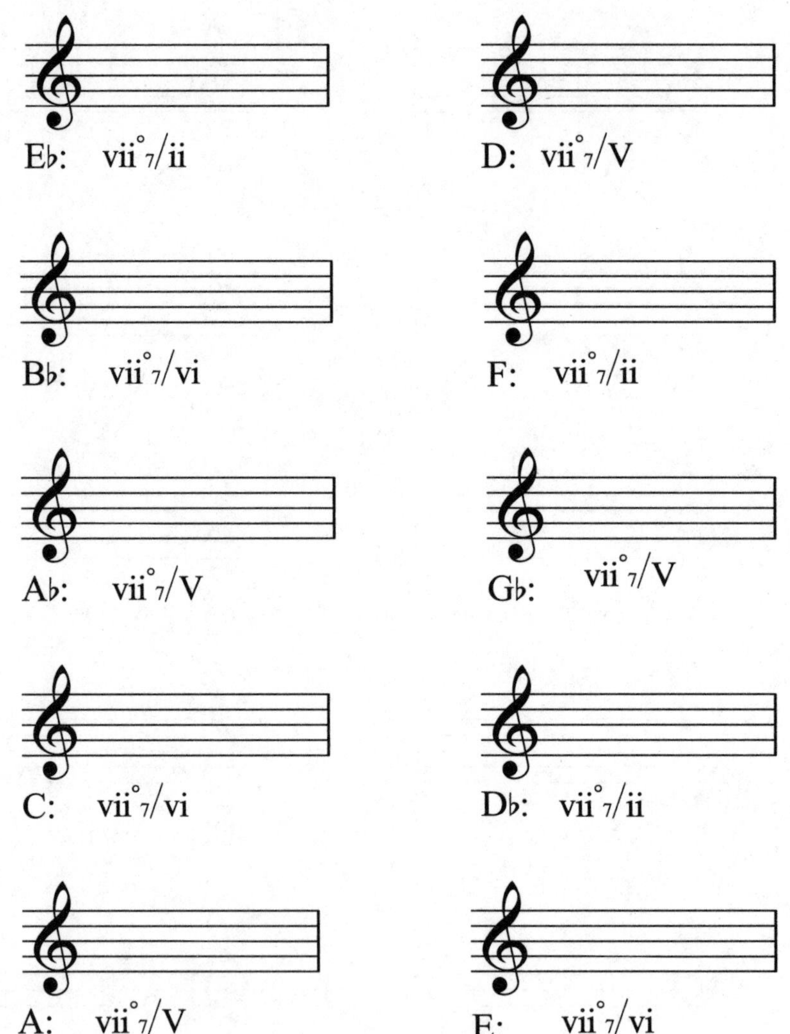

ETUDE 12.3 Etude Three

Realize the borrowed chords from the key and Roman numerals below

ETUDE 12.4 Etude Four

The following example modulates. Indicate the start and ending keys and circle the first chord in the new key.

**Example harmonized by J.S. Bach*

ETUDE 12.5 Etude Five

Using the space provided, write down the chords that are shared in the key of A and E major

CHAPTER 13

Jazz Harmony

You have already dealt with harmony on many different levels in this book. Yet, in modern times, harmony has diverged into a very unique art form that is truly American: jazz. Although jazz harmony is reminiscent of traditional tonal harmony, it looks and feels quite different. Now it's time to look at what makes jazz harmony unique since it's a crucial part of the history of music.

What Is Jazz?

Jazz is a very young genre of music that continues to evolve and reshape itself at a breathtaking pace. Every ten years or so, jazz seems to reinvent itself; the rate of change is astounding. Jazz is categorized by several important elements. One is instrumentation: bass, piano, drums, saxophone, and trumpet come to mind. The other main part is improvisation. It's actually the strongest component of playing jazz: improvising melodic solos over chord changes. It's one of the things that truly sets jazz apart. Now, look at the elements of jazz as they relate to music theory.

IN TIME

Jazz is one of the few purely American art forms that do not directly come from the European tradition. Instead, it was slowly formed from its origins in gospel music and the blues music of the Deep South. It quickly grew into art music through the great jazz innovators such as Louis Armstrong, Miles Davis, Charlie Parker, and John Coltrane, to name a few.

How is jazz different from other styles of music? Primarily, improvisation and instrumentation are the aspects that are unique to jazz. Consider jazz in relation to other styles of music. Does jazz use scales, diatonic chords, triads? How does its harmony work? What are the essential ingredients of jazz? The rest of this chapter is devoted to breaking jazz into its small parts.

Jazz Harmony

Jazz harmony is unmistakably rooted in the tradition of music theory. It relies on melodies that are harmonized with chords. The principal difference between jazz harmony and other harmony is its use of chords that are taller than triads—taller as in vertically, on the page, like the G13 chord shown in **FIGURE 13.1**.

TRACK 83

FIGURE 13.1 G13 Chord

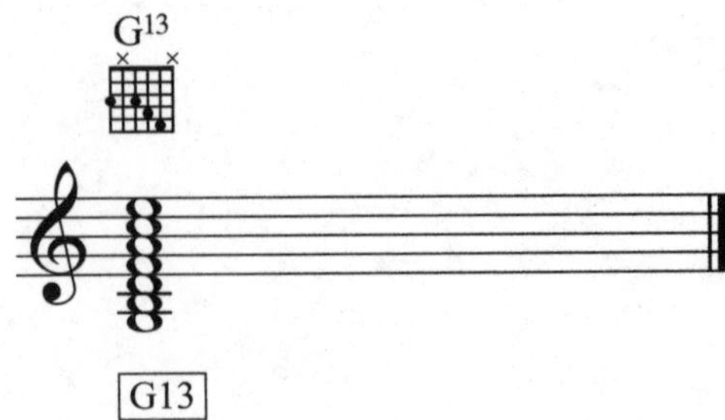

The G13 chord is considered a tall chord because it's tall on the page. It fits into a class of chords called extended chords. To understand extended chords, you need to understand extended intervals. This book's earlier discussion of intervals didn't say much about extended intervals, but jazz harmony requires it. You need to know what a thirteenth really is and what extended intervals are.

Extended Intervals

By now, intervals should be a common part of your music theory experience. Funny how there's more to learn about them. Intervals have shown you the exact distance between any two notes. Up until now, you have not distinguished intervals larger than an octave. You heard about them, but you never saw them put into practice.

Do a quick review: After you pass the octave (which is also called an eighth), you distinguish these larger intervals with, you guessed it, larger numbers. Any interval larger than an octave is considered an extended interval. However, there are some intervals that are never extended.

Music theory does not distinguish the distance of a third or a fifth differently, no matter what octave it is in. Much of this has to do with historical practice, but the real reason lies in triadic harmony.

Since the majority of jazz chords include extended intervals, just remember the rule of nine in order to decipher what a ninth from C is, for example. In jazz, the seventh chord is the smallest unit you will see, and typically, taller chords are more common than seventh chords, so you'll need to know extensions in order to succeed.

If you start stacking thirds on top of one another, you get this order: C–E–G–B–D–F–A–C. Or as intervals: root, third, fifth, seventh, ninth, eleventh, thirteenth, and root.

Using the rule of nine from Chapter 2, the extended intervals (ninth, eleventh, and thirteenth) spell the same as a second, fourth, and a sixth; they are just an octave away. The reason you don't see tenths and seconds (thirds and fifths) is that when you stack thirds, those intervals simply don't come up. Once you get to thirteen, the next third brings you back to the octave.

The other reason that thirds and fifths are not counted as extended intervals becomes clear when you hear them compared to other intervals (such as seconds versus ninths). To most ears, thirds and fifths sound the same no matter what octave they occur in. This is not to say that they sound identical, but the difference is so minute that you don't need another name for them based on whether they are more than an octave apart. A second sounds very different than a ninth. Try this out on your instrument.

Extended Chords

Now that you know about extended intervals, you need to look at extended chords. You learned about four families of chords: major, minor, diminished, and augmented. When sevenths are added into the equation, you get a fifth chord family: dominant chords (major triads with minor sevenths). These basic five chords and their extensions make up the majority of jazz harmony. To get by in jazz, you need to understand major, minor, and dominant extensions first. You will deal with diminished (which is typically note extended) and augmented chords later.

Extended Major

The basic jazz major chord is the major seventh chord. As you recall, a major seventh chord is a major triad with a major seventh interval added to it. In addition to the seventh, you see major chord extensions. Major chords can be written the following ways and still fall under the umbrella of major and, thus, substitute for each other:

- C Major 7th
- C Major 9th
- C Major 11th
- C Major 13th

The formula for these chords is pretty simple to spot: root (major) extension. Any chord that follows that formula is in the major seventh family. For example: F Major 9th is a major seventh chord, but F9th is something else because it lacks the necessary major component in its name. Knowing these basic rules will make life much less confusing, as jazz deals with chord symbols more often than actual written voicings. That's right, in jazz, you turn symbols into sounds.

In jazz, all major chord extensions take their notes from the major scale built off the root. A D Major 13th chord will take all of its notes from the D major scale. This is important because the spelling of the individual notes has to follow the home scale or the chord won't sound right. In practice, advanced jazz musicians often alter the notes in very tall chords, but that's a matter of personal taste.

Extended Minor

The basic jazz minor chord is the minor seventh chord. As you recall, a minor seventh chord is a minor triad with a minor seventh interval added. In addition to the seventh, you see minor chord extensions. Minor chords can be written the following ways and still fall under the umbrella of minor and, thus, substitute for each other:

- C minor 7th
- C minor 9th
- C minor 11th
- C minor 13th

The formula for these chords is pretty simple to spot: root (minor) extension. Any chord that follows that formula is in the minor seventh family. For example: F minor 11th is a minor seventh–type chord, simply extended.

In jazz, all minor chord extensions take their notes from the Dorian scale built off the root. A D minor 13th chord will take all its notes from the D Dorian scale. This is important because the spelling of the individual notes has to follow the home scale or the chord won't sound right. In jazz, the home scale for minor chords is the Dorian mode, not the expected natural minor scale. This is one of the places where jazz starts to pull away from traditional harmony: its use of modes for harmonic and melodic purposes.

Extended Dominant

The basic jazz dominant chord is the dominant seventh chord. As you recall, a dominant seventh chord is a major triad with a minor seventh interval added to it. In addition to the seventh, you see dominant chord extensions. When used in practice, many jazz players will simply call these chords seventh chords and leave off the moniker *dominant* as it's implied. Dominant chords can be written the following ways and all still fall under the umbrella of dominant and, thus, substitute for each other:

- C7th
- C9th
- C11th
- C13th

The formula for these chords is pretty simple to spot: root extension. Any chord that follows that formula is in the dominant seventh family. For example: F11th is a dominant seventh–type chord, simply extended to the eleventh.

Typically, with dominant chords comes chordal alterations. An alteration is some sort of change to the fifth or ninth of the chord. An altered dominant chord may read like this:

- C7♭9♯5

Even though that chord looks kind of scary, it's still very plainly dominant because at its core, it's a C7 with other stuff added to the end of it. You will look at this in more depth in the section titled "Substitutions and Enhancements."

In jazz, all dominant chord extensions take their notes from the Mixolydian scale built off the root. An E13th chord will take all its notes from the E Mixolydian scale. This is important because the spelling of the individual notes has to follow the home scale or the chord won't sound right. In jazz, the home scale for dominant chords is the Mixolydian mode, not the major scale (that's reserved for major seventh chords). This is another example of modal use in jazz.

Other Chords?

What about diminished and augmented? Well, in jazz, the diminished seventh chord is very common, and it is written exactly as you'd expect to see it: C°7. The other type of diminished chord, the half diminished chord, is often found in jazz, but it rarely goes by its classical symbol of Cø7. The symbols for full and half diminished simply look too close to each other. To rectify this, half diminished chords are written as "Minor 7♭5" chords, which gets you to the same chord and completely avoids confusion with the other diminished chord. Almost 99.9 percent of the time, you can assume that a diminished chord is a fully diminished seventh chord.

As for augmented chords, they appear as you'd expect them to, in the two varieties you studied in Chapter 8: Cmaj7+ (C–E–G♯–B) and C7+ (C–E–G♯–B♭). You can extend an augmented chord, but it's pretty rare. For most things, if you can decipher the major, minor, dominant, diminished, and augmented chord symbols, you're almost there.

Jazz Progressions

If you want to study the harmony of jazz, you're going to have to head to Tin Pan Alley. Jazz players used songs from the Great American Songbook as vehicles for jazz improvisation. They played the melodies instrumentally (or sang them if a vocalist was involved) at the start of the tune; this is called playing the head of the tune. Once that was done, the chords that formed the harmony of the song remained while the soloist improvised a new melody; this is called blowing on the changes. At the end, they'd play the melody one last time and that was it.

> Tin Pan Alley was the gathering place of a group of composers who wrote in the late nineteenth and early twentieth centuries and created the Great American Songbook, which is simply a collection of Broadway songs and other tunes that defined American music during this period. Stephen Foster, Cole Porter, and Jimmy Van Heusen are all significant contributors to this genre.

Because jazz players favored these songs so much, their melodies and harmonies became the foundation for jazz harmony. These songs became the songs that all jazz players know and play today; they are aptly referred to as standards. The harmonies of these songs have some regular patterns that appear over and over again, and thankfully can be studied. Start with the diatonic progressions.

The Diatonic Progressions

In jazz, if you simply take the diatonic major scale and harmonize each chord up to the seventh, you can learn a lot about how jazz harmony functions. **FIGURE 13.2** shows the A♭ major scale harmonized in seventh chords.

FIGURE 13.2 Harmonized Scale in 7ths

A♭maj7 B♭m7 Cm7 D♭maj7 E♭7 Fm7 Gm7♭5 A♭maj7

I7 ii7 iii7 IV7 V7 vi7 vii° I7

A♭Maj7 B♭min7 Cmin7 D♭Maj7 E♭7 Fmin7 Gmin7♭5 A♭Maj7

You'll be happy to learn that the basic jazz progressions are diatonic and still follow the chord ladder. Start with the mighty jazz progression of the ii–V–I.

In jazz, nothing is more common than the ii–V–I progression. Look at **FIGURE 13.3**.

TRACK 84

FIGURE 13.3 The ii–V–I

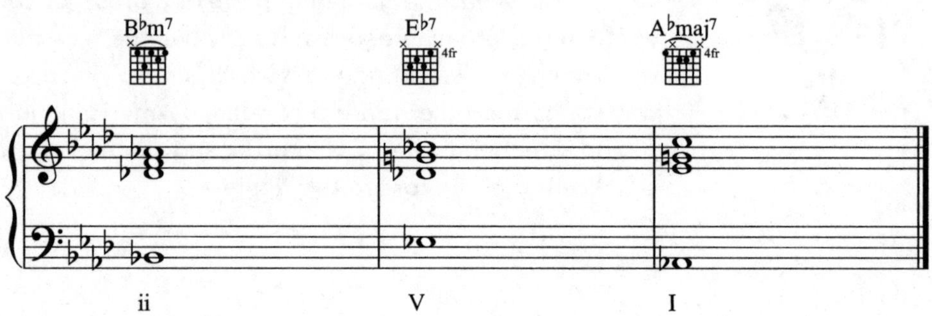

If jazz harmony were distilled to one central point, it would be the ii–V–I progression. It's simply all over jazz music. Sure, it gets more complicated, but the ii–V–I is the basic harmonic unit that all jazz players use.

What's interesting is that a ii–V–I is a substituted IV–V–I (as ii and IV substitute for each other), which is just a I–IV–V (remember those simple primary chords) reordered. Why change the IV to ii? By doing so, you create three different chords: a minor seventh chord, a dominant seventh chord, and a major seventh chord. That sound became the sound that made jazz sound different than other styles of music.

Add some extended chords and you get a very distinctive jazzy vibe out of this progression. See **FIGURE 13.4**.

TRACK 85

FIGURE 13.4 Jazzed Up ii–V–I

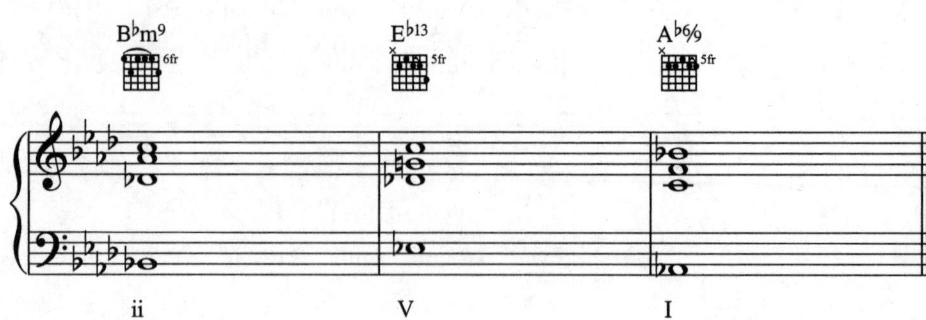

Add a few more chords before the ii, and you reach the other common jazz progression, the iii–vi–ii–V–I. See **FIGURE 13.5**.

FIGURE 13.5 Longer Jazz Progression

TRACK 86

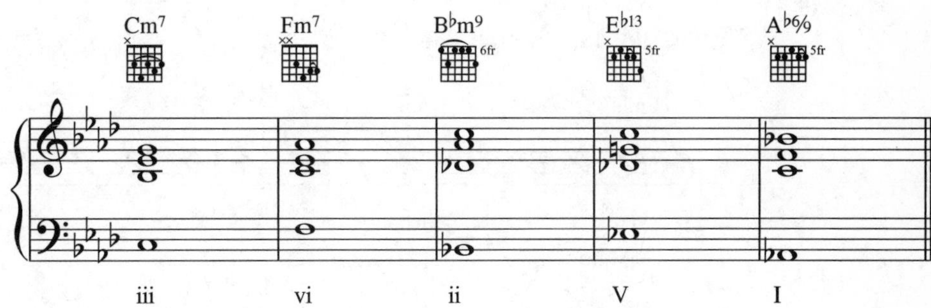

Minor Progressions

There is a minor key equivalent to the ii–V–I progression in major. It's still a two–five–one, but the qualities of the chords change. Instead of Dm7–G7–Cmaj7 (in the key of C major), the progression becomes Dm7♭5–G7–Cm7 (**FIGURE 13.6**).

FIGURE 13.6 ii–V–i in a Minor Key

TRACK 87

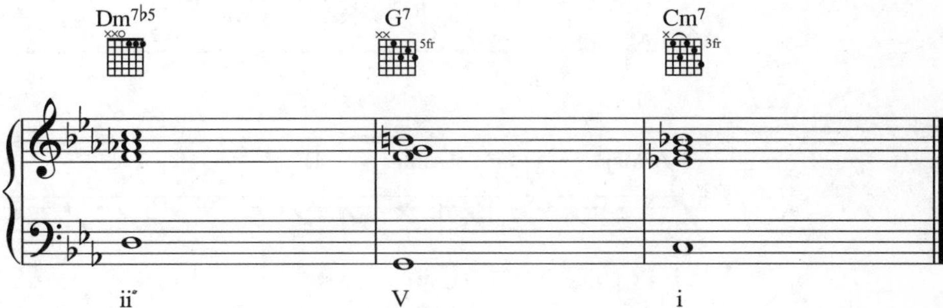

This progression is easy to spot because you also have three distinct chords, with a dominant chord in the middle. Look for the min7♭5, that's usually the signpost that screams, "Hey, minor two five coming," and see if the chords that follow it line up.

Now, look at how a real jazz tune is put together. **FIGURES 13.7** and **13.7A** present a very common standard, without the melody, just the changes (jazzspeak for the chords).

FIGURE 13.7 A Real Tune

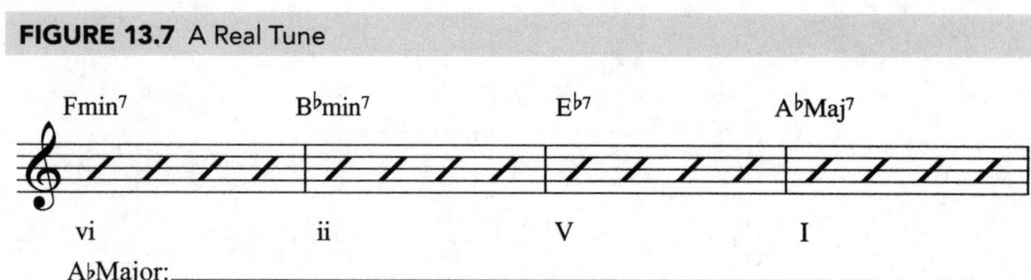

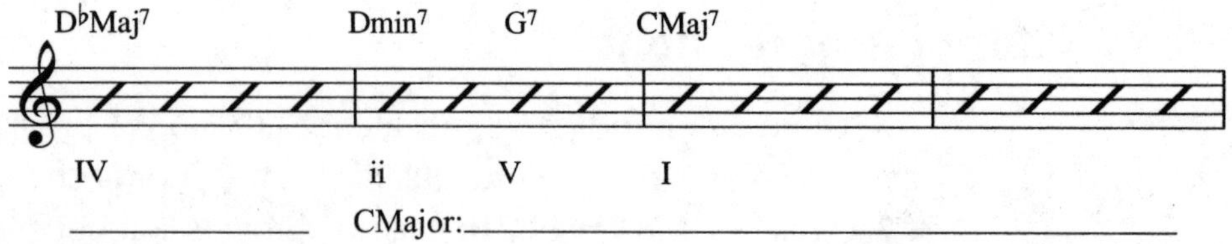

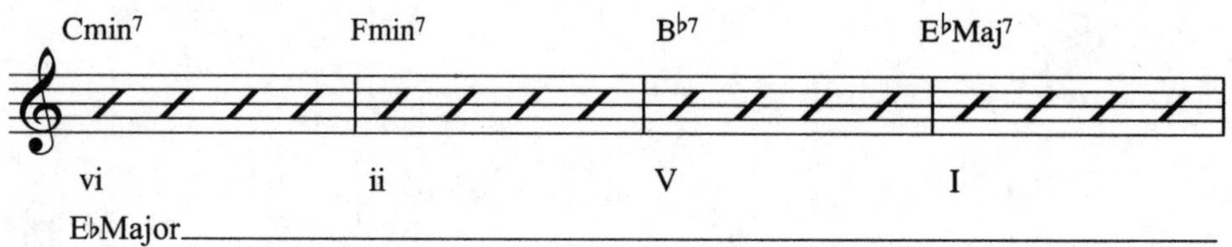

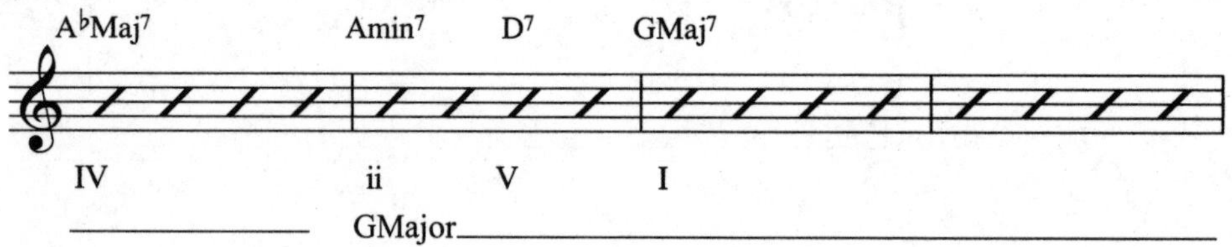

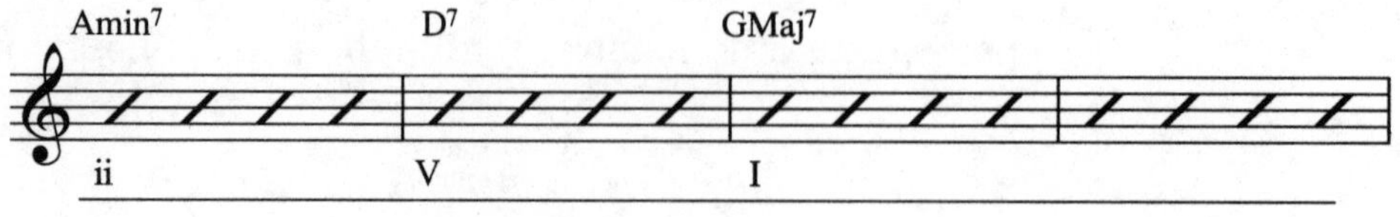

FIGURE 13.7A A Real Tune

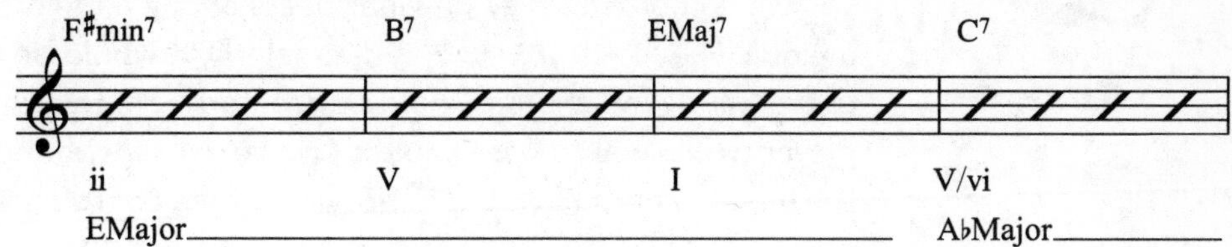

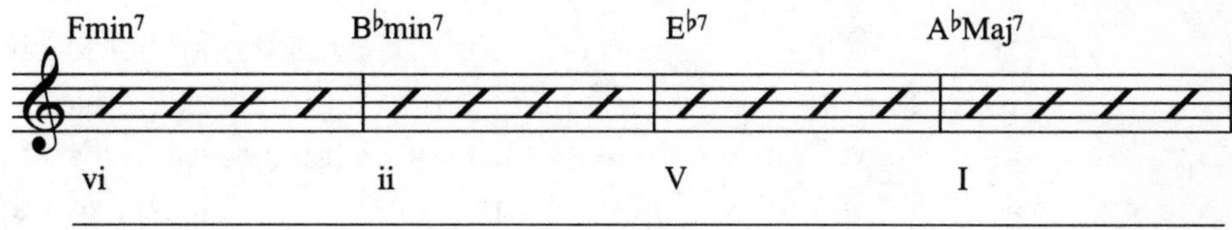

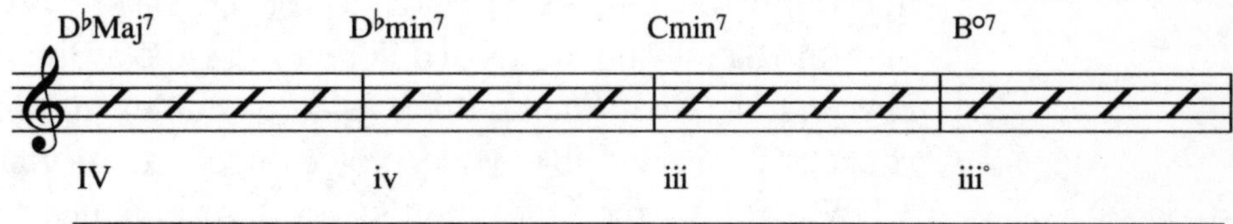

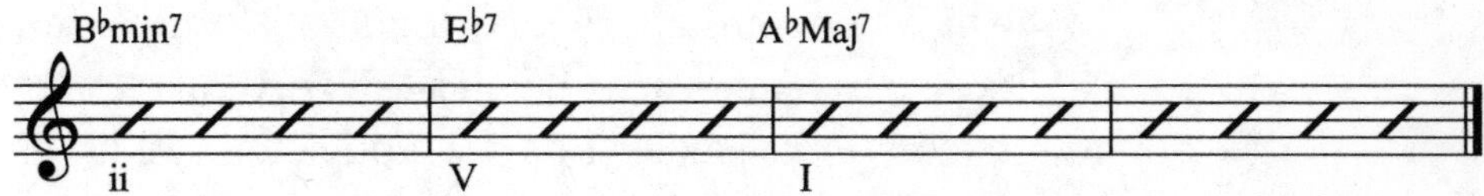

Notice the analysis under the chords. There are loads of ii–V–I progressions, in many keys, both major and minor. This is very standard practice for jazz (changing keys often), but beyond that, the progressions are fairly simple; it's just modulating often.

FIGURE 13.7 is essentially a lead sheet. This skeletal form of music tells you what chords to play on what beats and, if a melody is present, the melodic line. If **FIGURE 13.7** had a melody, it would be enough for an entire band. The chords would be created from the symbols, the bass player would walk a bass line that made sense with the chords, and the melodic players would improvise on the chord changes.

Substitutions and Enhancements

One of the cornerstones of jazz is the ability to change aspects of the harmony as you see fit. Listen to ten different versions of the stalwart standard "Autumn Leaves," and you will hear strikingly different approaches to a tune that is known by practically every jazzer in the known world. The reason that you can change things up so much lies in the essence of jazz substitution.

As you saw in **FIGURE 13.7**, jazz harmony is expressed as written chord symbols. The player has to realize these chord voicings and play them in her own way. There is no set way to voice C Major 7 on the piano or guitar; there are literally hundreds of different ways to play the same chord (see *The Everything® Guitar Chords Book* as an example). You rarely get the written voicings; it's always up to you to voice the chords as you see fit.

When you voice the chords, you can enhance the chords; actually, you're expected to do so. Think of it as supersizing. You see a C Major 7th chord, but that's really just a suggestion. It's telling you that you need to play a chord in the family of C Major 7th, but you are free to extend it as you see fit. C Major 7th could just as easily be C Major 9th; it's up to you. This is one of the nice freedoms afforded to you as a jazz musician.

It's also true in reverse; if you see a very tall chord, you have the chance to reduce it to its smallest part. If you see an F13th chord, you can say to yourself, "Okay, it's just an extended dominant seventh chord, I can reduce that chord to F7." Doing so isn't wrong; actually, it's pretty common. The only thing to ponder is why you would see such a tall chord. Sometimes composers put them in there for a very good reason. Often a chord exists because it supports a particular melody note (the melody is the thirteenth). You should try to learn to play every chord you see, but that's another story. Reducing is fine, with one notable exception: alterations.

Chord Alterations

A chord alteration, as discussed earlier, is tampering with the fifth or ninth of the chord in some way. You typically see this on a dominant chord, although you could see it anywhere. Chord alterations are not something that you can typically ignore. They are always there for a good reason. Usually they support a melody note of some sort.

Here are some conditions to keep in mind when dealing with altered chords.

- When in doubt, play them as written.
- Alterations to the fifth must be played as they affect the core triad.
- Alterations to the ninth don't have to be played as long as you reduce to a seventh chord and leave the ninths out altogether.
- It's probably not a good idea to extend an altered chord any higher than written. Altered chords can have funny extensions that are not clear and expected. When in doubt, play what you have.
- Always look at the melody that goes with the altered chord. Is the melody note the reason for the alteration? If not, why alter the chord at all? Maybe it's altered for harmonic color and beauty and not necessarily function.

These tips will assist you in understanding why you see altered chords, when to use them, and how to play them.

Lots of dominant chords are altered because as dominant chords, they typically function as V chords in jazz, so they will resolve to I. Because they are V chords and they resolve to I strongly anyway (because of the pull between the third and the seventh), composers and players like to alter them as the alterations have little effect on the V chord's proclivity to resolve. You simply end up with a more colorful chord, which is a very jazzy thing.

Blues Forms

Now that you have heard about chords and harmony, it's time to cover the blues, a basic ingredient in jazz. Jazz grew from the blues and still relies on the blues as a standard form and song style. The blues is just plain cool. Everybody's got the blues at one point or another. Jazz folks have the blues pretty often. In addition to the standard American Songbook tunes that everyone knows and loves, the blues remains a very important form for jazz players. Every self-respecting jazz composer has written a blues tune or two or three or four. The blues exists in two varieties: minor blues and major blues. Each blues song is exactly twelve bars (or measures) long. Blues songs follow a strict repeating harmonic formula, so it's easy to transpose them into any key, and in general, they are easy to learn to play.

12-Bar Major Blues

The 12-bar blues is taken from the traditional blues you might hear in the blues clubs or by someone like B. B. King, but jazz players have adapted the harmony just a little bit. Take a look at what a traditional 12-bar blues piece looks like in **FIGURE 13.8**.

FIGURE 13.8 Traditional 12-Bar Blues

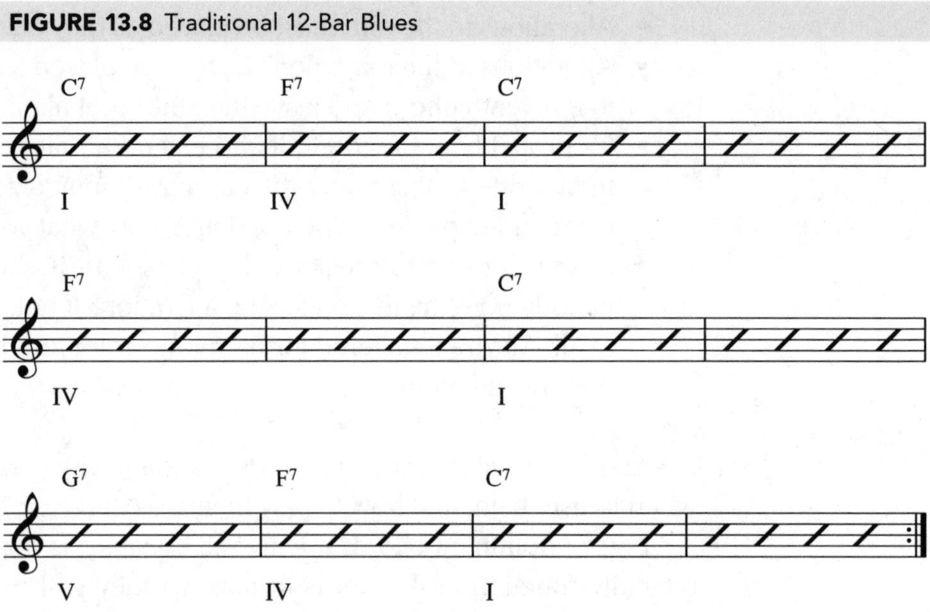

Now, contrast that with the blues that most jazz players play, shown in **FIGURE 13.9**.

FIGURE 13.9 Jazz Blues

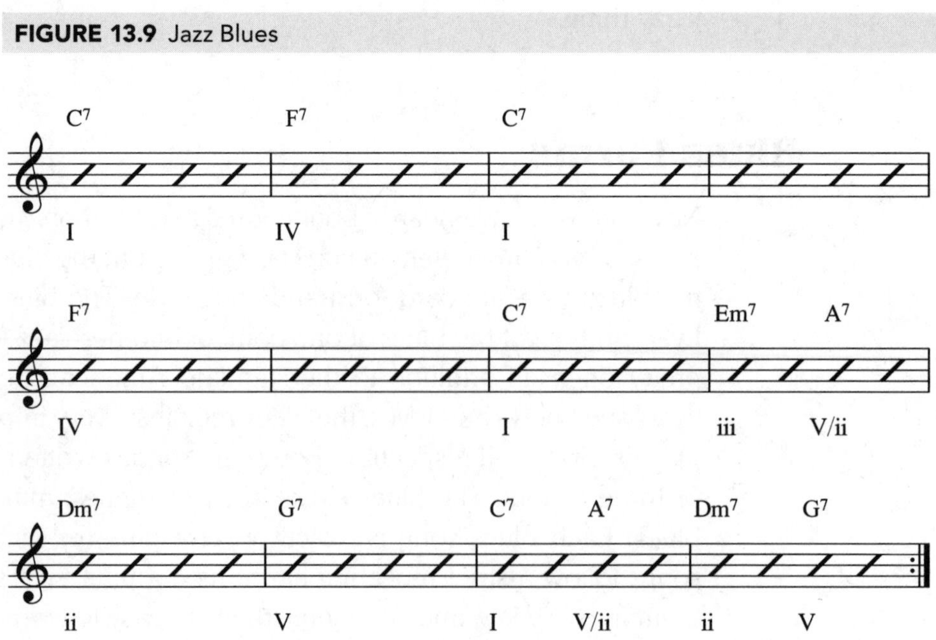

The last five measures are where you see a change. Instead of the traditional blues V–VI–I ending, the standard jazz ii–V–I progression is thrown in. Preceding that ii chord, a V/ii is thrown in to set up the progression and make life a bit more interesting for the improviser.

Notice how the Roman numeral harmony, chord symbols, and guitar chords are given for each example. This way, you can transpose the chords into any key. The B♭ blues is definitely one of the most used, standard jazz/blues keys, so it's a very good one to start with.

Here's a list of jazz tunes that are based on the 12-bar major blues:

- "Now's the Time" (Charlie Parker)
- "Blue Monk" (Thelonious Monk)
- "Straight, No Chaser" (Thelonious Monk)
- "Billie's Bounce" (Charlie Parker)
- "Tenor Madness" (Sonny Rollins)

There are a million more, but this will get you started. Make sure to transpose them into different keys. If you don't play harmonies, learn some melodies (all the jazz blues have heads, so learn those).

12-Bar Minor Blues

The final variant of jazz blues is called the minor blues, and you guessed it, it's in a minor key. Take a look at the minor blues in **FIGURE 13.10**.

FIGURE 13.10 Minor Blues

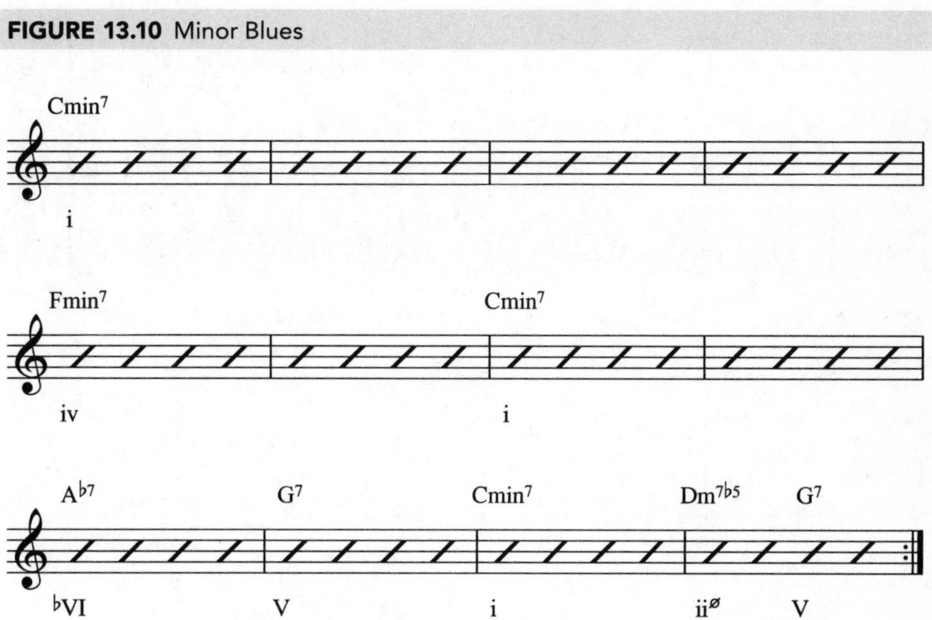

You see some basic harmony, such as i and iv chords, the expected dominant V chord that you need for minor keys. The chord that is slightly off is the ♭VI chord that precedes the V chord in bar nine. That's simply what makes a minor blues work the way it does; it is a definite difference between the major and the minor.

If you're looking for jazz tunes to play, check out a "real book," which is a takeoff on the "fake books" that include melodies, basic chords, and lyrics so musicians can improvise with any song. There are tons of real books available, and each is a repository of hundreds of jazz lead sheets with melodies, words, and chord changes. It's a great place to study and learn some great music.

Also, you'll notice a turnaround in the last bar of a Dmin7♭5, G7. This turnaround sets the i chord up in bar one so the tune can loop around. The progression is the minor version of a ii–V–i progression, as you learned earlier in the chapter.

That wraps up your general overview of jazz harmony. Sure, there's more to look at, but this will get you more than started. If you have a real interest in jazz, there are some great books that deal with jazz harmony, or consult a good jazz teacher. Either way you look at it, nothing beats listening to as much music as humanly possible.

ETUDES

ETUDE 13.1 Etude One

Reduce the complex chords to basic 7th chords.
For extra credit, name the complex chords!

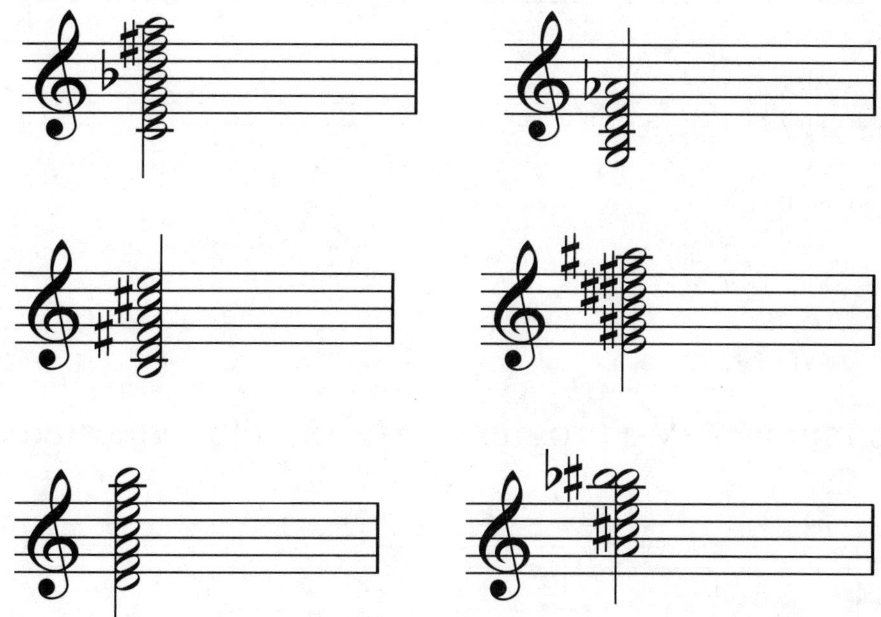

ETUDE 13.2 Etude Two

Realize major ii-V-I progressions from the requested key

ETUDE 13.3 Etude Three

Realize minor iiø-V-i progressions from the requested key

ETUDE 13-4 Etude Four

Add Roman numerals to analyze this chord progression

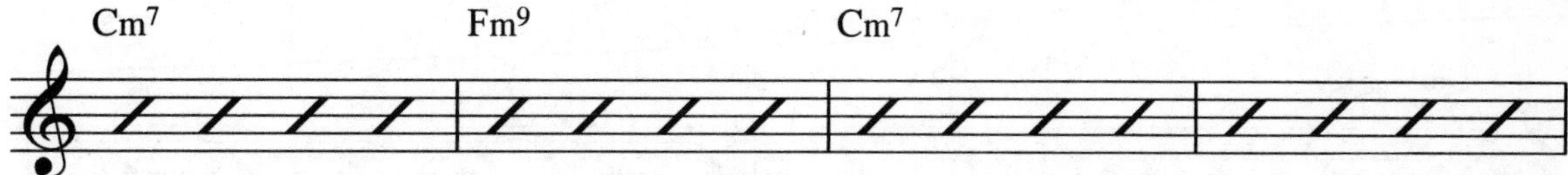

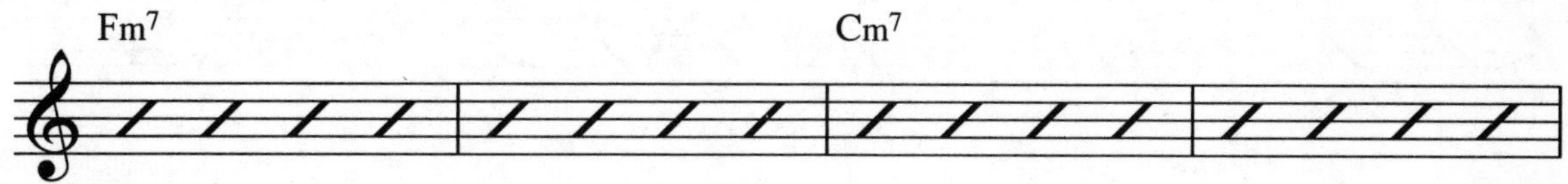

How many major and minor ii-V progressions can you find? Analyze and circle them in the following example.

CHAPTER 14

Transposition and Instrumentation

One of the most confusing and maligned aspects of music theory is the nature of transposing instruments. Few topics frustrate students more. Transposing isn't difficult, only misunderstood. When you learn about the instruments and their transpositions, you also can learn about their musical range, how to write for them, and how to analyze music that contains mixtures of transposing versus nontransposing instruments. It is important in the study of music to know that what you see isn't always what you hear.

What Is Transposing?

Suppose Josh plays the alto saxophone and Trish plays the clarinet. They get together and jam one day. Josh writes a short melody on the sax, notates it, and hands it to Trish to play along with. To their shock and amazement, the resulting sound is terrible. What was supposed to be two instruments playing the same melody in concert ended up as a cacophony! Confused, they set out to understand why alto sax and clarinet can't read the same melody. What they discover is that transposing and the natural keys of instruments has caused this musical calamity. All their lives, Josh and Trish were taught that C is C and D is D and so on. Unfortunately, this is not always true; it depends which instrument you are looking at.

Concert Pitch

The pitch of any note is a mathematical event. Notes exist as vibrations of air. The speed at which they vibrate can be measured and is expressed in hertz (Hz). The only true measure of a note is its frequency in hertz. A large group of instruments plays in concert pitch, meaning that when they play or read a note on the musical staff, they are getting the mathematically correct answer. When a piano plays a middle C, it's playing a note with a frequency of 261 Hz—it's an exact thing; the piano is playing concert pitch. Here is a list of popular instruments that play concert pitch, also called C instruments:

- Violin, viola, cello, bass
- Piano
- Harp
- Guitar/bass
- Flute/piccolo
- Oboe
- Bassoon
- Trombone
- Euphonium
- Tuba
- Pitched percussion (except glockenspiel)

All the instruments in this list play in concert pitch. There are some exceptions: Guitar and bass transpose an octave down to keep their music in the staff, but they are still considered concert. The piccolo and glockenspiel read an octave lower than they actually play, which also keeps these high-pitched instruments within the range of the staff for reading comfort.

What Does Transposing Mean?

Here is a list of the common instruments that transpose:

- Clarinet
- Soprano, alto, tenor, and baritone saxophone
- French horn
- Trumpet, baritone horn
- English horn

There are other transposing instruments, but these are the most common ones.

A great example of a concert pitch is an orchestral tuning note. When a symphony orchestra tunes up, the oboe player plays a concert A note and the rest of the orchestra tunes up to this note. Most metronomes that provide a tuning pitch also provide the same concert A (A = 440 Hz).

A transposing instrument reads the same music as other instruments. The only difference is that when a tenor sax plays a written C, the note that comes out would not register as a C on a tuner or match a C on a piano. An entirely different note comes out! A concert B♭ is heard when a trumpet plays a written C—this is what is meant by transposition. Look at the example in **FIGURE 14.1**. If you play a short melody for the tenor sax on the top staff, what you actually hear is the bottom staff.

FIGURE 14.1 Transposing Melody

Do you start to see the possibility for confusion? If you didn't know about transposing, you might be very confused. Just think about poor Josh and

Trish. Amazingly, transposing isn't always taught in the study of an instrument. Most students just learn to read the notes in front of them. But you are here for more than just playing! You want to understand what you are looking at, and if a score has multiple instruments on it, you can't trust your eyes. You have to know what you're really looking at.

Why Does This Happen?

Good question. Why can't we all just get along—er, play in the same key? There are two possible reasons that certain instruments transpose and others don't. The first is history. Brass instruments rely heavily on the overtone series to make their notes happen. Brass instruments used to add crooks, which were additional pipes, to play in different keys. The French horn was a good example of this. In time, as the instruments evolved and valves were added to the brass instruments, the additional crooks were no longer necessary. Certain instruments evolved into certain keys and stayed there. It's now been so long and there has been so much music written that it would be very painful to change.

Think you're immune to this? Play in a rock band? Imagine this: You play in a blues band and you bring in a sax or trumpet player to expand your sound. When it comes time to teach the melodies, what are you going to tell the musician to play? If she wants to solo on the E blues your guitar player is so fond of, exactly what will you say? You need to know how transposition works.

The second reason is best shown in the saxophone family. There are four saxophones in common use today: soprano, alto, tenor, and baritone. Each of the four saxophones transposes differently. The reason that it's done this way has less to do with history and more to do with the ease of the player. Each of the four saxophones, while physically differing in size, has the exact same system of keys that Adolphe Sax invented in the 1800s. The sax transposes four different ways so that any sax player trained on any one of the instruments could play any of the saxophones without having to relearn anything. Each saxophone reads the same treble clef melody, and the composer makes sure that each part is transposed correctly on paper for the proper sonic result. Some other instruments also do this.

Transposing Chant

For too many years, students have been baffled, perplexed, and generally confused as to how to transpose correctly for instruments. Now you will learn a chant that will help you make sense of it. The answer lies in knowing the full name of the instrument and the chant.

Each instrument has a key name. But a trumpet isn't usually called a B♭ trumpet, is it? *Trumpet* usually suffices. Knowing the full name of each instrument is one key to understanding how it transposes. The other key is the chant, which goes like this: *The instrument's key name is the note that you hear in concert pitch when that instrument reads its written C.* (Thank you, Dr. Scott Lavine!) Put that to use, using the B♭ trumpet again in **FIGURE 14.2**, which has a key name of B♭. To understand how the chant helps, add this information into your chant: The instrument key name (in this case, B♭) is the note you hear in concert pitch when that instrument (trumpet) reads its written C. Simply, when a trumpet plays a written C, you hear a B♭.

FIGURE 14.2 Trumpet Transpose

This means that whatever note is written for trumpet will come out exactly one whole step below what is written. So what can composers do to fix this? They simply write the trumpet part up a whole step, in a written D. The trumpet player will read and play the D, yet a perfect C will come out in concert key.

Sound down; write up. For most transposing instruments, this is the case. There are a couple of zany exceptions, but you don't need to worry about them right now. For the most part, you write parts up and they sound down. Just remember the chant.

B♭ Instruments

There are a few common instruments that exist in the key of B♭ together and thus transpose the same way (see **FIGURE 14.3**). They include the B♭ trumpet, B♭ clarinet, and B♭ soprano saxophone. Each instrument follows the same rule: Whatever they read comes out a whole step down.

FIGURE 14.3 B♭ Transpose

There is another B♭ instrument: the B♭ tenor sax. It's a little bit different than the others—it transposes an octave and a whole step down. When a tenor sax plays a C, you indeed hear a B♭, but it's a full octave lower than the other B♭ instruments (see **FIGURE 14.4**). To write parts that sound correct, write the part up a whole step in the case of clarinet, trumpet, and soprano sax. In the case of tenor sax, write it up an octave and a whole step (or a major ninth). The other instrument that follows this same transposition is the B♭ bass clarinet.

FIGURE 14.4 Tenor Sax Transpose

E♭ Instruments

There are two common instruments that are in the key of E♭: the E♭ alto saxophone and the E♭ baritone saxophone. Being in the key of E♭ means that when these instruments read a written C, an E♭ concert pitch is heard. The E♭ alto saxophone transposes a major sixth away from where it's written (see **FIGURE 14.5**). So a melody written in concert pitch would have to be transposed up a major sixth to sound correct on the alto saxophone.

FIGURE 14.5 Alto Sax Transpose

The baritone saxophone is also in the key of E♭; the only difference is that the baritone is a full octave below the alto sax, so it transposes at the intervals of a major sixth and an octave (or a major thirteenth). For a melody written in concert key to sound correctly on a baritone sax, it must be written a major thirteenth up (see **FIGURE 14.6**). Remember, it sounds down, but it must be written up.

FIGURE 14.6 Baritone Sax Transpose

F Instruments

Two instruments transpose in the key of F: the French horn and the English horn. Both the French horn and the English horn (which is a tenor oboe) transpose in the same way, exactly a fifth away. If a composer writes a melody in concert key and wants the French horn and English horn to play correctly, he must write the melody up a perfect fifth for it to sound correct (see **FIGURE 14.7**).

FIGURE 14.7 French / English Horn Transpose

Octave Transposes

The guitar and bass are unique transposing instruments; both play in concert key. That is, when guitar and bass play the note C, an electronic tuner would register the note C. But the guitar and bass octave transpose; that is, the pitch they read is an octave higher than the sound that comes out of their instruments. This is a slightly unusual practice. The reason for this makes perfect sense, however, if guitar and bass did not transpose like this, their music would be extremely low on the staff. Most of the notes they played would be many ledger lines below the staff—and you know how annoying it is to read that way. Guitar and bass raise their notes an octave higher to keep the majority of the notes on the staff for ease of reading.

You could go your whole life never knowing this and never notice. But if you ever have to write a unison line for guitar or bass, you'll know exactly what to do (see **FIGURE 14.8**).

FIGURE 14.8 Guitar Transpose

There are other instrument transpositions that you haven't learned about here. There are clarinets in A and trumpets in D, and French horns can be in almost any key possible. As long as you realize that the name of the instrument is the note you hear (in concert pitch) when it plays a written C, you will know how to read and understand that instrument.

Analyzing Scores

At this point, you've gotten pretty far into chords and theory and can make your way through myriad musical situations with confidence. You've analyzed your favorite pop songs and more with ease, and now you've decided to step up. Wanting to analyze the score of a symphony orchestra, you went to the library to see what was available. You decided to go German and checked out one of Beethoven's nine symphonies. Now, you'd like to know what's going on in his head; he is a genius, after all. So you crack open the score for the Ninth Symphony and see that there are a lot of instruments in it. Here's what you see in the score listing of required instruments:

- Piccolo
- Flute
- Oboe
- Clarinet (in B♭, C, and A)
- Bassoon
- Contrabassoon

- French horns (in D, E♭, B♭, and bass B♭)
- Trumpet (in B♭ and D)
- Trombones
- Percussion, including pitched percussion (timpani)
- Violin
- Viola
- Cello
- Bass
- Four-part choir

Well, that's quite a list. What's even worse is that there are instruments that you don't recognize. What's an A clarinet? Horns in D, E♭, B♭, and bass B♭? What is going on?

Welcome to a full symphony score of the nineteenth century. A conductor/composer would only view scores like this: transposing scores. You are looking at what the players read on their music stands. You are going to have to transpose the parts into concert pitch to figure out what's there, and you'll have to do it basically at first sight.

Begin by picking a few single chords to analyze in the fourth movement. (The fourth movement contains the famous "Ode to Joy" that everyone knows and loves.) Now, the Ninth Symphony is very long, so only two measures (in the key of D minor) are being looked at here.

Although you have the full listing of instruments, Beethoven does not use them all at the same time. The section you are looking at features only flute, oboe, clarinet, bassoon, contrabassoon, horn in D, horn in B, trumpet in D, timpani, violin, viola, cello, and bass. Take a look at the excerpt in **FIGURE 14.9**. (On the CD, the voices are played with a synthetic symphony orchestra. Try listening to a real recording of this monumental piece.)

It's pretty impressive-looking, right? The chords in question are highlighted on the staff. To start, you need to figure out which instruments are in concert key and which ones need to be transposed. This is actually easier than you think. Remember the listing of instruments (which is also on the score excerpt)? If the instrument isn't concert pitch (that is, it transposes), it will tell you in its name, such as B♭ clarinet and so on.

TRACK 88

FIGURE 14.9 Beethoven's Ninth Symphony Excerpt

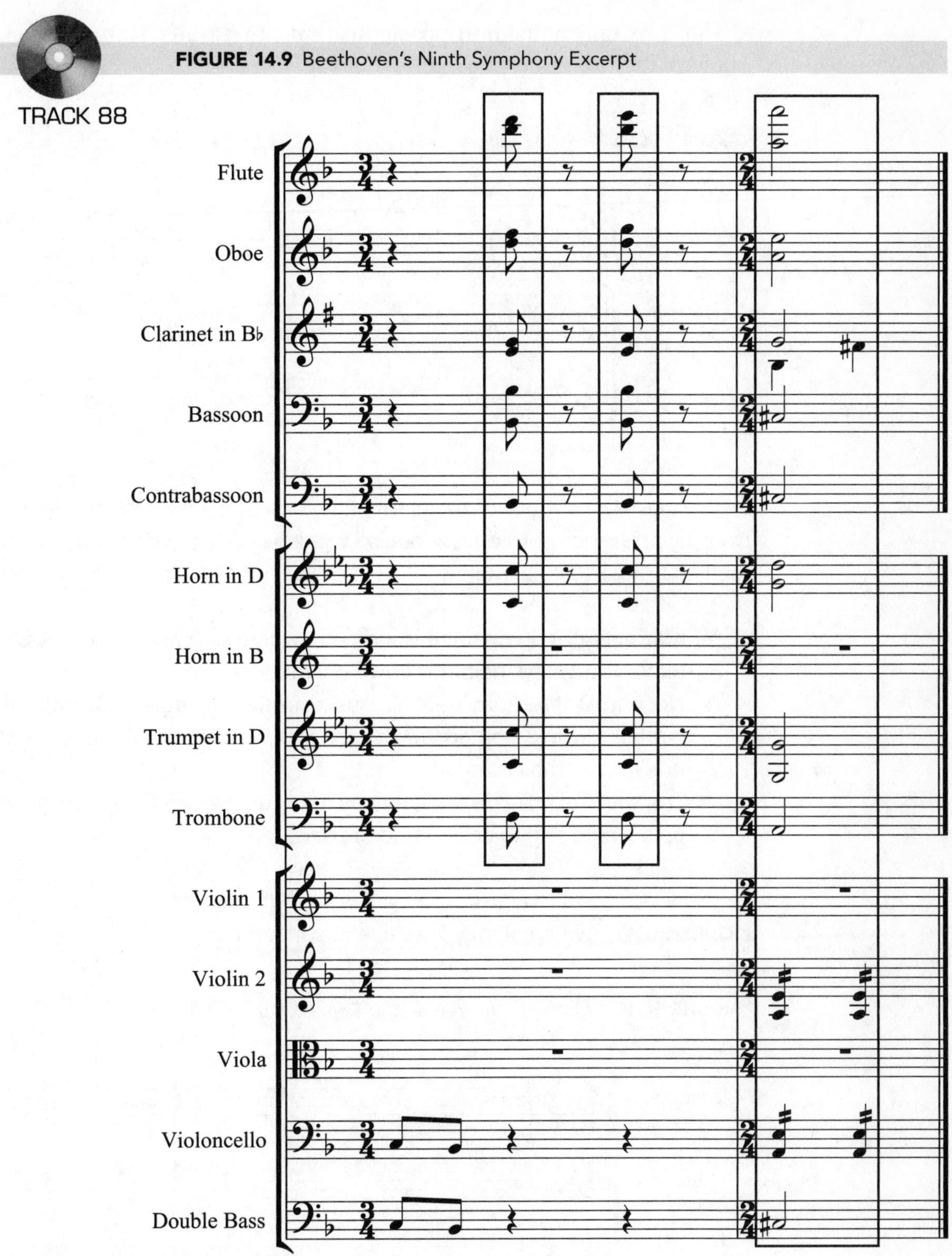

So, look only at the transposing instruments (**FIGURE 14.10**) and figure out what they are really playing.

FIGURE 14.10 Transposing Instruments

FIGURE 14.10 segregates the clarinet, French horns, and the trumpet. Go over their transpositions one by one so you know what to do to each instrument to bring it to concert key.

- Clarinet in B♭. Everything is written a whole step higher than concert pitch. Transpose the notes down a whole step.
- Horn in D (the horn in B isn't used in this example). Everything is written a whole step down. To read it in concert pitch, transpose the notes up a whole step.
- Trumpet in D. This is the same as the French horn in D; transpose it up a whole step to get to concert pitch.

Now you need to adjust those notes so that they read in concert pitch. **FIGURE 14.11** shows what they look like in concert pitch.

FIGURE 14.11 Transposing Instruments in Concert Pitch

Now throw them back in the score in concert pitch and start analyzing. **FIGURE 14.12** presents the full score in concert pitch.

FIGURE 14.12 Full Score in Concert Pitch

Start reading from the bottom up and put some chords together. Remember that the bass and the contrabassoon are the lowest-sounding pitches, so you can get your roots from there. Amazingly enough, when you analyze the piece, you come to these three chords (see **FIGURE 14.13**).

FIGURE 14.13 Chord Analysis

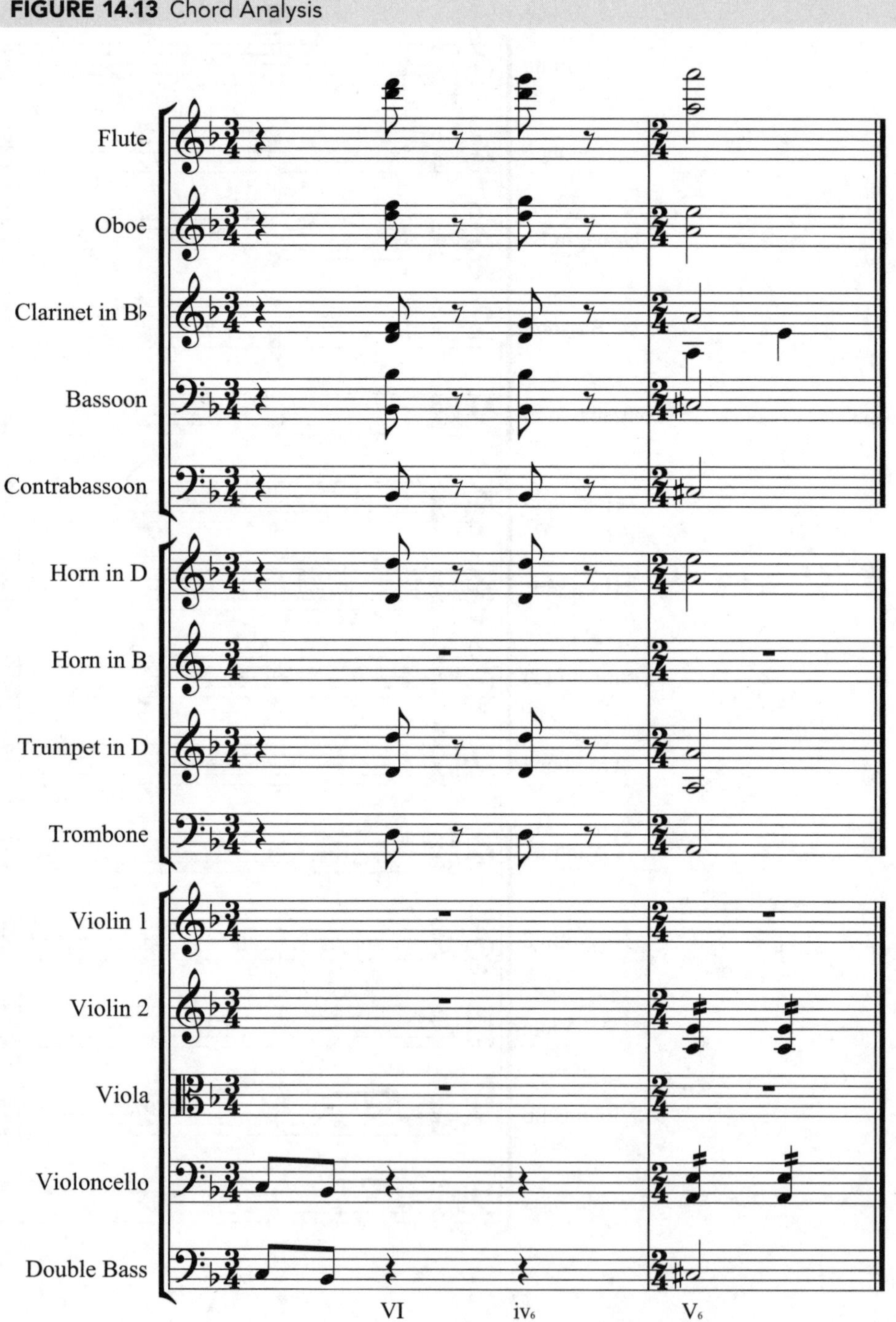

B♭, G minor, and A triads! Triads! What, were you expecting more? There are so many instruments in an orchestra that you'd figure there would be many different notes. Wrong. The basic foundations of harmony don't change. Beethoven was a tonal composer, and in those times, tonal meant triadic and seventh chords. So, all in all, it's just a matter of taking a three-note chord and voicing it throughout a huge orchestra, doubling notes in different instruments to create the sound. When you analyze this music, you can still break it down to the small parts and thankfully figure out what's going on—as long as you know what notes the instruments are actually playing.

Realizing that a full orchestra is playing only fairly simple triads and seventh chords is a bit of a revelation. For some, it can make the act of symphonic composing less impressive. Have no fear; the real genius in writing for large groups is not what chords are present, as chords are just the culmination of melodies that intersect vertically. The brilliance is in writing for different groups of instruments and making them sound cohesive.

Instrument Ranges

As long as you're studying these instruments so deeply, you might as well learn the ranges of the instrument families. You might be looking to theory for help in your compositions, and there is nothing more useful than understanding what you can and can't write for certain instruments.

The following charts show the ranges for just about every instrument you should know. You can see their ranges from the extreme top to the extreme bottom. No chart will ever truly take the place of studying scores and reading some great orchestration books, but it will save you from making some silly mistakes (like writing in the wrong key or writing completely out of an instrument's range).

FIGURES 14.14, **14.15**, **14.16**, and **14.17** contain the charts for easy reference.

FIGURE 14.14 Vocal Ranges

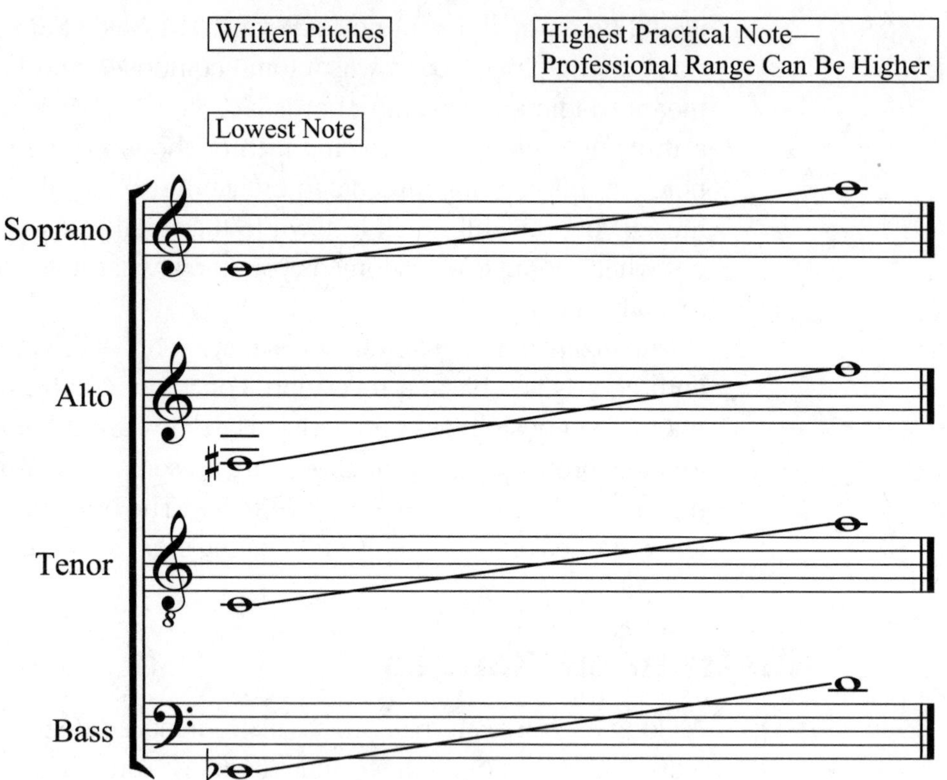

FIGURE 14.15 String Ranges

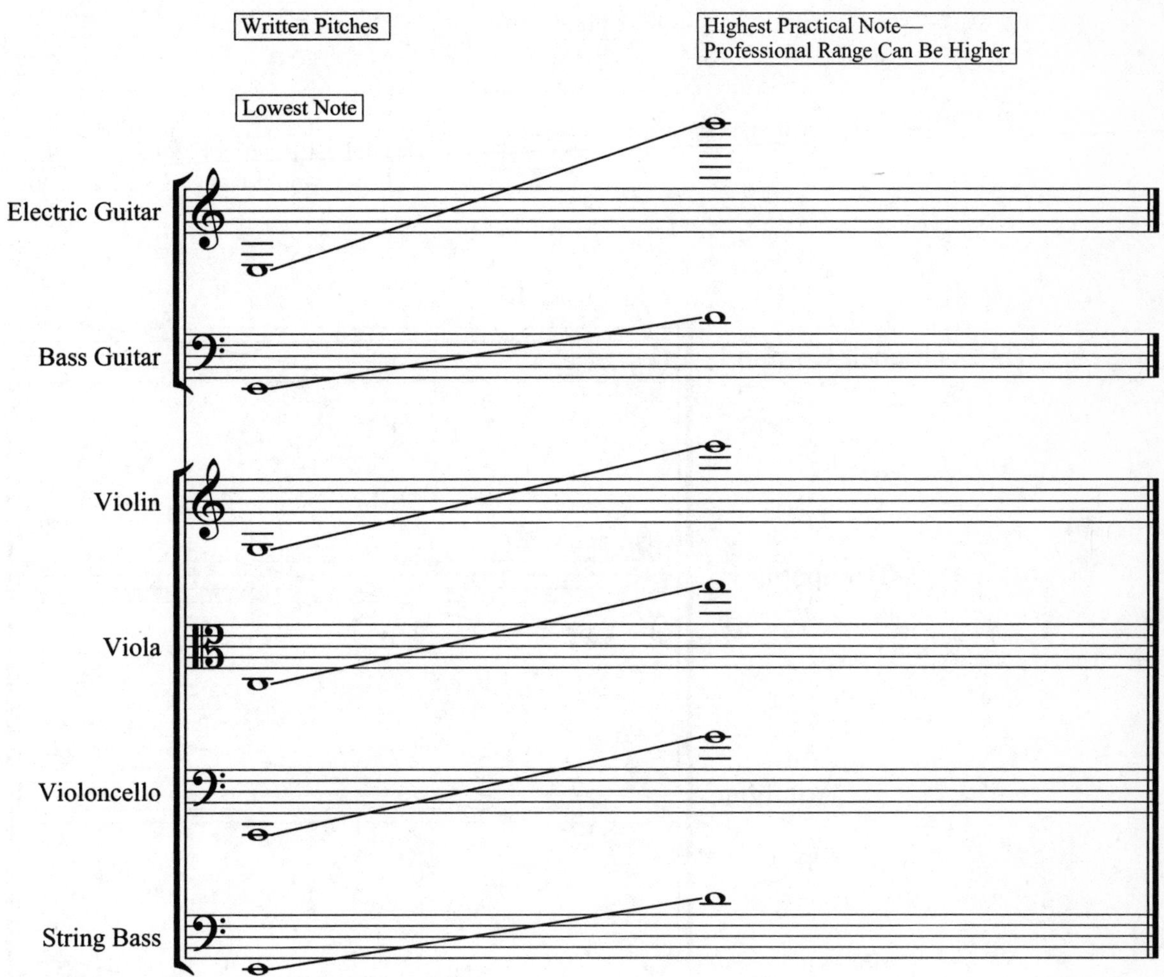

FIGURE 14.16 Brass Ranges

Written Pitches

Lowest Note

Highest Practical Note—
Professional Range Can Be Higher

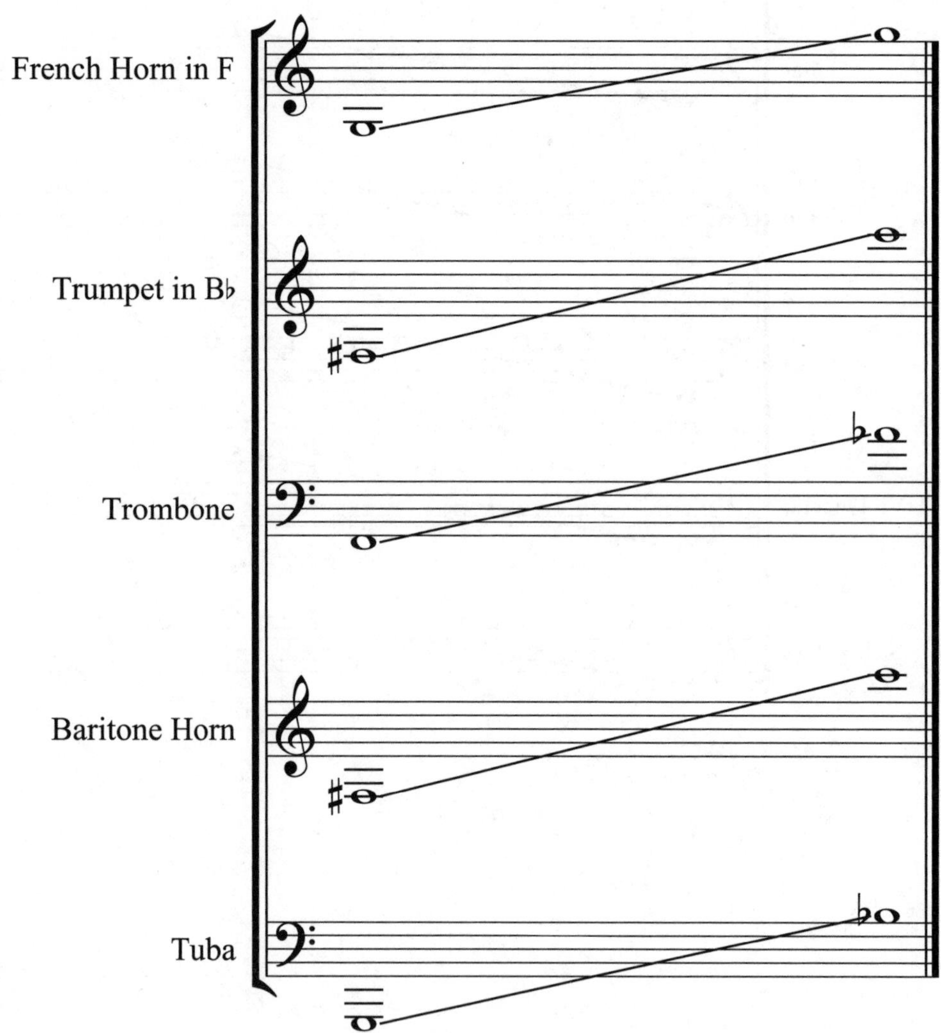

FIGURE 14.17 Woodwind Ranges

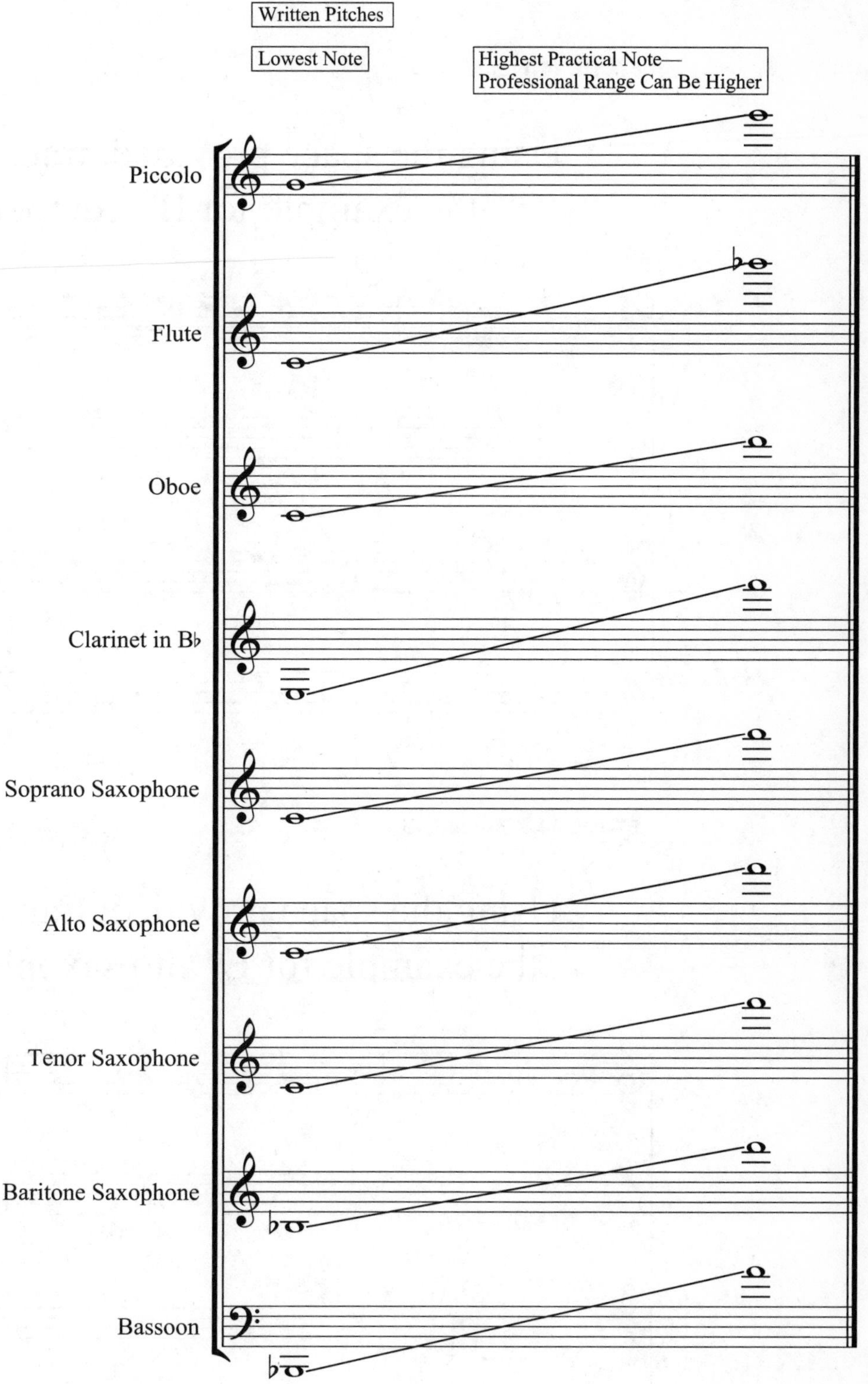

ETUDES

ETUDE 14.1 Etude One

Using the space provided, transpose the example for B♭ trumpet

ETUDE 14.2 Etude Two

Using the space provided, transpose the example for E♭ alto saxophone

ETUDE 14.3 Etude Three

Using the space provided, transpose the example for horn in F

ETUDE 14.4 Etude Four

Using the space provided, transpose the example for guitar

ETUDE 14.5 Etude Five

Arrange the following excerpt for a quartet of flute, B♭ clarinet, horn in F and Violoncello. Transpose as needed.

APPENDIX A

Glossary

4/4 time: Also called common time; is abbreviated by the symbol c; denotes that four beats are found in each measure

12-Bar Major Blues: A set progression of chords that takes twelve bars or measures to complete and resolves to a major or dominant chord

12-Bar Minor Blues: A set progression of chords that takes twelve bars or measures to complete and resolves to a minor chord

Aeolian Mode: A major scale played from its sixth note (also the minor scale)

Arpeggio: A chord played one note at a time

Augmentation Dot: Also called a dot; increases the duration of the dotted note by one half

Augmented Interval: Any interval that is one half step larger than major or perfect

Bass Clef: A symbol used for instruments that have a lower pitch, commonly called the F clef

Borrowed Chords: A chord that exists in the parallel major or minor key that you can borrow in your present key

C Clef: A clef that has two semicircles that curve into the middle of the staff and point toward middle C

Chord: Three or more notes sounded simultaneously

Chord Alterations: Chords that have their fifths or ninths altered

Chord Progression: The movement of chords from one point to another

Chord Substitution: When one chord can take the place of another chord

Chord Tones: Melodic notes that are contained within the supporting harmony

Circle of Keys: A visual organization of all the possible musical keys

Clef: A symbol that sits at the beginning of every staff of music and that defines which note is where

Common Chords: Chords that are shared between two different keys

Compound Meter: Meter that breaks itself into groups of three notes

Concert Key: Instruments that adhere to the physical definitions of pitch (i.e., A = 440 Hz)

Concert Pitch: Instruments that play in concert key

Deceptive Resolution: A substitution when one chord resolves to an unexpected resolution, typically when the tonic is expected and not heard

Diatonic: Using the notes from only one scale/key to make chords or melodies

Diminished Interval: Any interval that is one half step smaller than a minor or perfect interval

Diminished Scale: A symmetrical scale built on repeating intervals, always half steps and whole steps; two varieties: one that starts with the pattern whole-step, half-step intervals, and one that uses half-step, whole-step interval patterns

Dominant: The fifth chord or tone of a scale

Dominant Seventh Chord: A major triad with a minor seventh interval added

Dorian Mode: A major scale played from its second note

Eighth Note: A rhythm that receives half of one count; its duration is one-half of a beat

Enharmonic: Where two notes sound the same yet are different notes on paper

Extended Chords: Chords that contain ninth, eleventh, or thirteenth intervals

First Inversion: Whenever the third of the chord is in the bass

Fully Diminished Seventh Chord: A diminished triad with a diminished seventh interval added

Grand Staff: When the bass clef and the treble clef are grouped together; often used for piano

Half-Diminished Chord: A diminished triad with a minor seventh interval added

Half Note: A rhythm that receives two counts; its duration is two beats

Half Step: The smallest interval; its proper name is a minor second; also called semitone

Harmonic Minor: A minor scale with the seventh note raised one half step

Harmonic Rhythm: The speed at which the harmony progresses from chord to chord

Harmonization: Using chords and melodies together; making harmony by stacking scale tones as triads

Instrument Ranges: The lowest and highest notes a particular instrument can physically play

Interval: The distance from one note to another

Inverted Chords: Any chord or triad in which the root is not the lowest-sounding pitch

Ionian Mode: The major scale

Key: Defines the basic pitches for a piece of music

Key Signature: Indicates that a certain note or notes are going to be sharp or flat for the entire piece

Lead Sheet: Simplified shorthand for a musical piece found in jazz

Leading Tone: The seventh note of a major scale; a tone that pulls heavily to the tonic

Locrian Mode: A major scale played from its seventh note

Lydian Mode: A major scale played from its fourth note

Major Intervals: Intervallic distances of seconds, thirds, sixths, and sevenths

Major Scale: A seven-note scale based on the interval pattern of WWHWWWH

Major Seventh Chord: A major triad with a major seventh interval added

Mediant: The third chord or tone of a scale

Melodic Harmonization: Harmonizing a melody with chords or other melodic lines

Melodic Minor: A minor scale with the sixth and seventh notes raised up one half step

Minor Intervals: Intervallic distances of seconds, thirds, sixths, and sevenths that are exactly one half step smaller than a major interval

Minor Scale: A seven-note scale based on the interval pattern of WHWWHWW

Minor Seventh Chord: A minor triad with a minor seventh interval added

Mixolydian Mode: A major scale played from its fifth note

Mode: The notes of a major scale starting from any note but the expected tonic

Modulation: The art of shifting the tonal center to another key and staying there

Orchestration: The art of arranging music for multiple instruments

Passing Tones: Melodic notes that are not contained within the supporting harmony

Pentatonic Scales: A scale that contains only five notes; can be major or minor

Perfect Intervals: Intervallic distances of unison (no interval at all), fourth, fifth, and octave

Perfect Pitch: The natural ability to name a note just by listening to it; also called absolute pitch

Phrygian Mode: A major scale played from its third note

Primary Chords: The I, IV, and V chords of any major key

Quarter Note: A rhythm that receives one count; its duration is one beat

Relative Minor: The minor key that is shared within a major key signature

Relative Pitch: The learned ability to name and recognize chords and intervals by ear comparatively, not absolutely

Resolution: The feeling of rest in a harmony

Roman Numerals: A standard way for music theorists to name and help analyze chords and chord progressions

Root Position: A chord that has its root as the lowest-sounding pitch

Scale: A grouping of notes together that makes a key

Second Inversion: Whenever the fifth of the chord is in the bass

Secondary Chords: The ii, iii, and vi chords of any major key

Secondary Diminished Chords: Any diminished chord that is not functioning as a true leading-tone chord

Secondary Dominant Chords: Any dominant chord that is not the fifth chord of a key; a dominant chord that resolves to any chord other than tonic

Semitone: *See* Half Step

Seventh Chord: Any triad with an added seventh interval

Simple Meter: Meters containing groupings of two or four notes

Solar Harmony: The system of harmony that revolves around the tonic chord being the most important harmony

Subdominant: The fourth chord or tone of a scale

Submediant or Superdominant: The sixth chord or tone of a scale

Supertonic: The second chord or tone of a scale

Tablature: A graphical system that guitar players use for reading numbers instead of notes

Tertian Harmony: Harmony based on chords built from third intervals

Third Inversion: Whenever the seventh of the chord is in the bass

Tonic: The first chord or tone of a scale

Transposing: Changing the key of a melody while keeping its intervallic relationship intact

Transposing Instrument: Any instrument that plays in a key other than concert pitch

Treble Clef: A symbol that circles around the note G, commonly called the G clef

Triad: A three-note chord, built with third intervals

Tuplets: A grouping of odd groups of notes divided equally into one or more beats

Voice Leading: The art of connecting chord to chord in the smoothest manner possible

Whole Note: A rhythm that receives four counts; its duration is four beats

Whole Step: The distance of two half steps combined; its proper name is a major second

Whole-Tone Scale: A symmetrical scale built entirely with whole steps

APPENDIX B

Recommended Books and Websites

Books

Black, Dave, and Tom Gerou. *Essential Dictionary of Orchestration.* Los Angeles: Alfred Publishing Co.

Gerou, Tom, and Linda Lusk. *Essential Dictionary of Music Notation.* Los Angeles: Alfred Publishing Co.

Harnsberger, Lindsey C. *Essential Dictionary of Music.* Los Angeles: Alfred Publishing Co.

Kennan, Kent. *Counterpoint.* Upper Saddle River, NJ: Prentice Hall.

Kennan, Kent, and Donald Grantham. *The Technique of Orchestration.* Englewood Cliffs, NJ: Prentice Hall.

Piston, Walter. *Harmony.* New York: W. W. Norton & Company.

Roeder, Michael Thomas. *A History of the Concerto.* Portland, OR: Amadeus Press.

Stolba, K. Marie. *The Development of Western Music: A History.* Madison, WI: Brown and Benchmark.

White, John D. *Comprehensive Musical Analysis.* Metuchen, NJ: Scarecrow Press.

Websites

Ricci Adams' musictheory.net (*www.musictheory.net*)

One of the best online resources for music theory

eMusicTheory.com (*www.emusictheory.com*)

A great website that offers subscription-based resources for students and teachers

The Mutopia Project (*www.mutopiaproject.org*)

An online community project that publishes public domain music in PDF and Lilypond format for free; a great resource for students and teachers to study important musical works

Sibelius.com (*www.sibelius.com*)

Makers of the Sibelius brand of score-writing and music-theory software for Windows and Macintosh

Virginia Tech Multimedia Music Dictionary (*www.music.vt.edu/musicdictionary*)

An excellent general music-theory site

APPENDIX C

Reference Material

All Chromatic Major Scales

All Chromatic Natural Minor Scales

All Chromatic Natural Minor Scales (continued)

All Chromatic Harmonic Minor Scales

All Chromatic Melodic Minor Scales

All Chromatic Melodic Minor Scales (continued)

All Modes from a C root

All Seventh Chords from C

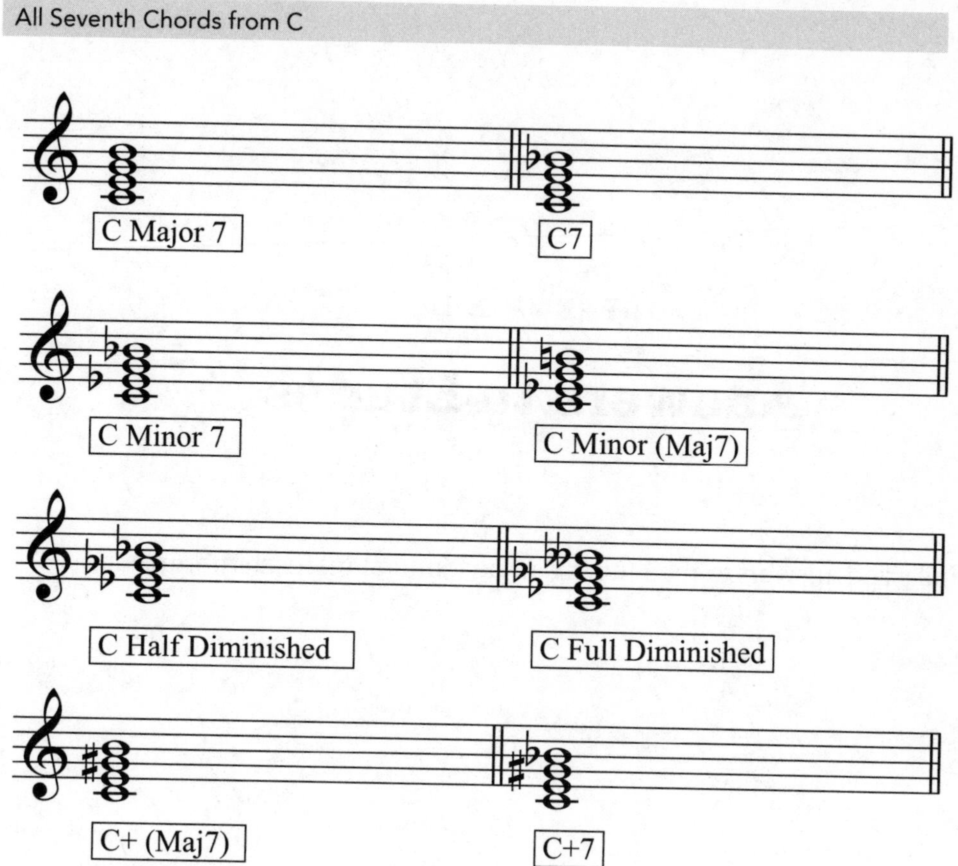

APPENDIX D

Answers to Etudes

Full-sized answers to the Etudes can be found at marcschonbrun.com.

Answer to Etude 1.1

Name the following treble clef notes

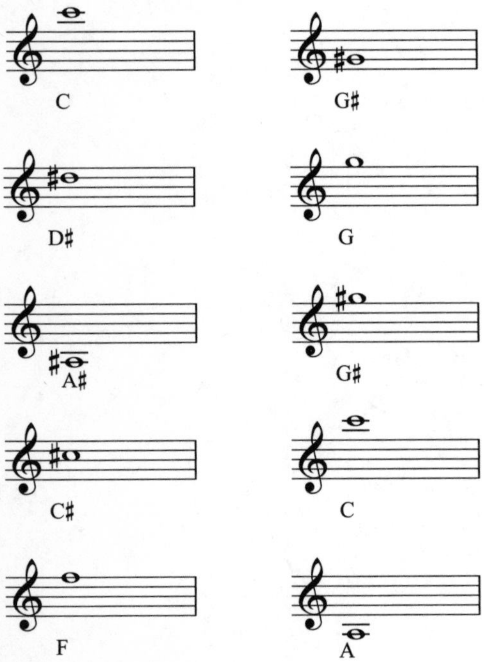

C G♯

D♯ G

A♯ G♯

C♯ C

F A

Answer to Etude 1.2

Name the following bass clef notes

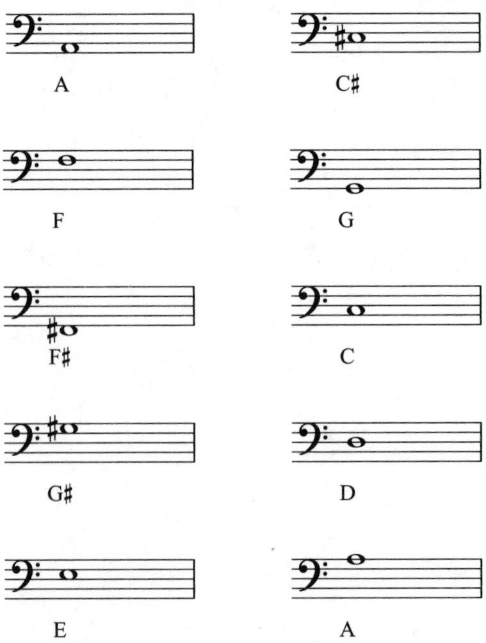

A C♯

F G

F♯ C

G♯ D

E A

Answer to Etude 1.3

Name the following alto clef notes

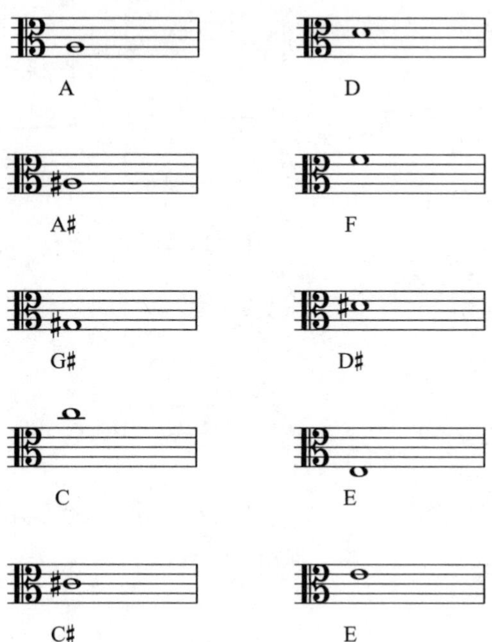

Answer to Etude 1.4

Count the beats in the following measures.
Circle if the measure has too few or too many notes
for the given time signature.

Answer to Etude 1.5

Add rests to make each example add up

Answer to Etude 2.1

Name or write the following major intervals

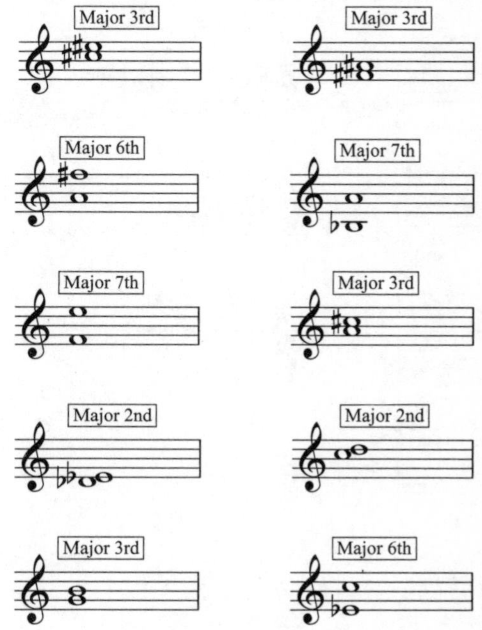

Answer to Etude 2.2

Name or write the following minor intervals

Answer to Etude 2.3

Name or write the following perfect intervals

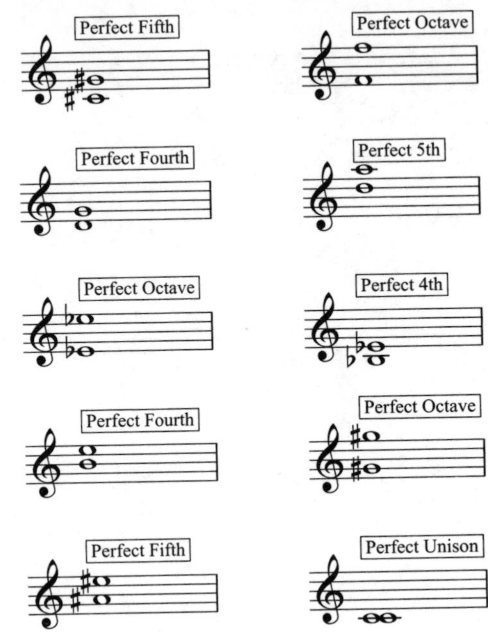

Answer to Etude 2.4

Name or write the following augmented & diminished intervals

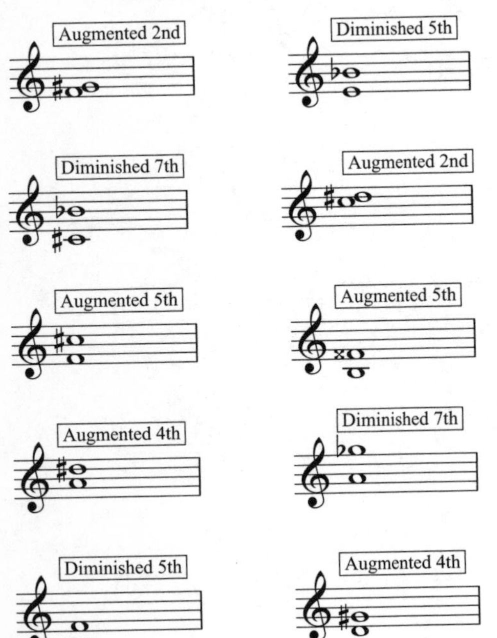

Answer to Etude 2.5

Name the original and inverted intervals

Answer to Etude 3.1

Spell major scales from the starting note

Answer to Etude 3.2

Spell major scales from the starting note

Answer to Etude 3.3

Can you find the mistake in each major scale?

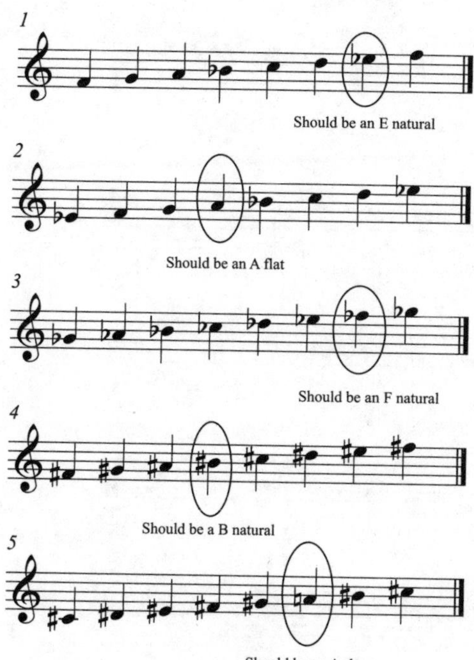

Answer to Etude 3.4

In the following examples, find the half steps

Answer to Etude 3.5

In the following examples, notate the scale tones (1-7) beneath the notes

Answer to Etude 4.1

Spell minor scales from each note

Answer to Etude 4.2

Spell harmonic minor scales from each note

Answer to Etude 4.3

Spell melodic minor scales from each note

Answer to Etude 4.4

Find the mistakes in the following minor scales

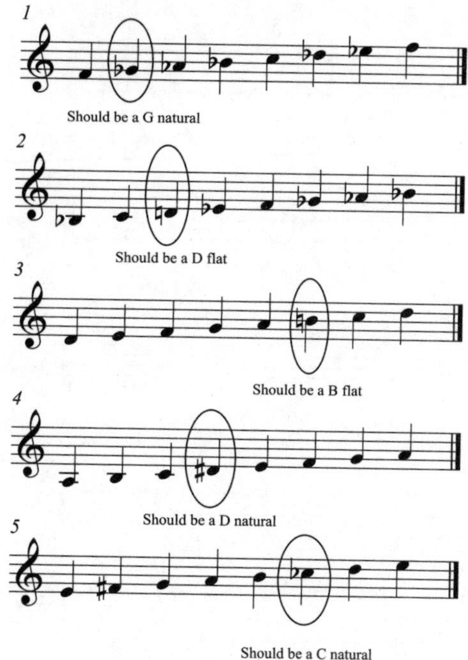

Answer to Etude 4.5

Change the following major scales to minor

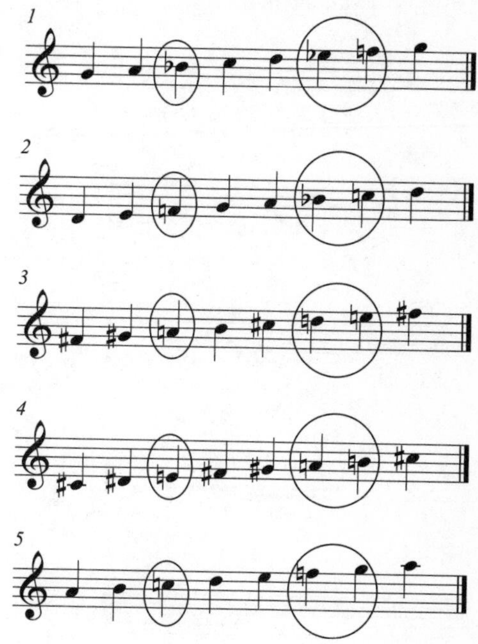

Answer to Etude 5.1

Name the following major key signatures

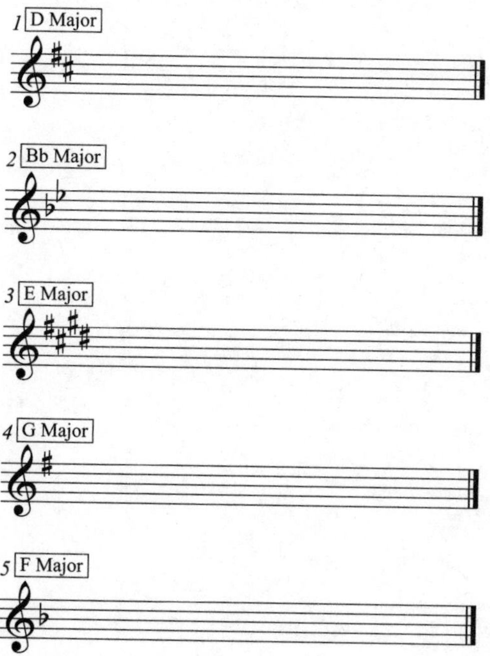

Answer to Etude 5.2

Name the following minor key signatures

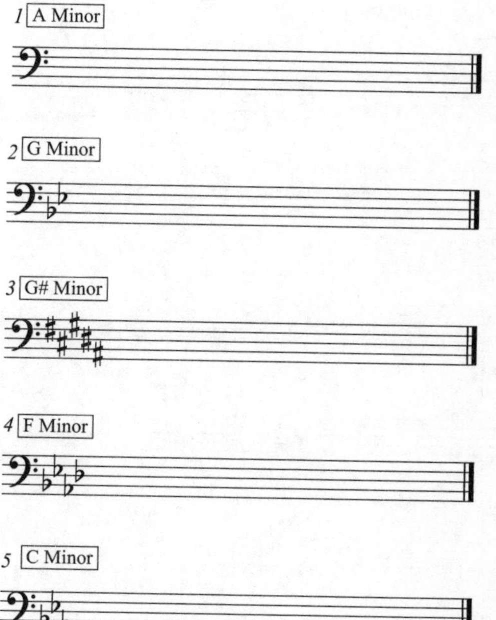

Answer to Etude 5.3

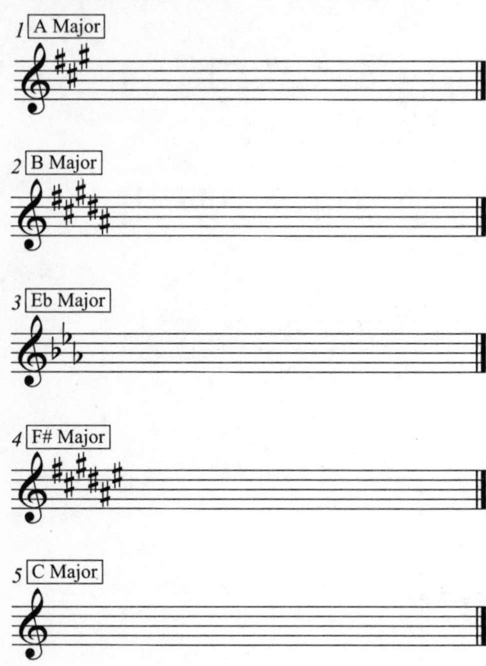

Answer to Etude 5.4

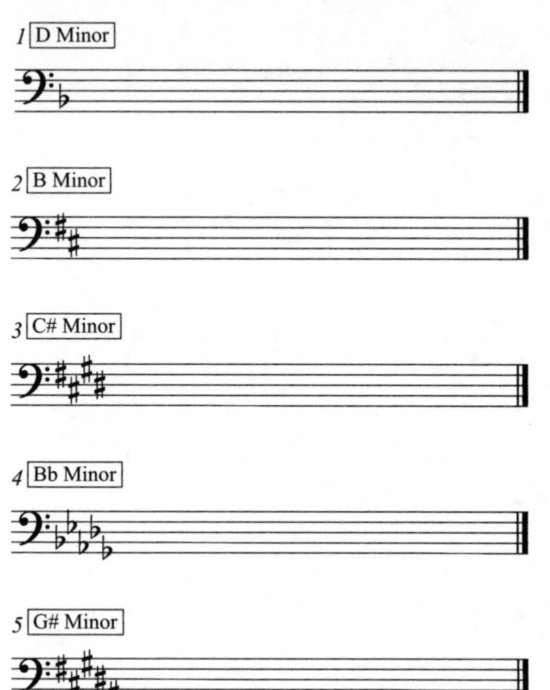

Answer to Etude 5.5

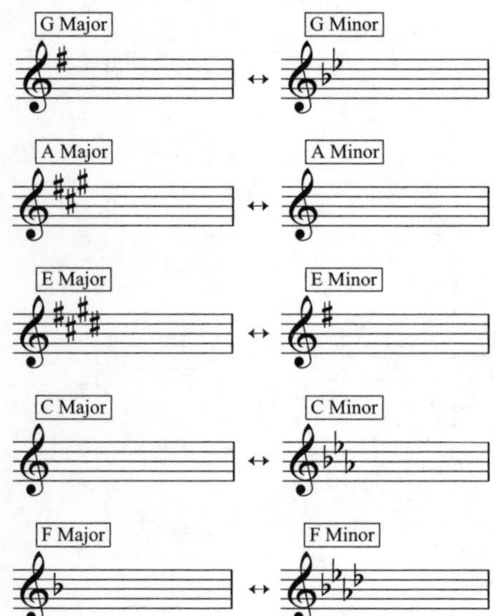

Answer to Etude 6.1

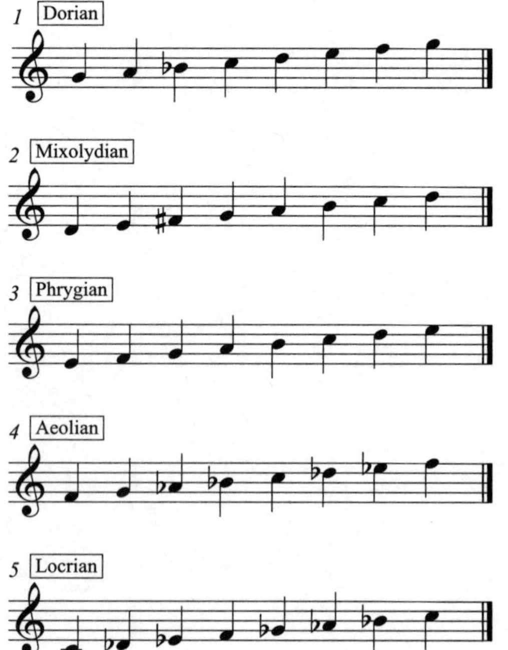

Answer to Etude 6.2

Spell modal scales from each note

Answer to Etude 6.3

Spell major pentatonic scales from each note

Answer to Etude 6.4

Spell minor pentatonic scales from each note

Answer to Etude 6.5

Spell the following scales from each note

Answer to Etude 7.1

Write major triads from the following notes

Answer to Etude 7.2

Write minor triads from the following notes

Answer to Etude 7.3

Write diminished triads from the following notes

Answer to Etude 7.4

Write augmented triads from the following notes

Answer to Etude 7.5

Write major scales from the following notes, harmonize with triads and name the chords.

Answer to Etude 8.1

Create major and minor seventh chords from the following notes

Answer to Etude 8.2

Create dominant seventh chords from the following notes

Answer to Etude 8.3

Create half and fully diminished seventh chords from the following notes

Answer to Etude 8.4

Transform the root position triads to inverted triads from the following chords

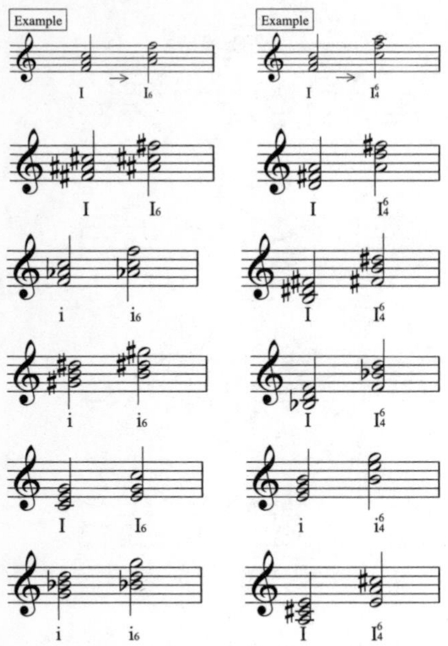

Answer to Etude 8.5

Transform the root position dominant seventh chords to inverted seventh chords from the following chords

Answer to Etude 9.1

Circle the primary chords and name the chord progression with Roman numerals

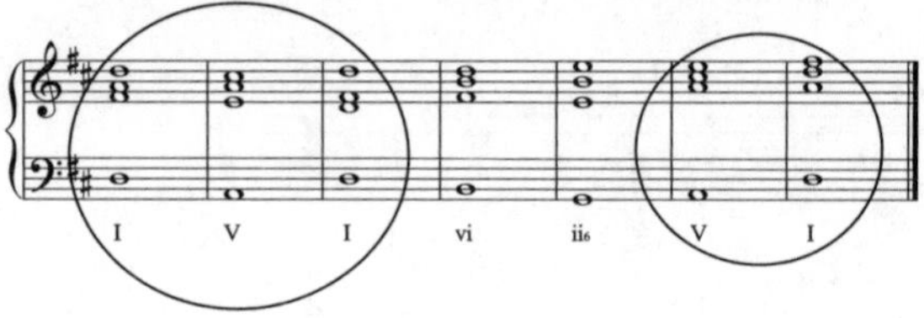

Answer to Etude 9.2

Circle the secondary chords and name the chord progression with Roman numerals

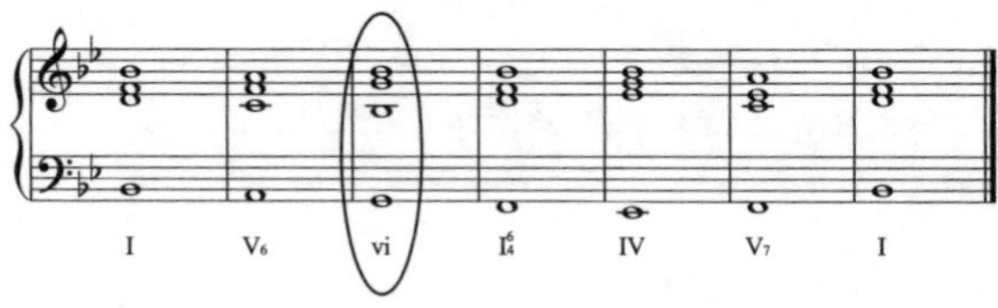

Answer to Etude 9.3

Using the chord ladder, find a substitute chord for the ii chord and insert it in the progression below

Note: The voicing of your IV chord may be different than above. All that matters is that you chose a IV chord and use the notes B♭-D-F instead of the ii chord. Also note the altered voicing of the original V and I chords to avoid voice leading issues.

Answer to Etude 9.4

Circle the chord that breaks the progression from moving completely in fifths

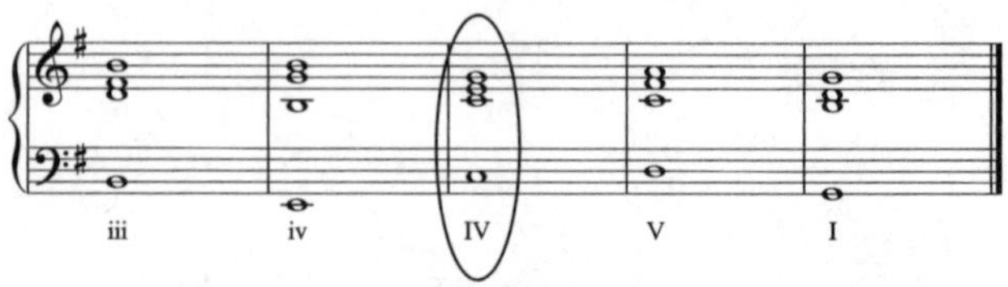

Answer to Etude 9.5

Circle the deceptive resolution in the following chord progression

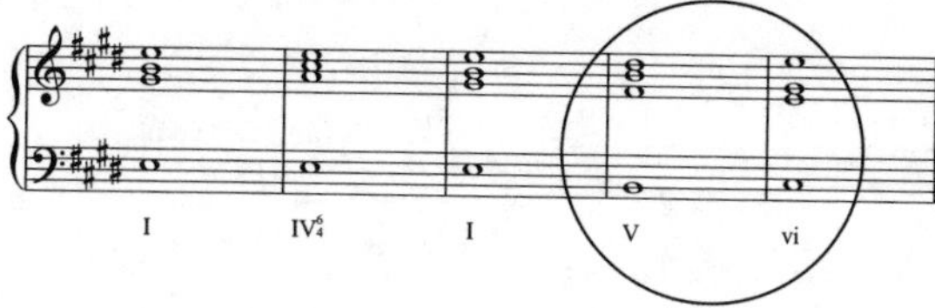

Answer to Etude 10.1

In the following examples, indicate the leading tone and its resolution to the tonic with an arrow

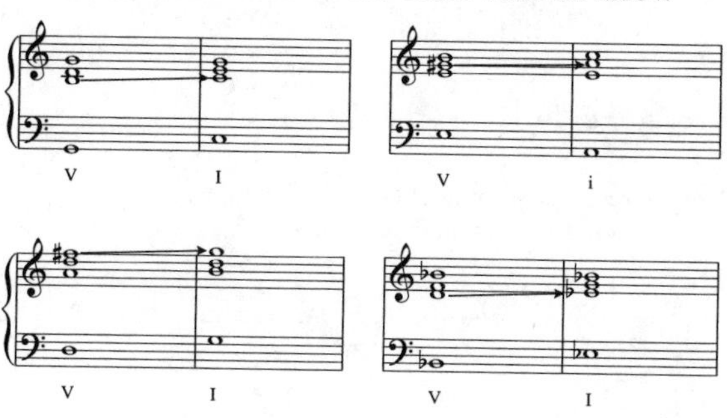

Answer to Etude 10.2

Using arrows, indicate the proper resolution of the tritone in the following V7 chord

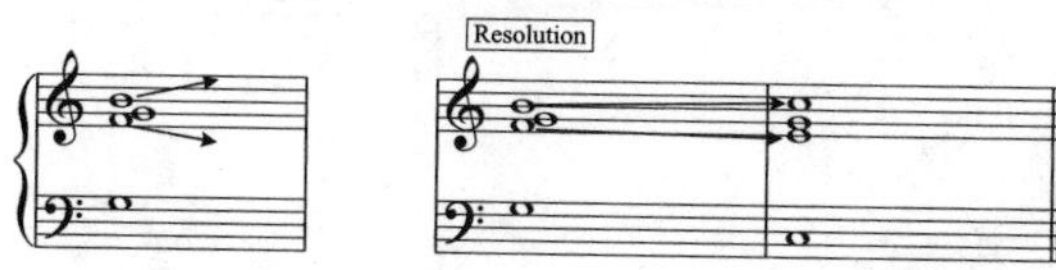

Answer to Etude 10.3

The following minor chord progression has a mistake in it. Can you find it and correct it?

In most minor progressions, the V chord is made major or dominant. Adding the G# to the 3rd measure completes the cadence from V to i in A minor.

Answer to Etude 10.4

Transpose the example progression from major to the parallel minor, altering the notes as needed

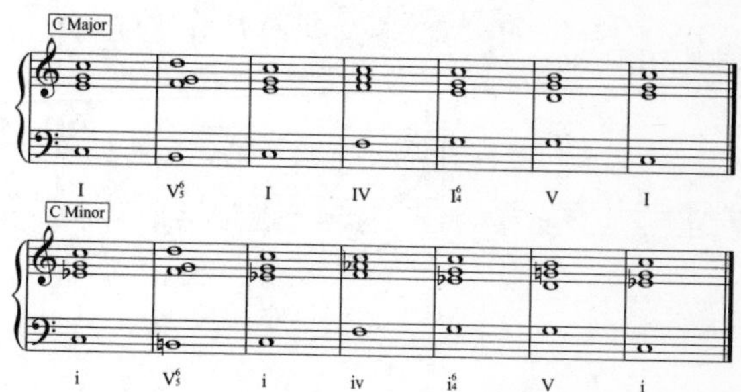

Answer to Etude 10.5

Using the Roman numerals and the provided bass notes, realize the chord progression below

There's no single correct way to voice lead any progression. The answer above is just one example. Check that all of your chords are spelled correctly, even if they are voiced differently from this answer.

Answer to Etude 11.1

In the key of B♭, indicate which chords harmonize with the note E♭

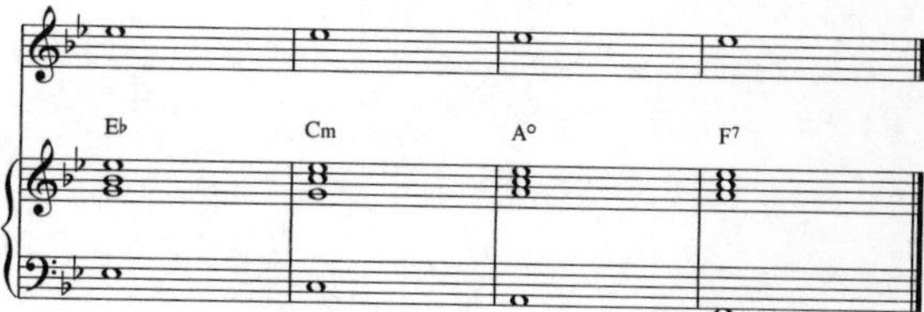

Answer to Etude 11.2

For the following harmonized melody,
circle the chord tones

Answer to Etude 11.3

In the following harmonized melody,
circle the non-chord tones

Answer to Etude 11.4

Harmonize this melody with diatonic 3rds and 6ths

Answer to Etude 11.5

Harmonize the following melody with only diatonic chords

Again, this is just one example of a suitable harmony. Send me a copy of your example if you want someone to look at your work.

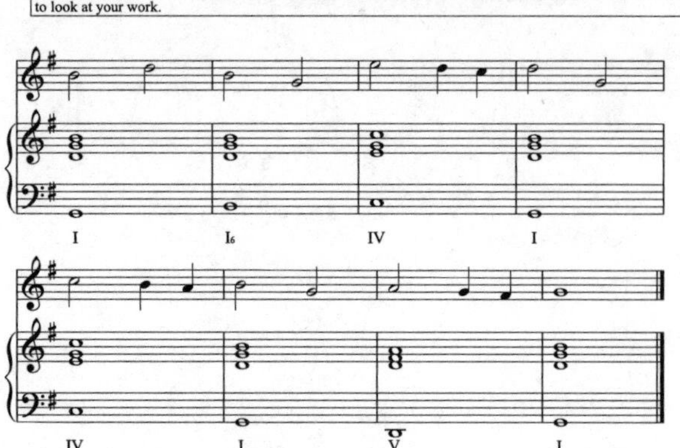

Answer to Etude 12.1

Realize the secondary dominant chords from the key
and Roman numerals below

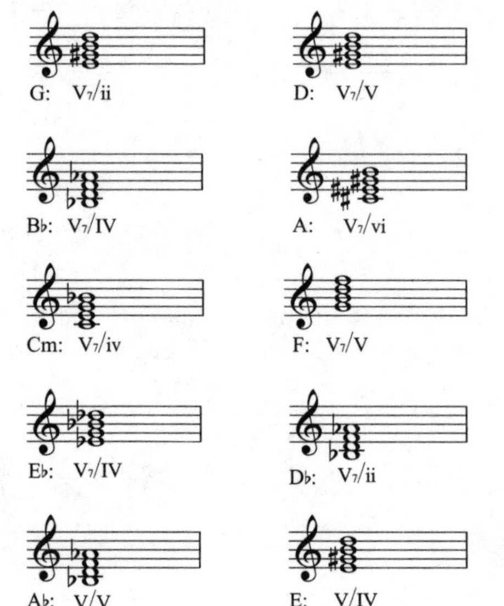

Answer to Etude 12.2

Realize the secondary diminished chords from the key and Roman numerals below

Answer to Etude 12.3

Realize the borrowed chords from the key and Roman numerals below

Answer to Etude 12.4

The following example modulates. Indicate the start and ending keys and circle the first chord in the new key.

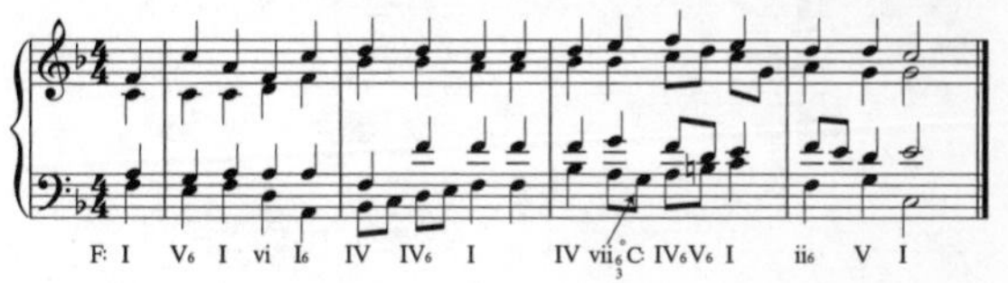

Answer to Etude 12.5

Using the space provided, write down the chords that are shared in the keys of A and E major

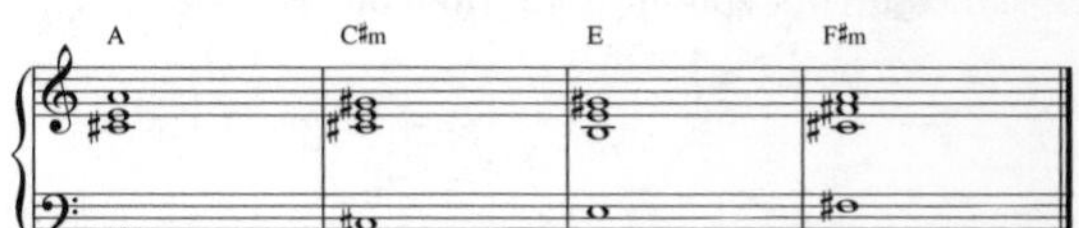

Answer to Etude 13.1

Reduce the complex chords to basic 7th chords. For extra credit, name the complex chords!

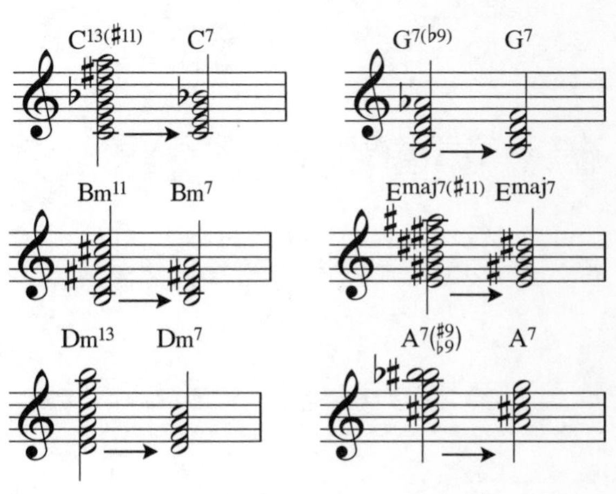

Answer to Etude 13.2

Realize major ii-V-I progressions from the requested key

**This answer contains inverted chords to smooth the voice leading. Your answers can be in root position as long as they have the same pitches (in a different order is fine).*

Answer to Etude 13.3

Realize minor iiø-V-i progressions from the requested key

**This answer contains inverted chords to smooth the voice leading. Your answers can be in root position as long as they have the same pitches (in a different order is fine).*

Answer to Etude 13.4

Add Roman numerals to analyze this chord progression

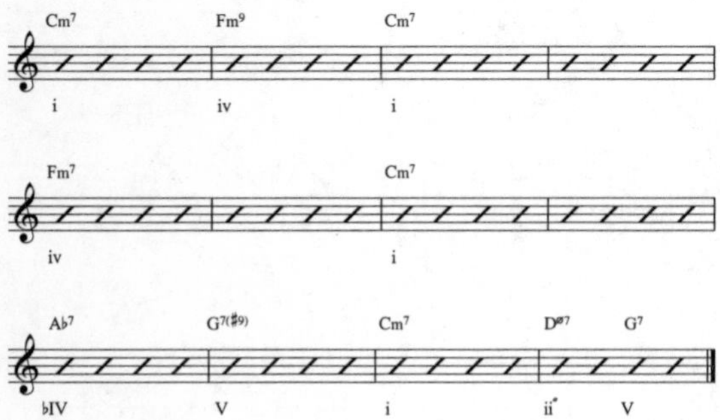

**This is a standard minor blues form*

Answer to Etude 13.5

How many major and minor ii-V progressions can you find? Analyze and circle them in the following example.

Answer to Etude 14.1

Using the space provided, transpose the example for B♭ trumpet

B♭ trumpet sounds a major second lower than written concert pitch

Answer to Etude 14.2

Using the space provided, transpose the example for E♭ alto saxophone

**E♭ alto saxophone sounds a major sixth lower than written concert pitch*

Answer to Etude 14.3

Using the space provided, transpose the example for horn in F

**Horn in F sounds a perfect fifth lower than written concert pitch*

Answer to Etude 14.4

Using the space provided, transpose the example for guitar

**Guitar sounds an octave lower than written concert pitch*

Answer to Etude 14.5

Arrange the following excerpt for a quartet of flute, Bb clarinet, horn in F and Violoncello. Transpose as needed.

Index

YOU SHOULD CAREFULLY READ THE FOLLOWING TERMS AND CONDITIONS BEFORE USING THIS SOFTWARE PRODUCT. INSTALLING AND USING THIS PRODUCT INDICATES YOUR ACCEPTANCE OF THESE CONDITIONS. IF YOU DO NOT AGREE WITH THESE TERMS AND CONDITIONS, DO NOT INSTALL THE SOFTWARE AND RETURN THIS PACKAGE PROMPTLY FOR A FULL REFUND.

1. Grant of License

This software package is protected under United States copyright law and international treaty. You are hereby entitled to one copy of the enclosed software and are allowed by law to make one backup copy or to copy the contents of the disks onto a single hard disk and keep the originals as your backup or archival copy. United States copyright law prohibits you from making a copy of this software for use on any computer other than your own computer. United States copyright law also prohibits you from copying any written material included in this software package without first obtaining the permission of F+W Media, Inc.

2. Restrictions

You, the end-user, are hereby prohibited from the following:

You may not rent or lease the Software or make copies to rent or lease for profit or for any other purpose.

You may not disassemble or reverse compile for the purposes of reverse engineering the Software.

You may not modify or adapt the Software or documentation in whole or in part, including, but not limited to, translating or creating derivative works.

3. Transfer

You may transfer the Software to another person, provided that (a) you transfer all of the Software and documentation to the same transferee; (b) you do not retain any copies; and (c) the transferee is informed of and agrees to the terms and conditions of this Agreement.

4. Termination

This Agreement and your license to use the Software can be terminated without notice if you fail to comply with any of the provisions set forth in this Agreement. Upon termination of this Agreement, you promise to destroy all copies of the software including backup or archival copies as well as any documentation associated with the Software. All disclaimers of warranties and limitation of liability set forth in this Agreement shall survive any termination of this Agreement.

5. Limited Warranty

F+W Media, Inc. warrants that the Software will perform according to the manual and other written materials accompanying the Software for a period of 30 days from the date of receipt. F+W Media, Inc. does not accept responsibility for any malfunctioning computer hardware or any incompatibilities with existing or new computer hardware technology.

6. Customer Remedies

F+W Media, Inc.'s entire liability and your exclusive remedy shall be, at the option of F+W Media, Inc., either refund of your purchase price or repair and/or replacement of Software that does not meet this Limited Warranty. Proof of purchase shall be required. This Limited Warranty will be voided if Software failure was caused by abuse, neglect, accident or misapplication. All replacement Software will be warranted based on the remainder of the warranty or the full 30 days, whichever is shorter and will be subject to the terms of the Agreement.

7. No Other Warranties

F+W MEDIA, INC., TO THE FULLEST EXTENT OF THE LAW, DISCLAIMS ALL OTHER WARRANTIES, OTHER THAN THE LIMITED WARRANTY IN PARAGRAPH 5, EITHER EXPRESS OR IMPLIED, ASSOCIATED WITH ITS SOFTWARE, INCLUDING BUT NOT LIMITED TO IMPLIED WARRANTIES OF MERCHANTABILITY AND FITNESS FOR A PARTICULAR PURPOSE, WITH REGARD TO THE SOFTWARE AND ITS ACCOMPANYING WRITTEN MATERIALS. THIS LIMITED WARRANTY GIVES YOU SPECIFIC LEGAL RIGHTS. DEPENDING UPON WHERE THIS SOFTWARE WAS PURCHASED, YOU MAY HAVE OTHER RIGHTS.

8. Limitations on Remedies

TO THE MAXIMUM EXTENT PERMITTED BY LAW, F+W MEDIA, INC. SHALL NOT BE HELD LIABLE FOR ANY DAMAGES WHATSOEVER, INCLUDING WITHOUT LIMITATION, ANY LOSS FROM PERSONAL INJURY, LOSS OF BUSINESS PROFITS, BUSINESS INTERRUPTION, BUSINESS INFORMATION OR ANY OTHER PECUNIARY LOSS ARISING OUT OF THE USE OF THIS SOFTWARE.

This applies even if F+W Media, Inc. has been advised of the possibility of such damages. F+W Media, Inc.'s entire liability under any provision of this agreement shall be limited to the amount actually paid by you for the Software. Because some states may not allow for this type of limitation of liability, the above limitation may not apply to you.

THE WARRANTY AND REMEDIES SET FORTH ABOVE ARE EXCLUSIVE AND IN LIEU OF ALL OTHERS, ORAL OR WRITTEN, EXPRESS OR IMPLIED. No F+W Media, Inc. dealer, distributor, agent, or employee is authorized to make any modification or addition to the warranty.

9. General

This Agreement shall be governed by the laws of the United States of America and the Commonwealth of Massachusetts. If you have any questions concerning this Agreement, contact F+W Media, Inc., via Adams Media at 508-427-7100. Or write to us at: Adams Media, a division of F+W Media, Inc., 57 Littlefield Street, Avon, MA 02322.